CONTEMPORARY AFRICA:
DEVELOPMENT, CULTURE AND THE STATE

CONTEMPORARY AFRICA:
DEVELOPMENT, CULTURE
AND THE STATE

Morag Bell

Copublished in the United States with
John Wiley & Sons, Inc., New York

Longman Scientific & Technical
Longman Group UK Limited,
Longman House, Burnt Mill, Harlow,
Essex CM20 2JE, England
and Associated Companies throughout the world

*Copublished in the United States of America with
John Wiley & Sons Inc., 605 Third Avenue,
New York, NY 10158*

© *Longman Group Limited 1986*

First published 1986
Reprinted with corrections by Longman Scientific & Technical 1987

British Library Cataloguing in Publication Data
Bell, Morag
  Contemporary Africa: development, culture
  and the state.
  1. Africa . . . Economic conditions . . . 1960-
  2. Africa . . . Civilization . . . 20th century
  I. Title
  330.96'0328   HC800

ISBN 0-582-30090-8

Library of Congress Cataloging-in-Publication Data
Bell, Morag.
  Contemporary Africa.

  Reprint. Originally published: London; New York: Longman, 1986.
  Bibliography: p.
  Includes index.
  1. Africa--Politics and government--1960-   .
2. Africa--Economic conditions--1960-   . 3. Africa--
Economic policy. 4. Africa--Social conditions--
1960-   . I. Title.
  DT30.5.B44   1987   306'.096   87-2707
  ISBN 0-470-20656-X (USA Only)

Produced by Longman Group (FE) Ltd
Printed in Hong Kong

FOR MY PARENTS

CONTENTS

LIST OF FIGURES

LIST OF TABLES

PREFACE

To write another book about development in Africa would seem to be both presumptuous and unnecessary. Existing literature reflects the work of disciplines spanning the full range of the social sciences and encompasses contrasting viewpoints. One might wonder what more could be said by a subject, geography, with its derivative theories and relatively recent contribution to development thought. This book is written by one (among many geographers) committed to the field of development for whom active involvement in both theory and practice represents a necessary but difficult challenge. It was inspired by an interest in the wider debate over development and underdevelopment, in particular by the approach of political economy, and also by a realisation that change involves more than politics and economics. Africa's cultural traditions and the richness of its cultural variety are brought into sharp relief for even the casual visitor to the continent. It is this cultural context which plays an active role in both the formulation of development projects and in their implementation.

The aims of this book are modest. To introduce to the student of African affairs an approach in which the interplay between politico-economic structure and culture is regarded as central to our understanding of changes in the organisation of space. There will be those who claim that the book deals inadequately with culture or is limited in its interpretation of political economy. The focus arises from the author's experience as a frequent visitor to and researcher in different parts of the continent. It is written by an outsider and as such does not pretend to encompass fully the significance of the links between structure and culture but by one who feels that much of the existing literature does not give these links the importance they deserve. This is an introductory text pointing the way towards filling this gap.

In researching and writing the book, progress would have been slow without the generous help and co-operation of many colleagues and friends too numerous to mention. My special thanks are due to Dr. Bill Gould of Liverpool University. His material help, positive suggestions and editorial assistance have been invaluable. Many members of my own department at Loughborough University have encouraged me throughout, especially Professor Robin Butlin to whom I am most grateful, and Dr. Denis Cosgrove for his critical observations on parts of the text. The ideas for this book have been prompted by my work with two groups of scholars: as a member of the WEDC (Water and Engineering for Developing Countries) Group at Loughborough University under the leadership of Professor John Pickford, and as a researcher with the National Migration Study in Botswana organised and co-ordinated by Dr. Carol Kerven and John Case. The benefits and intellectual stimulus I have gained from working with these groups are immeasurable. In this context I should like to thank Dr. Wendy Izzard for her detailed comments on Chapter 8 and acknowledge the Botswana Government for allowing me to publish certain factual details. The staff of Loughborough University Library, and in particular Mona McKay, provided an excellent service. My thanks are also due to Anne Tarver who produced the maps and to Gwynneth Barnwell for her help, notably with the bibliography. Finally, I am indebted to Jenny Jarvis. This work could not have been completed without her patient co-operation, understanding and professional skill in the preparation of the manuscript. Any errors of fact and interpretation are the author's alone.

Morag Bell
Loughborough
January 1985

ACKNOWLEDGEMENTS

We are grateful to the following for permission to reproduce copyright material:

Edward Arnold Ltd for our figs 4.1, 4.2, 4.4 from figs 53, 56 71 (Fage & Verity 1978); Cambridge University Press for our tables 5.2, (Rajana 1982), 7.4 (Warwick 1982); Cambridge University Press and the Organisation for Economic Co-operation & Development for our table 5.1 (Kirkpatrick & Nixson 1981, Lewis 1980); Commission of the European Communities for our fig 5.2 from *The Courier* (1984); Earthscan for our table 7.1 (Agarwal et al 1981); Heinemann Educational Books Ltd for our table 3.2 (Kpedekpo 1979), our fig 2.3 from fig 37.1 (Livingstone & Ord 1980); Longman Group Ltd for our fig 7.1 from fig 1.1 (Woods 1982); Oxford University Press for our fig 8.3 (Colclough & McCarthy 1980); Ravan Press (Pty) Ltd for extracts from pp xi, 19, 51, 59–60, 60, 81–82, 102 *Families Divided: The Impact of Migrant Labour in Lesotho* by C Murray (1981); The Scandinavian Institute of African Studies for our table 2.5 from table 1 (Isaksen 1981); United Nations for our tables 2.4 (United Nations 1983), 3.3 (United Nations 1984); University of California Press for our fig 6.1 from *Bureaucrats, Politicians and Peasants in Mexico: A Case Study in Public Policy* by M S Grindle (1977); Yale University Press for our table 2.2 from p 325 (Young 1982).

Chapter 1

FRAMEWORK FOR GEOGRAPHICAL STUDY

Introduction

It is the combination of unity and diversity on the continent of Africa which makes the task of the geographer both challenging and difficult. Our concerns are with the organisation of space as reflected in, for example, the changing use and misuse of the environment, spatial variations in social organisation and landscape, and patterns of inequality. The task is enormous and can be approached from alternative theoretical perspectives. The approach adopted here is intended as a complement to existing regional and systematic texts on Africa written by geographers (for example, Mabogunje 1980a; O'Connor 1978; Udo 1982). It draws upon and seeks to integrate literature in the related social sciences into geographical explanation, in particular the focus of political economy on state structures and institutions with the interest of sociology and social anthropology in culture.

The geographical focus of the book is sub-Saharan Africa, an area penetrated by colonial capitalism in the nineteenth century since when its social, economic and political structures have been interrelated with the international community. Our study area is therefore characterised by broad uniformities – a colonial history, links with the international economic system – but also local variation – the legacy of diverse pre-colonial societies, contrasting environmental conditions and post-colonial political ideologies. It is to maintain this underlying sense of unity in diversity that South Africa is excluded from the analysis. As Allen and Williams point out (1982: xv) 'In its level of development (notably industry and agriculture), in the completeness of the proletarianisation of its African population, and in the sophistication and effectiveness of its state, South Africa is anything but typical of Africa in general.' Its extensive influence on the continent cannot, however, be ignored and is discussed within the broader regional context of Southern Africa.

There is a tendency in geographical study to be constrained by physical entities defined in terms of political boundaries. The concept and physical expression of the modern nation state is alien to the traditions of many African people. Nevertheless, it is arguably the most significant politico-economic and spatial division of the continent within which distinct social processes operate, with effects reaching far beyond the boundaries of that unit. The contemporary nation states were created at the time of European colonial penetration, and the institutions established to manage them have since then had an important influence on the spatial concentration of economic activities and hence on patterns of social and spatial inequality within the African states. In explaining the similarities and differences between countries it is therefore important to explore the state structures and agencies whose decisions influence the organisation of space (Fig. 1.1). But change within countries must in turn be related to the international system of production and exchange by which they were created and with which they remain interlinked. Disparities in income and welfare, the poverty of much of African agriculture, the prospects offered by rural development, the nature and implications of rural-urban demographic, social and economic interactions cannot be explained without reference to the constraints within which national governments operate.

External presence and influence in Africa in the form of direct foreign investment, foreign aid and international trade profoundly affect the spatial distribution of economic opportunities and social provision within countries. It is in making this essential link between the international scale and change at national and intra-national levels that theoretical discussion and debate derived from the literature of political economy are essential to the geographer. As Wellings and McCarthy (1983: 339) point out with respect to southern African human geography, we must not be mere technicians 'seemingly capable of functioning independently of the theoretical and political debates and advances' proceeding around us.

Decision-making, inequality and the question of scale

Central to the debate over African development and underdevelopment is the significance of changes in African society brought about by colonial capitalism. The values and ideals enshrined in the European institutions which penetrated the continent challenged those of traditional society. Within each newly created colonial state the change in organisation of production influenced the nature and location of economic opportunities, the form of the urban hierarchy and the internal structure of urban centres, the physical character of the rural landscape, and disparities in income and welfare within and between rural and urban areas. New social categories emerged, notably social classes defined in economic terms (Amin 1971; Sklar 1979). Since independence an indigenous political and bureaucratic élite, schooled within the environment of alien European institutions, but influenced by their own ideologies, have governed African countries. Thus three common threads can be identified in an otherwise highly complex process of social change: 'the rise of the modern state, the emergence of national communities and of nationalist ideologies and sentiments, and the formation of new strata, notably bureaucrats, bourgeoisies and intelligentsia' (Smith 1983: 1).

For the geographer an awareness of this politico-economic structure is important and should influence interpretation of space and the spatial dimension of inequality. Geographic space is not merely a formal unit for delimiting statistical data, it is a variable to be explained. Much discussion in development

2

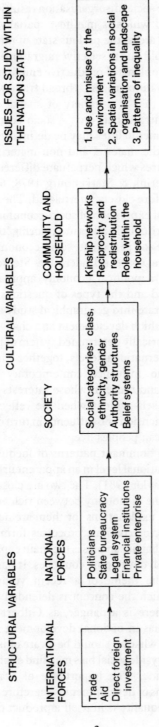

Figure 1.1 The context of geographical study

literature centres around the social disorganisation resulting from the penetration of the money economy and which is manifest spatially in a number of ways: drought and famine in rural areas, the parlous state of much African agriculture, the disruption of the household due to selective migration which changes the social role and status of women, problems of productive employment in rural and urban areas and housing problems in towns. As a broad framework for analysing these issues it can be suggested that at a variety of spatial scales – inter-regional, rural-urban, intra-rural, intra-urban etc. – socio-economic disparities have arisen. These disparities or inequalities may be defined as 'the unequal access of individuals and groups to the material and non-material resources of society' resulting from social structures which perpetuate differences in influence, status and material wealth (Hinderink & Sterkenburg 1978: 6). Socio-economic and spatial inequalities are therefore closely interrelated. The geographer's role is not merely to describe the spatial expression of socio-economic inequality within and between countries. More particularly it lies in exploring 'the nature and evolution of the structures which cause and perpetuate socio-economic inequality in relation to any particular geographical space' (Hinderink & Sterkenburg 1978: 6).

Thus the adoption of a political economy approach by the geographer influences the focus adopted and the types of questions asked. In particular it highlights the need to integrate into geographical study analysis of the politico-economic structure within which development and change take place. This must include reference to the historically determined system of production and division of labour at national and international levels, together with the key groups, both internal and external, who influence contemporary policy decisions, the interactions between them and those in whose interests actions are taken. The importance of this task is self-evident when we reflect that these forces do themselves have a spatial dimension and influence in turn our conceptualisation of the space within which African peoples live.

In much of Africa two dominant patterns of inequality can be identified. They are reflected at intra-national level in an apparent urban bias and within this in a bias against the poor (Taylor 1981). The two are closely interrelated but not synonymous (for example, the dichotomy between rich and poor cuts across the rural-urban divide); but the explanations for them are not necessarily different. Space as a surrogate for socio-economic processes forms the basis of Michael Lipton's (1977) hypothesis that urban bias is the main explanation of 'why people stay poor' in the post-colonial developing countries. It has become the subject of much debate and forms the theme of a recent volume of the *Journal of Development Studies* in which the concept is defended and misinterpretations clarified (Lipton 1984). There is a danger, as Gilbert (1982) points out, in assuming that any spatial bias in national development is merely a product of distance constraints. Rather what we should be aware of is that as the majority of poor people live in the countryside social bias may find expression at intra-national level in a rural-urban divide. The importance of scale in influencing our perceptions of spatial patterns of development is therefore emphasised and with it a recognition that spatial inequality is in itself a product of social processes.

4

In considering the mechanisms which perpetuate or seek to reduce inequality within African countries, the geographical and political focus at which these unequal relationships – rural-urban, rich-poor – come together is the centre of power and decision-making, the capital city. National decision-makers are overwhelmingly urban-based. They interact externally in a North-South relationship with agencies of the more developed countries, and internally with powerful groups whose interests span rural and urban areas but who in turn tend to be urban-based. The strength and significance of the patterns of inequality identified within and between countries are strongly influenced by the ways in which these interactions are reconciled at the centre.

Politico-economic structure and the cultural context

It is at this point that we must return to the discussion of uniformity and diversity in Africa. It is accepted that the entry of an alien mode of production has introduced new social categories derived from alien values and practices, together with new ways of dividing territories (nation state, administrative district) including patterns of inequality not hitherto identified (rural-urban). But social processes do not operate in a uniform manner either within or between countries. Neither powerful groups within African society nor the ordinary people behave in a manner which conforms directly with the expectations of the alien mode. To take but a few examples, national ideologies, changes in fertility and mortality, rural-urban interactions reflect a complex combination of values, ideals and obligations. It is this evidence which leads us to question in geographical study the extent to which African society is suffused with Western values and priorities.

In questioning this assumption it is not intended in this text to explore in detail the extent to which decision-making at the centre and the social and spatial outcomes are informed by a class analysis. The concept of class in Africa is a topic of much controversy and debate and although class relations are much used in the literature of radical political economy to explain uneven development, as Allen and Williams (1982: xix) remind us, 'class membership is only one of several ways in which people identify themselves collectively, and forms one of the sources of collective action'.

The dangers of adopting without question conventional development paradigms in the African context must be avoided. As Anthony Smith points out (1983: 1):

Throughout the world, economic growth and social change have taken place within very varied political and cultural contexts, and hence such apparently uniform developments as technical advance, rising material standards and output, rapid urbanisation, the commercialisation of agriculture, the redistribution of wealth and the provision of a

5

wider range of social services for the population, take on a different significance and have consequences according to this political and cultural context.

It is an awareness of this context which is critical to our explanation of the changing geography of Africa but which is frequently inadequately acknowledged. A major limitation of the Marxist paradigm, for example, is the tendency to interpret non-capitalist modes as 'merely parasitic adjuncts' to the capitalist mode (Hyden 1980: 249). Such a criticism is forcefully expressed by Hyden (1980: 23) as follows:

> capitalism has modified the social structures of Africa, but the latter are still influenced by the peasant mode of production which continues to exist in a controversial relationship with capitalism. They constitute two contending modes of production. A study of Africa's political economy [*and the organisation of space with which it is associated*] cannot start from the assumption that one has submerged the other. Instead the task must be to explain the structural anomalies that this situation gives rise to. [italics added]

At the base of this text is a recognition that in order to make sense of the changing geography of African states, we must understand the complexities and diversities of their politico-economic structure and the cultural values, beliefs and ideals, both national and local, by which the system is sustained. While the loyalties and behaviour patterns expected of individuals have changed with the creation of the nation state, it should not be assumed that the economic rationality and individualism of Western society are necessarily dominant. Moreover, in acknowledging the importance of cultural issues it should not be assumed that culture is of significance only at community level, the scale of particular interest to social anthropology. Culture mediates all political, economic and social processes. It influences on the one hand, national policy-making and, on the other, the response of the African people to changes in their environment.

A sensitivity to the cultural dimension of Africa's politico-economic structure is therefore essential. It is through an awareness of the role of culture that standard social and spatial categories are refined. Divisions of African society based on ethnicity and gender remain important in shaping attitudes, values and the roles which people perform. In addition, the loyalties of kinship and, within this, obligations to the family unit, both of which operate within and between rural and urban areas, are a persistent influence on the behaviour patterns of particular groups.

By considering those social categories which are important to the African people our approach to space is also modified. Culture influences the use made of space by individuals and groups as they accommodate themselves to the constraints of the politico-economic system within which they live. It helps to explain spatial variations in fertility and mortality. Cultural values influence the

6

use made of environmental resources in economic activities and the efforts made by individuals to overcome the constraints imposed by space on the maintenance of their social relations. It is through evidence such as this that our interpretations of, for example, the rural-urban divide are modified and refined.

Outline of the book

It is the purpose of this text to demonstrate that by understanding the relationship between politico-economic structure and culture, the somewhat elusive link between macro-scales and micro-scales may be forged and that our explanations of the changing geography of Africa may in turn be refined. Three assumptions underlie the approach adopted. First, while it may be argued that the influence of culture on behaviour is most easily identified at the level of individual and community (the so-called micro-scale), it is also significant at the political and spatial centre of power where the competing forces which control the spatial distribution of and access to economic opportunities and social provision are resolved. Second, the African people are not passive victims of the processes of change. Within the limits set by the broader political economy, the behaviour of individuals, conditioned by their own established norms and values, does in turn shape and reproduce the system. Third, culture is not static and immutable. Through the influence of external forces and the interactions between modes of production, cultural norms and practices, both national and local, are themselves modified and changed.

Chapters 2 and 3 discuss the structural and cultural contexts within which we may study the changing geography of Africa. Chapter 2 outlines alternative theories of development and underdevelopment including the relative importance attached to internal and external forces. From this discussion the importance attached to the African state created out of colonially defined boundaries is emphasised, and within this spatial unit there is a need to focus on the key actors, at both internal and international levels, who have fashioned social and spatial change. Central to the discussion are the concepts of neo-colonialism and dependency and with these the importance of the emerging social classes in influencing the nature of change. Chapter 3 provides a counterbalance to this approach by stressing that a structural analysis is in itself inadequate to explain the changing geography of African states. The interaction between structure and culture is acknowledged at two levels: in exploring the political and economic forces at the centre in relation to the decisions made and their social and spatial outcomes; and in understanding the behaviour of the African people, their responses to changes in their environment including the opportunities presented and the constraints imposed. Subsequent chapters build upon the ideas and concepts presented in these two contextual chapters.

In Chapter 4 an historical background to the contemporary geography of

Africa is outlined. While a central theme is the importance of developments in Europe in stimulating change within the continent it is also stressed that the effects were not uniform across the continent and that in explaining the legacy of colonialism, of critical importance is the interaction which took place between colonial and indigenous value systems. It is demonstrated that it was the nature of this interaction which moulded the political and economic organisation of space inherited on independence, together with the emerging regional disparities and social inequalities within and between rural and urban areas.

Chapters 5 and 6 consider the role of the State since independence in altering these inherited structures. Chapter 5 continues into independence a theme outlined in Chapter 4, namely, that despite national sovereignty external forces continue to have a powerful influence on decision-making at the centre. The concept of a culture of dependency is, however, challenged at two levels. First, by reference to the indigenisation measures taken by individual governments to reduce the power of the multinational institutions in general and the European Economic Community in particular. Second, through the various regional groupings formed within the continent to counter foreign domination. At both levels it is, however, emphasised that in explaining the effectiveness of these measures in reducing regional disparities and social inequalities within countries, closer scrutiny is needed not only of the ability but, more particularly, of the willingness of the State to use these mechanisms in the interests of the majority. Chapter 6 concentrates on the ways in which African cultural beliefs and values have influenced the national ideologies of African leaders and the characteristics of spatial planning. With specific reference to rural development, administrative decentralisation and urban planning, it is demonstrated that the relationship between the State and traditional political and social structures has played a key role in both the approach adopted and the outcomes obtained.

The final two chapters focus directly on the effects of changes in the African political economy on the African people. By reference to the three demographic processes of fertility, mortality (Ch. 7) and spatial mobility, and in turn to the rural-urban interactions with which the latter is associated (Ch. 8), it is emphasised that the speed and direction of change has been neither easy to define nor simple to explain. Nor have individuals behaved in a manner expected of them within the new environment shaped by outside forces. Above all emphasis is placed on the role of culture in mediating demographic behaviour. In doing so reference is made to the two levels with which the geographer is principally concerned – macro-scale of continent, nation and region, and micro-scale of community and household. By means of specific case studies it is demonstrated that the pattern of loyalties and the cultural norms which operate at community and household level influence the demographic response to changing circum-stances, and condition in turn the means by which social change is achieved. Thus the importance of cultural beliefs, values and practices in reproducing and shaping the broader political economy is highlighted.

Finally, it should be emphasised that the themes and issues perceived to be important in this book together with the interpretations offered are presented from the perspective of an outsider. Much of the available literature on African development is by Western academics and planners brought up in an alien culture and whose interpretations are informed by their own background and experience. There is indeed a growing literature relating to foreign perspectives on Africa (for example, *Review of African Political Economy* 1982 no. 23). The cultural dimension is implicit in all studies of Africa. While the author's own background, as nothing more than a frequent visitor to and researcher on the continent, influences the material selected and the interpretations presented, reference is made in the course of the text to the community of African writers concerned to transmit the richness, the variety and the traumas of contemporary African life in the countryside and in the towns.

Further reading

For a discussion of the relationship between social and spatial inequality see in particular Gilbert (1982), Hinderink and Sterkenburg (1978) and Taylor (1981). The debate over rural-urban imbalances is raised in a special issue of the **Journal of Development Studies** 1984 vol. 2, no. 3, 'Development and the rural-urban divide'.

——— Chapter 2 ———

THE POLITICO-ECONOMIC STRUCTURE –
INSTITUTIONS, INTEREST GROUPS AND CLASS

Introduction

Most African states have now experienced some twenty years of independence in which indigenous leaders have attempted to mould their political economy and society. Political independence has produced a new generation of African politicians and widespread indigenisation of personnel within the bureaucracy. How far have these changes at the centre influenced the geography of Africa as expressed in social differences and regional change? National goals are expressed by politicians to be translated into specific programmes and projects by the bureaucracy for subsequent implementation at national, regional and local levels. In evaluating the outcomes space is frequently interpreted as a formal framework within which statistical units (states, regions, districts) can be delimited. Spatial inequality is then based on a description of differences between these units defined by quantifiable socio-economic phenomena.

In the continent, owing to data limitations, national units are most frequently used as a basis within which to chart progress and to make comparisons between states. On the basis of information recorded at this scale Killick (1980: 379) suggests 'it could well be argued that the economic differences among African countries are more important than the similarities'. However, Table 2.1 illustrates that despite the change in political control together with determined efforts at social and economic development, overall there is still much to be achieved. Moreover, when comparisons are drawn with countries beyond the continent in the main the African states do not score well. According to the United Nations, in 1975 eighteen African countries were among the 'least developed' nations. These were in West Africa: Benin, Chad, the Gambia, Guinea, Mali, Niger, Burkina Faso (formerly Upper Volta); in East and Central Africa: Burundi, the Central African Empire, Ethiopia, Rwanda, Somalia, Sudan, Tanzania, Uganda; and in Southern Africa: Botswana, Malawi and Lesotho. In 1977 the European Economic Community reported that there were twenty-one African countries south of the Sahara with a per capita income of below US $265 per annum ranging from Burkina Faso with a per capita income of $90 to the Comoros with a per capita income of $260. A further twenty-one countries had per capita incomes of between $265 and $820 while only two states had high incomes – Djibouti at $1720 and Gabon at $2240. The World Bank (1984) offers a further two-fold subdivision of developing countries with a population of 1 million or more (Fig. 2.1). Of the thirty-four low income countries with a per capita income of $390 or less in 1982 –

10

Table 2.1 Socio-economic indicators for selected African countries (Source: World Bank 1984: 218, 228, 258, 264, 266)

	GNP PER CAPITA (US DOLLARS)	LIFE EXPECTANCY AT BIRTH (YEARS)	INFANT MORTALITY (AGED UNDER 1) PER 1000 LIVE BIRTHS	DAILY CALORIE SUPPLY PER CAPITA AS % OF REQUIREMENT	AVERAGE INDEX OF FOOD PRODUCTION (1960–70 = 100)	ENROLMENT IN PRIMARY SCHOOL AS % OF AGE GROUP
	1982	1982	1982	1981	1980–82	1981
Ethiopia	140	47	122	76	82	46
Mali	180	45	132	72	83	27
Zaire	190	50	106	94	87	90
Malawi	210	44	137	94	99	62
Burkina Faso (formerly Upper Volta)	210	44	157	95	95	20
Uganda	230	47	120	80	86	54
Tanzania	280	52	98	83	88	102
Guinea	310	38	190	75	89	33
Niger	310	45	132	102	88	23
Ghana	360	55	86	88	72	69
Kenya	390	57	77	88	88	109
Mozambique	—	51	105	70	68	90
Sudan	440	47	119	99	87	52
Senegal	490	44	155	101	93	48
Lesotho	510	53	94	111	84	104
Zambia	640	51	105	93	87	96
Zimbabwe	850	56	83	90	87	126
Nigeria	860	50	109	91	92	98
Cameroon	890	53	92	102	102	107
Ivory Coast	950	47	119	112	107	76
Angola	—	43	165	83	77	—

the group which has suffered most severely since 1960 – some twenty-one were in Africa south of the Sahara. The second group of sixty middle income developing countries with an average per capita income of $1520 in 1982 included a mere twelve from sub-Saharan Africa: Sudan, Mauritania, Senegal, Angola, Lesotho, Cameroon, Zimbabwe, Liberia, Zambia, Congo People's Republic, Nigeria and Ivory Coast. Of these only Angola, Nigeria and Lesotho achieved the rate of economic expansion characteristic of that group as a whole.

It is apparent from these classifications, based as they are on national level statistics, that with a few notable exceptions strong similarities exist between African states with respect to their poor economic performance. Moreover, from the limited data available on the intra-national scale there is no widespread evidence of an improvement in living standards for all. Cohen and Daniel (1981: 221) point out, high infant mortality rates and high levels of illiteracy persist, and the exodus from rural areas has been accompanied by urban employment problems and agricultural decline. The unintended consequences of government policies have been serious. In spatial terms, while there is much poverty in both rural and urban areas, since the majority of poor people live in the countryside, Michael Lipton's hypothesis (Lipton 1977; 1984) regarding urban-biased development receives a measure of support.

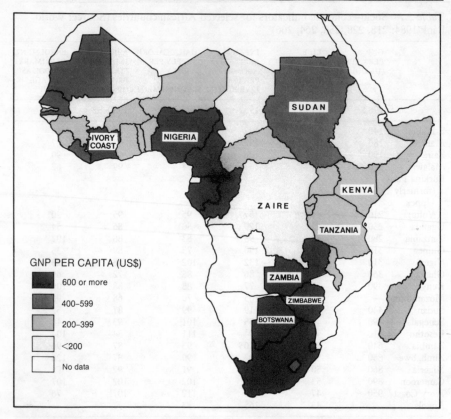

Figure 2.1 Gross national product in the countries of sub-Saharan Africa (data from World Bank 1984: 215)

Why this should be so is a key topic of debate in academic and planning circles both within the continent and outside it underlying which are important theoretical assumptions. (See, for example, Davidson 1975; Arrighi & Saul 1973; Gutkind & Waterman 1977; Saul 1979.) While identifying the conditions and diagnosing the symptoms of underdevelopment produces broad agreement, by contrast explanation of the causes raises some controversy. Clearly causation is a complex issue influenced by the ideological position and the approach adopted.

Underdevelopment – internal or external forces

At the base of the discussion is one fundamental question, namely, what is the relative importance of internal and external factors in causing the problems of poverty and in providing solutions? Do many of the problems stem from conditions and circumstances within African states; and within them can important, though of course only partial, solutions be found? By contrast are the roots of underdevelopment much broader, lying in conditions external to African states and in particular with the links between nations? These two types of explanation are not unrelated, differing in emphasis rather than in kind (Singer 1976). Nevertheless, the contrasting focus in each one has given rise to two broad types of explanation, namely, the liberal position widely associated with the so-called 'developmentalists' and the more radical perspective.

The liberal position

Debate among liberal academics and practitioners has focused on the post-independence practice of development within African states, the leadership structure, the strategies pursued and the problems of policy implementation. Discussions centring around the selection of incorrect choices or the wrong strategic thrust are widespread and related back to theoretical principles. These derive from a tradition of orthodox development theory dating back to the 1950s and 1960s which is reviewed in recent literature (Brookfield 1978; Harriss & Harriss 1979; 1981).

Early approaches were dominated by the concept of successive 'stages of economic growth' in which the process of development was seen as a linear path along which countries must pass (Rostow 1960). Underdevelopment was identified as a condition resulting from a lack of internal resources in which, through productive investment, economic growth would be achieved (Lewis 1955). At intra-national level the concept of economic dualism proved a persuasive prescription for economic development. Initially formulated by W. Arthur Lewis (1954) it considered the changes involved in the transition from a non-capitalist mode of production to a mature capitalist mode. Ranis and Fei (1961) formalised it as a normative model of rural-urban movement while Ann Seidman (1972) used it to describe the internal structure of the East African economies. In practical terms during the era of economic growth in the 1960s it encouraged state and private capital investment in the modern sector of African economies.

Since the end of the first development decade, however, the failure of conventional economic indicators to represent the plight of the vast majority of Third World populations and the inadequacy of traditional theory to account for these conditions have led to important changes in the 'Orthodox' tradition. Among the most significant is a recognition of the international dimension of development and underdevelopment, notably the detrimental effects of conditions external to the developing countries on their economic growth. With this the need has been acknowledged to reconcile sustained economic growth with a concern for the redistribution of income and assets in favour of the poor both at international and intranational levels (Chenery et al. 1974). The Brandt Report (*ICIDI* 1980),

13

published at the end of the second development decade, represented the culmination of this influential view. Thus there is no lack of awareness among liberals of the considerable difficulties faced by African states in their drive to realise their ideals: not only the problems of disunity, ethnic diversity and political instability (Akintoye 1980) but also the constraints to action at international level associated with patterns of trade, aid and foreign investment.

Perhaps the most significant and positive feature of this approach, however, is a concern not only with the problems faced by and the shortcomings of African regimes but also with constructive recommendation. A liberal belief in the value of intervention through the planning mechanism pervades this literature and has since the 1960s promoted efforts towards realistic solutions to the problems of persistent poverty. It was a concern at international level with income inequalities which led, for example, to the setting up in 1969 of the World Employment Programme by the International Labour Organisation (ILO) and, under its auspices, a Jobs and Skills Programme for Africa (JASPA). Advisory missions to African countries have followed – Zambia (1977). Swaziland (1977), Lesotho (1979), Tanzania (1980) – to assist national policy-makers to improve employment opportunities and income distribution. Perhaps the most widely documented of these is the employment mission to Kenya in 1972, the report of which (ILO 1972) in challenging the traditional emphasis on the material economy, became a blueprint for the so-called basic needs approach to development. (See, for example, *IDS Bulletin* (Brighton) 1978 Vol. 9, no. 4.) Since the early 1970s the International Bank for Reconstruction and Development (World Bank) has similarly embraced a philosophy of 'redistribution with growth' which is reflected in its frequent missions to the African countries (cf. World Bank 1974; 1975; 1978a) emphasising projects targeted directly on the rural and urban poor (Tendler 1982).

The radical perspective

In contrast to this liberal approach attempts have been made to explain the continued underdevelopment of Africa by reference to historical processes within a structuralist framework in which Africa's position in the world capitalist system is seen to be fundamental. Rather than offering an alternative development path this approach presents a critique of orthodox development theories and strategies by criticising their failure to take into account the international roots of African underdevelopment and hence their inability to prescribe viable solutions (Arrighi & Saul 1968; Leys 1975; Rodney 1972). The analysis has derived considerable impetus from the writings of Marx (1885, 1967), Lenin (1916, 1964) and Rosa Luxemburg (1913, 1951; 1921, 1972) on class exploitation, international capitalism and imperialism, while more recently the work of Baran (1957), Frank (1967; 1974) Bettelheim (1972) and Sunkel (1977) on the theory of non-colonialism and dependency has been influential.

14

These writers contend that the historical structure of relations between Africa and Europe, derived from the spread of international capitalism during the colonial period and based on unequal exchange, created economic dependence and an unequal social structure within the colonial territories. Despite the achievement of political independence it is suggested that the persistence of inter-national and intra-national inequalities derives from the fact that Africa's dependent position within the international capitalist system has not changed and is indeed maintained by the interests of the indigenous controlling élites. A pattern of investment, trade and aid exists and motives are ascribed which reinforce the inherited 'structures of domination' (Arrighi & Saul 1973: 7). Emphasis on class forces and class formation within the African territories is fundamental to this approach. While critical of the strategies adopted, as indeed are the liberals, proponents of the more radical persuasion regard these strategies as reflecting and reinforcing the power of the major interest groups, notably foreign capital in combination with the emerging indigenous élites. Motivations are ascribed to this small leading minority which are socially divisive and designed to benefit and preserve their interests at the expense of the majority. Genuine progress within the existing centre-periphery framework and state structure is therefore seen to be impossible. Twenty years ago Dumont's (1966) *False Start in Africa* predicted the exploitation of independent Africa betrayed by the new leadership intent on increasing their privileges. In a follow-up study based on the same framework, *Stranglehold on Africa*, Dumont & Mottin (1983) review the outcome – rural poverty and ever-increasing urban shanty towns – in selected states (Zambia, Tanzania, Senegal, Ivory Coast, Guinea Bissau).

This approach suggests that as a result of these structures the very conditions from which African leaders sought to break away on independence, namely, external control, economic dependence and internal inequalities, have persisted and perpetuated underdevelopment. A leading African nationalist Kwame Nkrumah (1965: ix) clearly articulated the feelings of the continent when, during the early years of independence, he emphasised the need to avoid 'neo-colonialism' where 'The State which is subject to it is, in theory, independent and has all the outward trappings of international sovereignty. In reality its economic system and thus its political policy is directed from outside.' Ironically these are the very conditions which are consistently identified by radical academics. Concepts such as 'neo-colonialism' and 'false decolonisation' have become the accepted terminology to describe the contemporary political economy of the continent (cf. Arrighi & Saul 1973; Cabral 1973; Fanon 1967; Saul 1979).

Development theory and the geographer

What is the relevance of this theoretical discussion to the geographer? If we interpret space as a structure created by society then there are a number of issues with which we should be concerned. These include changes in both the administrative and economic organisation of space as a result of the penetration of forces from beyond the continent and their interaction with internal structures (Mabogunje 1980a). The impact of spatial reorganisation on the lives of the African people is also a central concern. In this regard identifying changes in social and spatial access to the means of production and to social provision is of critical importance and with this, the patterns of social and spatial inequality which have emerged. Equally important is the way in which individuals and groups use space within the constraints of the politico-economic system to maintain social interaction and to sustain their economic activities – through migration, the organisation of settlement and the use of environmental resources.

Investigation of issues such as these requires that we explore the range of social processes which operate at contrasting but interlocking geographical scales to influence the organisation and use of space. It is in this context that theoretical discussion within the social sciences informs our explanations. From the two contrasting theoretical perspectives outlined above a number of themes emerge. Both approaches stress the importance of the key actors in the process of decision-making – the African leadership, the strategies defined, the role of the bureaucracy and the problems of policy implementation. Both stress the need to place these decision-makers within the broader international economic system including the constraints to action imposed by foreign trade, international aid and direct foreign investment within the African states. From the radical perspective we derive two additional concerns. The importance of historical processes in explaining the contemporary problems of African development and underdevelopment are stressed and in particular the influence of capitalist penetration on the African economy and society. The role of different interest groups in influencing the direction and speed of change is linked to class formation and used in turn to explain persistent problems of poverty and inequality.

How then do we proceed? While the primary concerns of this book are the changes which have taken place in Africa since independence, we must also be aware of the legacy on which contemporary African political economy and society is based. The nature of the links between past processes and present circumstances needs to be established and for this reason we can with justification begin with the past – not only to satisfy the intellectual curiosity of the student of African affairs but also because of the contemporary relevance of historical processes.

Historical processes

Central to the academic debate over Africa's contemporary economic and social problems is the apparently dialectical relationship between Western development and African underdevelopment. It has been discussed at the continental level (cf. Ake 1981a; Rodney 1972), within regions of the continent (Amin 1973; Brett 1973;

Szentes 1976) and within individual countries (Howard 1978; Williams 1976). Two points are at issue, first the extent to which the expansion of Western capitalism was due to exploitation of the African territories and second how far foreign penetration into Africa produced distorted, dependent economies and disrupted the social system. In assessing the former Laclau (1971) argues that capitalist expansion depended on the maintenance of pre-capitalist modes of production in peripheral areas. But it must be borne in mind that the degree of investment in and trading with the continent varied greatly between African countries and was relatively small overall during much of the colonial period in comparison with elsewhere. The types and scale of activities and investments must therefore be scrutinised for different colonial territories. Such a focus links with the second point, namely, the economic and social structures which evolved under foreign political control.

Models of internal economic structure

The economic structure of the African territories within which export production expanded has been a topic of major interest. It is widely argued that a dual economy became characteristic comprising two competing sectors – one dominant and serving colonial interests but dependent for its proper functioning on exploitation of the second, namely, the traditional sector (Gutkind & Wallerstein 1976). Arising from this pattern a model of dialectical dualism has been envisaged – very different from that originally proposed by Lewis (1954) – in which the second sector through conflict with and penetration by the first gradually became distorted though nevertheless conserved. The debate focuses not on the sphere of exchange and international links typical of dependence theory, rather it concentrates on the sphere of production, that is, the modes and social relations of production operating within the African territories which gave rise to the system of exchange. The non-capitalist modes were not destroyed through capitalist penetration, rather they were transformed in different ways through interaction with the capitalist mode to meet the varying needs of capitalist production – notably peasant products and labour power. This process of interaction and transformation took different forms across the continent and has prompted various attempts to classify what Cliffe (1976) refers to as 'the articulation of modes of production' in socio-economic and regional terms.

Political and economic institutions

Other studies have concentrated on the key actors, both internal and external, involved in Africa's transformation. Some have sought to determine the precise function of the colonial administration in this economic transformation through

17

an investigation of its relationship with private foreign investment and the indigenous population. In West Africa the work of Amin (1973), Howard (1978) and Smith (1979) is of this nature. Smith (1979) in a case study from Nigeria questions the conventional belief that in West Africa the State played merely an 'enabling role' by opening up the existing economic potential of the peasant farmer to international capital and trade. She argues strongly that economic and political processes were directly linked, with the colonial government actively intervening to control the changes which took place. In East Africa several writers have concentrated on the particular influence of foreign firms including the large multinationals in the process of capital accumulation. Swainson (1980), for example, outlines their contribution to capital development after 1918 together with the underlying political conditions which influenced the direction of change in Kenya.

Class formation

Discussion of these institutions and agencies is closely linked with analysis of the new social forces which emerged as a result of foreign penetration and which became major stimuli for change within particular regions and countries. Many studies have sought evidence for the evolution of a class structure in African society under the influence of the capitalist mode of production (Amin 1971; Nkrumah 1970b). The emergence of explicit class divisions between different groups such as the bourgeoisie, the proletariat and the peasantry has been much discussed and the complexity of social change widely acknowledged (see Sandbrook & Cohen 1975). The role of different indigenous groups in the process of underdevelopment has also been studied. Leys (1978), for example, suggests that a key factor behind this process in Kenya was the growth of an indigenous African bourgeoisie who prevented the productive investment of the surplus locally. The changing characteristics of the African peasantry under foreign influence during the colonial period has also received attention (Bernstein 1978; Palmer & Parsons 1977) including the wide-ranging effects of their involvement in the migrant labour system (Arrighi 1970; Cohen 1975; Szentes 1964).

We shall return to these various themes and issues later. At this point it is sufficient to stress that for one reason in particular they warrant investigation: namely, their direct relevance to discussion of post-colonial Africa. The institutional structures introduced from outside affected the political organisation of space and the spatial concentration of economic opportunities and activities within countries. They determined the legacy on which newly independent governments had little option but to build. The nature of these externally induced structures and the contrasting interpretations of their social and spatial impact must be explored. In this context the relevance of concepts such as dualism and class formation becomes important as we seek to explain regional disparities in income and welfare and changes in the lives of the African peoples in both rural and urban areas.

Issues in independent Africa

It has been stressed by many writers (cf. Cabral 1973; Saul 1979) that the nature of the post-colonial state, under the influence of the international bourgeoisie in combination with the emerging internal classes, has been fundamental in perpetuating dependency and internal inequalities. 'The problem of the nature of the state created after independence is perhaps the secret of the failure of African independence' (Cabral 1973:83). Reference made to the 'State' here relates not to a narrow definition of the bureaucracy or to the public sector but to the broader political, economic and social institutions created out of colonially defined boundaries. By grounding the discussion firmly in the internal structures and institutions which have emerged from the decolonisation process a useful complement is provided to the global perspective characteristic of the dependency school and common ground is found with the more liberal position outlined above.

From the viewpoint of the geographer focus on the state is also important for two main reasons. In seeking to identify the major agents of change – the critical decision-makers, the leading interest groups whose attitudes, values and practices have influenced the environment of Africa, its economy and society since independence – the post-colonial state provides an essential context for such investigations. This derives not from a geographical obsession with spatial structure and regional division, that is, from the belief that space is the context for society, rather it arises from the conviction that spatial patterns and inequalities are societal in origin. The political economy does indeed have a profound influence on the spatial organisation of the material economy. In view of this the post-colonial state represents an important spatial unit through which to elucidate the interacting forces which have both maintained and sought to change the character of the continent since independence.

On this issue there is in fact broad agreement between those of a liberal and radical persuasion which leads to the second main reason for focusing on the state, namely that it provides an important point of contact between alternative development perspectives. It provides a framework within which to discuss the controversial issues surrounding decolonisation and dependency. What is clear from contemporary literature is that evaluations of post-colonial change in Africa can be made on several different levels and from different focuses. For example, the political economy of individual states cannot be fully explained without reference to the broader continental and international context including changes in the costs of energy and capital, in world demand for raw materials and in technology transfer. At the same time lack of progress is partly due to internal politics which have shaken the stability necessary for effective development planning. The inherent institutional structure and resource base have in turn constrained the decision-making process. The policies themselves and their implementation at regional and local levels are also open to criticism. The nation state provides a useful point of reference within which these different scales and

19

focuses of discussion can be accommodated and resolved. As Shaw (1982: 241) suggests 'African states are not robots that merely react to external inputs and instructions'. They are the point at which both supra-national and intra-national forces come together.

Development policy – political processes

Analysis of regional inequality, of rural change and urban development, of how people make a living and organise their lives within these different environments cannot be explained without reference to the broader set of forces by which their environment is shaped, in particular the ideals surrounding the formulation of government policy and the constraints on government action. Certain writers, notably Fanon (1967), in assessing the conditions under which individual states attained political freedom sought at the time to use this evidence as a predictor of their future success in achieving full economic independence from the metropolitan powers. In doing so nationalist rebellion and an associated mass movement for freedom were regarded as critical in preventing 'false decolonisation'. On the basis of this argument Cliffe (1975: 140), in reviewing the independence period of the two East African states, Kenya and Tanzania, suggests that the former with the experience of violent conflict arising from the settler economy should have been more successful than the latter whose political freedom followed the more general African pattern of 'decolonisation in areas which have not been sufficiently shaken by the struggle for liberation'. In the light of some twenty years of political independence in these two states and in African countries in general it is apparent that patterns of social and economic change have been shaped by the prevailing ideology and practices of those with political influence and economic power. However, these have been conditioned not only by historical circumstances and the form in which liberation was achieved but also by contemporary internal and international events.

The links between ideology, policy and practice can be characterised as follows. First, identifying particular political, economic and social goals depends initially on clarifying a particular blueprint for development (or ideology) defining desirable conditions and the means by which to achieve them. Second, commitment to achieving these goals depends upon an acceptable approach by which to translate ideology into practice through the institutional structure and resource allocation between sectors and regions. It is the gulf which has emerged between ideology, policy and practice which lies at the base of many contemporary problems within African countries and which has given rise to the theoretical debate outlined above.

As a framework within which to proceed, Fig. 2.2 summarises some of the issues and agencies which interact to influence government decision-making and policy implementation. In seeking to explain the social and spatial outcomes it is to these issues and agencies that our attention should turn. The colonial legacy of political, economic and social structures within the African states provides the

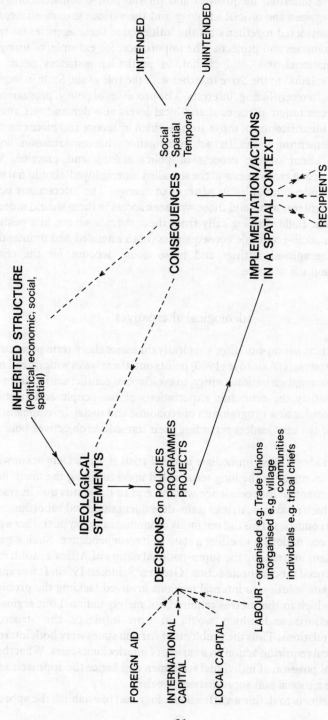

Figure 2.2 Structural framework

21

context for the inherited inequalities and for the post-colonial ideology. The relationship between the official ideology and the various groups affected by it needs to be considered together with the influence of these agencies on specific policies, programmes and projects. The importance, for example, of foreign aid, and of international and local capital, in particular instances needs to be considered in relation to the State together with the role of the State in mediating their various, often conflicting, interests. The processes of policy, programme and project implementation at regional and local levels also demand our attention, including the identification of those groups which influence and place constraints upon the implementing bodies. In such investigations due consideration should be given to the client in the process of policy-making and practice. Village communities, urban employees and the so-called 'unemployed' should not be seen merely as dependent variables in patterns of change. The interactions between those who control resources and those who seek access to them should indeed be a central concern. Following logically from these themes we are in a position to interpret their socio-economic consequences (both intended and unintended) in particular geographical settings and in so doing account for the changing organisation and use of space.

Ideological alternatives

On independence, nation-building was clearly the major short-term preoccupation of all African states. As Akintoye (1980) points out, there was a widespread need to preserve and strengthen national unity, to avoid social conflict arising from ethnic rivalries, to satisfy the economic expectations of the people and to mobilise popular support for new programmes of economic and social development. Thus the rhetoric of the new leaders regarding their immediate objectives bore strong similarities.

Over and above these immediate internal goals it was widely acknowledged that their achievement in the long term rested upon fulfilling the much broader objective of economic independence with an end to the status quo in trade and investment which rendered African states dependent upon and subordinate to the industrialised countries. This did not imply economic isolation but rather a greater equality between nations – in effect a state of interdependence. Such a goal was vitally important in stressing the supra-national nature of Africa's problems, and as a result the need for corporate action (Green & Seidman 1968). It was apparent that the ultimate solution to internal tensions involved tackling the problems of dependency which in themselves required not merely national but regional and continental efforts and which would in turn influence the structure of international relations. Thus the problems of African states were both interrelated and hierarchical requiring action on a variety of interlocking scales. What then was the ideological position of individual statesmen and hence the approach adopted towards these national and supra-national goals?

In their efforts to define an official ideology and to establish the appropriate politico-economic institutions African leaders had before them as a guide two markedly different approaches to development, each one based on a different set of assumptions and values concerning the types of changes to be encouraged and the methods employed to achieve them. The capitalist experience of Western countries, derived from the classical economics of Adam Smith through Keynesian macro-economics to post-1945 neo-classical theory, was influential in emphasising the importance of economic growth in development (Sunkel 1977). The basic assumption of this capitalist model is that private ownership of the principal means of production and free competition between owners for a share of the surplus provides the most efficient means of allocating scarce resources and achieving economic growth. Free competition ensures that the community as a whole benefits and as a consequence government influence should be supportive rather than inhibiting. It was under a system similar to this that African states had evolved during the colonial period.

Among the major obstacles to the economic growth and development of the newly independent countries of the continent, according to this model, was a lack of the three basic means of production: capital, technology and skills. The aim of the State should therefore be to encourage the import of capital, to stimulate local and foreign savings and investment and to ensure that capital accumulation be allowed to proceed unhindered. The role of state institutions should include providing positive incentives to investment through tax concessions, a flexible wages policy and provision of the necessary social and economic infrastructure including education and training facilities. The rationale behind such a strategy was that through the range of economic opportunities generated, living standards for all would rise. While such a system would inevitably reproduce Western class structures these should be regarded as beneficial since through private ownership of the principal means of production the economy would expand and benefit all. Cohen and Daniel (1981: 222) point out that this type of strategy 'has occurred in virtually all of Africa's capitalist-orientated nations', notably in Nigeria, Kenya and Ivory Coast.

The socialist or centralist approach also originated in Europe but emerged as a direct reaction to capitalism. Formulated by Marx and Engels in the nineteenth century in response to the problems of industrialisation which capitalist expansion had brought about, the first attempt to implement such a system was in the Soviet Union after 1917 and coincided with the country's era of rapid economic growth. After the Second World War a similar model was adopted in Eastern Europe and more recently in a growing number of developing countries such as Cuba, North Korea, and South Yemen, the primary assumption being that only through state ownership of the means of production and state control over the distribution of the surplus could a balance be achieved between rapid growth, greater equality and higher living standards for all. Such ideas were widely discussed in Europe during the 1940s and 1950s when future leaders such as Kwame Nkrumah and Julius Nyerere were studying in Britain and Senghor in France. The conditions of colonialism and the need for a post-colonial ideology provided a suitable environment for such ideas to flourish.

23

According to the socialist model African states were underdeveloped due to external control and the associated internal class divisions. They should therefore seek to socialise the economic relations of production through progressive state control over the means of production, either directly or indirectly through collectives or co-operatives. By this process the State should have the authority to plan output and distribution to ensure rapid economic growth and higher living standards for all. Coupled with internal reorganisation the State should also restructure its links with international capital in order to reduce external dependency. The Tanzanian experiment in socialism is perhaps the most widely discussed example within the continent. Reference should also be made to the doctrine of 'humanism' in Zambia (Kandeke 1977) and, since the late 1960s, to the Marxist-Leninist tradition of scientific socialism in such states as Congo-Brazzaville (1969), Somalia (1970), Benin (1974), Madagascar (1975), Ethiopia (1976), and the former Portuguese colonial empire (Mozambique, Angola, Guinea-Bissau) whose liberation movements were informed by Marxism-Leninism.

Young (1982) classifies African regimes today in a threefold typology (Table 2.2). He identifies those states which have pursued a market economy or capitalist policy though generally denying any ideological attachments to such a system. The second group he calls populist socialist comprising states which espouse a socialist orientation but either do not stress or expressly reject Marxism. The countries of the third group are identified by an explicit commitment to Marxism-Leninism as the state ideology. In drawing up this classification Young is careful to emphasise that it is based on the ideological selfascription of the regime's leadership. Various alternative typologies have also been offered. For example, Wiles (1982) draws a distinction between what he refers to as 'the new Communist Third World' including Angola, Mozamibique, Ethiopia and the People's Republic of South Yemen, and 'the Marginals' within which he includes Benin, the Congo, Madagascar and Somalia.

Table 2.2 Classification of selected African regimes (Source: Young 1982)

AFRO-MARXIST GROUP	POPULIST SOCIALIST GROUP	AFRICAN CAPITALIST GROUP
Angola	Ghana	Ivory Coast
Benin	Guinea	Kenya
Congo	Mali	Nigeria
Ethiopia	Tanzania	Malawi
Madagascar		Zaire
Mozambique		
Somalia		

Development planning – the bureaucracy

In studying individual states and making comparisons between states an important distinction is needed between ideology and politics. While the ideology of development has shifted only slightly in many countries since independence by contrast internal politics have proved to be highly volatile. The implementation of stated ideals has thus proved more difficult in practice. Nevertheless in spite of inter-state differences in national politico-economic orientation and internal political instability there has been a common commitment to state involvement in social and economic development through the planning mechanism (Seidman 1980). All African governments have recognised the need for central planning and in doing so have engaged in development planning which seeks to achieve long-term improvements in economic and social conditions.

Of course State planning in general and development planning in particular are not exclusive features of post-independence Africa. In 1919 Ghana (then the Gold Coast) had its first ten-year economic plan and indeed development planning became standard British colonial policy following the Colonial Development and Welfare Act 1940. However, it is apparent that the rationale behind and the scope of post-colonial planning is somewhat different from that of the colonial period. Indeed, since independence it has become an important symbol of political freedom. As Green (1965: 17) observed in the early years of African independence, 'the rapid post-war surge of colonial public expenditure plans was closely related to attempts first to counter the popularity of the nationalist movements and later to strengthen the economic infrastructure during the terminal colonial phase prior to independence'. They were therefore primarily concerned with public expenditure. By contrast post-colonial national planning 'is viewed by almost all African states as one of the standard attributes of sovereignty'. Faced with a common set of problems the planning mechanism was seen by the African leadership and the leading political parties as a necessary instrument for achieving their national goals. A Kenya Government document of 1965 (Republic of Kenya 1965:11) stated firmly that 'African socialism must rely on planning to determine the appropriate uses of productive resources [and] on a range of controls to ensure that plans are carried out'. Planning symbolised the effort needed to improve social and economic life and also represented a means by which to bring it about (Sutton 1961).

Plans and their implementation involve the bureaucracy both at national and local levels and require co-operation between ministries and departments at these alternate scales. Thus to be effective the necessary institutional machinery and administrative structures had to be strengthened. As a result since independence the bureaucracies have expanded with skilled personnel appointed and a range of ministries, departments and/or planning units set up to devise, co-ordinate and implement planning programmes. In some states, for example in Ghana, a separate Planning Commission was established after independence, while in Kenya a new Ministry of Economic Planning and Development was set up. A similar initiative was taken in Botswana in 1967 when the Ministry of Development Planning was created out of a small Economic Planning Unit which had been established within the Ministry of Finance shortly before independence. In order to improve co-ordination these two ministries were in fact merged in 1971 to form a new Ministry of Finance and Development Planning.

25

Dimensions of development planning

Several different levels and types of development planning have been employed by the African bureaucracies and distinguished on the basis of their scope and the time scale over which they operate. Livingstone and Ord (1980) identify three main levels (Fig. 2.3). While not all forms operating at these different levels are directly spatial in nature, each one through its impact in particular sectors, economic activities or social groups, influences both social and spatial disparities in income and welfare.

Macro-planning is concerned with the economy as a whole at the national level. It has given rise to long-term perspective plans which outline the broad direction of the economy over a period of some fifteen to twenty years. Within this framework medium-term plans covering periods of four to seven years have become a regular preoccupation of the African bureaucracies. In the early 1960s five of the economically larger states – Ghana, Kenya, Nigeria, Tanzania and Uganda – launched major five- to seven-year Development Plans and in the case of Ghana, Tanzania and Uganda they formed the first components of longer perspective plans. The Tanganyika First Five-Year Plan for Economic and Social Development 1964–69 (United Republic of Tanganyika and Zanzibar 1964) was linked with fifteen-year projections up to 1980, while in Uganda a fifteen-year perspective plan from mid-1966 to mid-1981 was accompanied by the Second five-Year Plan, Work for Progress, 1966–71 (Republic of Uganda 1966).

Secondary-level planning has been adopted in many states to formulate

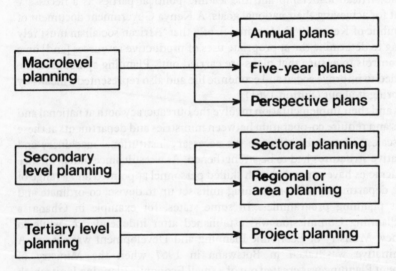

Figure 2.3 The three levels of planning (after Livingstone and Ord 1980: 542)

policies for the development of specific sectors of the economy (sectoral planning) such as agriculture, industry, education and social services. The details of such strategies have frequently been worked out by officials in the main operational ministries with responsibility over the sectors concerned – for example, the Ministries of Agriculture, Commerce and Industry, Education and Health – the plans approved then being communicated to officers of the respective ministries in the field. Responsibility for co-ordinating these separate strategies and activities has been with the central ministries involved in national planning.

The critical importance of inter-sectoral and, by implication, interministerial co-ordination to solve particular problems has become increasingly apparent during the last two decades and has promoted new initiatives within the bureaucracy. Co-ordinated rural development has become a major issue in many countries to overcome the problems of agricultural decline and rural poverty. As a result appropriate machinery has been required to co-ordinate the activities of the various operational ministries involved. In Botswana a top level Rural Development Council was established in 1972 for this purpose comprising permanent secretaries of the operational ministries concerned plus representatives of local government together with a representative of the private bodies involved in rural development. The Council was assigned the responsibility of reviewing all plans for rural development, for advising ministries on appropriate initiatives and making recommendations to Cabinet. A separate Rural Development Unit within the central Ministry of Finance and Development Planning was set up to service this Council. In Botswana's latest National Development Plan 1979–85 (Republic of Botswana 1980), an additional complementary strategy to rural development, namely, employment creation is being emphasised. A similar top-level council has been created to provide impetus to this strategy together with a secretariat in the form of a new Employment Policy Unit based once again in the Ministry of Finance and Development Planning.

Reference made above to planning for a rural environment links with the other main branch of secondary-level planning, one with a specifically spatial dimension, namely, regional/district or area planning. Although all forms and levels of activity within the planning process have an impact on the organisation of space this type of state intervention is specifically geographical in orientation. (It is discussed in detail in Ch. 6.)

Finally, reference should be made to tertiary-level planning which focuses on the detail of individual projects within or between sectors including their identification and appraisal and the procedures for implementation at local level. Responsibility for these various tasks has to varying degrees involved the central ministries, the operational ministries and regional/district officers depending on the scale and scope of the projects concerned. In the case of large-scale multi-sectoral schemes such as the major river basin schemes in Nigeria special river basin authorities have been set up.

Bureaucratic influence from national to local level is clearly an important dimension to be considered in assessing regional change within African states. The different levels of planning identified above are in theory complementary and indeed the medium-term development plans produced at regular intervals by African states since independence have incorporated statements derived from secondary and tertiary planning. For the observer of African affairs a key question is the effectiveness of the rhetoric and the institutional machinery established. In answering such a question two issues arise, namely, the validity of the assumptions on which bureaucratic intervention is based and the political commitment to that intervention. Implicit in development planning is the belief that the State can enable improvements to be made at local level by establishing the appropriate institutional machinery. Leys (1972: 75) wrote more than a decade ago, however, that the conventional plan document is merely useful in 'providing politicians with a magic book to brandish at political meetings or at consultations with aid donors'. Conyers (1982: 3), by contrast, stresses that in recent years planning has moved from an isolated activity to become 'part of a complex process of 'development'' involving close interaction between policy-making, planning and implementation. It is against the background of debate such as this that the geographer seeks to understand the social and spatial outcomes of state planning and in doing so provides a link between activities in the capital city and the countryside. Forging this link depends, however, on yet another dimension – the international.

Africa and the international community

Changing patterns of economic activity, of income distribution and welfare both within and between the African countries cannot be explained solely in terms of internal forces. Critical in development theory is the need to relate national and intra-national change to the forces at work within the broader international community. Powerful institutions in the form of foreign private investors have sought to exploit the resource potential of the continent and in doing so have had a significant impact on the economic organisation of space through their control over the means of production and investment decisions. Reference should also be made to the structure of Africa's foreign trade and with it to the concept of unequal exchange which pervades development literature. The efforts made through selected international bodies including the major aid agencies to modify the terms of trade and with these the internal economic structure of African states are also important. External forces have affected patterns of social differentiation and spatial concentration within countries and in turn the cultural landscape. The significance of such changes depends, however, upon the context within which they are analysed. This must include underlying theories concerning the relationship between foreign influence and development.

Much theoretical debate centres around the nature and desirability of foreign presence in Africa including the relationship between the structure of Africa's foreign trade and development. External interactions have on the one hand been encouraged as an important stimulus to growth and criticised on the other hand as a source of continued international and internal inequalities. Adedeji (1981: 20) offers the following description of the African territories at the time of political independence:

> Colonies were even more firmly locked into a dependent relationship with one metropolitan country. Their economies were increasingly geared to the export production of a very limited range of commodities and the importation of a wide range of consumer goods. The manufacturing sector was therefore severely restricted. Africans were restrained by virtue of racial discrimination, educational disabilities and financial circumstances from participating in effective decision-making processes, and – particularly where mining and European-managed agriculture dominated – were often barred from the most profitable areas of production and trade.

His words highlight the inequalities in access to the means of production and decision-making within African states which he relates to three dimensions of external dependence. These are, first, trade dependence – a heavy reliance on exports to generate national income, the geographical concentration of this trade, the commodity specialisation of exports and a reliance on imported manufactures; second, resource dependence in the form of foreign capital and skills in the export sector; and third, direct economic dependence – a monopoly of leading economic positions controlled by foreign investors and, by implication, a lack of citizen control over major economic decisions (Livingstone & Ord 1980). These interpretations of Africa's interactions with the international community are both critical and pessimistic. But are they accurate? Is the state merely a passive victim of external forces?

External demand, vulnerability and economic growth

Since the colonial period the exchange of goods through international trade has comprised a significant share of the national income of African states. Moreover, the export earnings acquired from exchanging locally produced goods for foreign goods continues to be a critical source of the finance needed to raise domestic production and incomes. Thus international trading relations are vital in influencing internal social and economic change.

The role of international trade in the development process forms part of a broader discourse over outward-looking and inward-looking development strategies (Morton & Tulloch 1977). Two issues in particular preoccupy economists studying the theory of international trade. First, on the supply side, the factors which influence the kinds of goods and services a country imports and exports. This is associated with the theory of comparative advantage of the classical economists, Adam Smith and David Ricardo, which argues that trade specialisation acts as an important 'engine of growth'. The second issue concentrates on the demand side and is concerned with a country's ability to profit

29

from trade as determined by the terms of trade. It is on this issue that the greatest dissatisfaction has been expressed by the developing countries as a whole and the African states in particular (Table 2.3).

International circumstances continue to influence the commodity composition of imports and exports and the geographical concentration of foreign trade. As in the colonial period, African countries remain primary exporting economies. The value of primary production as a source of foreign exchange and in relation to overall output is confirmed by data on export earnings from a range of commodities and by comparing the contribution of the major industrial sectors to gross domestic product (GDP). Table 2.4 indicates the limited range of primary commodities on which the African countries depend. The exploitation of land resources for agriculture either through peasant production or plantations is clearly critical to income generation.

It should be pointed out that, although it is contrary to orthodox economic theory, 'specialisation' in primary production and a reliance on a few primary exports as a major source of foreign exchange have come to be regarded as an

Table 2.3 Terms of trade of selected African countries (Source: World Bank 1984: 234)

	(1980 = 100)	
	1979	1982
Chad	100	99
Ethiopia	139	74
Mali	107	102
Zaire	113	81
Malawi	111	106
Burkina Faso (formerly Upper Volta)	113	97
Uganda	103	74
Tanzania	105	86
Somalia	116	111
Benin	115	75
Central African Republic	99	90
Niger	112	89
Togo	108	112
Ghana	136	61
Kenya	108	87
Sierra Leone	121	84
Sudan	98	85
Mauritania	101	97
Liberia	121	92
Senegal	110	89
Zambia	118	72
Zimbabwe	81	105
Nigeria	67	103
Cameroon	119	71
Ivory Coast	119	91
Congo, People's Republic	74	110
Angola	74	104

Table 2.4 Leading primary exports of selected African countries in 1980 as a percentage of the total exports of each country (Source: *United Nations Statistical Yearbook* 1981)

	FOOD AND BEVERAGES	RAW MATERIALS	FUELS	VEGETABLE OILS
Central African Republic	28.4	54.3	—	—
Ghana	75.5	14.8	—	—
Ivory Coast	59.9	15.0	4.4	2.1
Kenya	38.8	2.3	33.3	3.2
Nigeria	2.9	—	94.8	—
Sierra Leone	9.7	60.8	—	—
Tanzania	41.4	15.5	—	—
Burkina Faso (formerly Upper Volta)	34.5	47.9	—	—
Zambia	—	91.1	—	—

unsatisfactory basis for economic development (Myint 1980). Nevertheless, since independence this specialisation has also contributed to a dramatic improvement in the economic fortunes of selected countries. In a world where mineral and energy resources are highly prized the discovery and development of these natural resources, either by foreign companies or by joint state-foreign enterprise, have substantially altered the balance of economic power between states and made an important contribution to the post-independence economic growth of the countries concerned. The exploitation of Nigeria's oil and natural gas deposits since the early 1960s and those of the Congo since the late 1970s are important illustrations. Botswana represents a further illustration.

Mineral exploitation began only in 1967 in Botswana with copper and diamonds, the latter controlled by the major South African mining corporation De Beers. Since then a dramatic change has taken place in the sectoral contribution to GDP and in the size of the GDP as a whole. In 1965 GDP per capita was at a world low of US$86 while by contrast in 1977/78 it had risen to US$547, well above the African average and comparable with Nigeria. Isaksen (1981) in a study of the changing composition of GDP between 1964 and 1978 clearly illustrates the vulnerability of an economy such as Botswana in a semi-arid environment which until relatively recently depended in large measure on agricultural production for its wealth. He points out that on independence (in 1966) the low GDP figure resulted from a calamitous drought which destroyed much of the country's valuable cattle herd (beef then being the country's principal export) and severely affected subsistence agriculture with serious consequences for the majority of the population. However the restoration of normal rainfall in 1966/67 and hence the revival of the livestock sector resulted in a growth of GDP at a spectacular average rate of 10.6 per cent between 1965 and 1969. Isaksen then outlines further developments during the 1970s and notably the decline in the contribution of agriculture as the mining sector has expanded (Table 2.5), an important structural change which has reduced the country's dependence on the vagaries of the environment.

In spite of these changes the continued fragile base of this primary exporting

31

Table 2.5 Changes in GDP in Botswana, 1965–77 (Source: Isaksen 1981: 10)

	1965 to 1968/69	1968/69 to 1973/74	1973/74 to 1977/78	1965 to 1977/78
Per cent annual real increase in GDP	10.6	22.0	—	11.4
Total increase in GDP (P million at current prices)*	18.3	146.3	135.7	300.3
Contribution of the following sectors to this total increase				
Agriculture	12.1	46.0	–2.4	55.7
Mining and related sectors	—	37.9	38.0	75.9
Government	5.8	8.7	33.6	48.1
All other sectors	0.4	53.7	66.5	120.6

*The national currency in Botswana is the Pula(P). P = US$1.27.

economy is reflected in its dependence on fluctuations in world market prices and on foreign capital and technology for mineral exploitation. External vulnerability has indeed been widespread among African states. Many have experienced a slow growth in export earnings from primary commodities and a deterioration in their terms of trade (Ake 1981a; United Nations Secretariat 1980; World Bank 1984). National income and government revenue have in turn been affected making the fulfilment of development plans more difficult.

International agreements and overseas aid

Attempts have nevertheless been made at the international level to improve trading relations. The General Agreement on Tariffs and Trade (GATT), to which twenty-six African states[1] are contracting parties, provides a forum for discussion as does the United Nations Conference on trade and Development (UNCTAD). The former has sought to stimulate trade by, among other things, reducing protectionism in the North. Hitherto, success has been limited. Since 1964 UNCTAD has also sought to improve the terms of trade of the developing countries through, for example, measures to stabilise export earnings. At the fourth meeting held in Nairobi in May 1976 agreement was reached to establish a Common Fund to finance stabilisation schemes for a total of eighteen primary commodities. Of these, ten 'core' commodities singled out for priority are of

[1]Contracting parties to the GATT in sub-Saharan Africa as at March 1982 included Benin, Burundi, Cameroon, Central African Republic, Chad, Congo, Gabon, Gambia, Ghana, Ivory Coast, Kenya, Madagascar, Malawi, Mauritania, Mauritius, Niger, Nigeria, Rwanda, Senegal, Sierra Leone, Tanzania, Togo, Upper Volta (now Burkina Faso), Zaire, Zambia, Zimbabwe. The following countries maintained a *de facto* application to the GATT pending final decisions as to their future commercial policy: Angola, Botswana, Guinea-Bissau, Lesotho, Mali, Mozambique, Swaziland.

special importance to tropical Africa. Subsequent plenary sessions of UNCTAD (UNCTAD V in Manila in 1979, UNCTAD VI in Belgrade in 1983) have, however, failed to secure further important concessions. Reference should also be made to Africa's relationship with the European Economic Community (EEC). Under the first and second Lomé Conventions (1975–80 and 1980–85 respectively) preferential trading arrangements were formulated between the EEC and a group of ex-colonies comprising African, Caribbean and Pacific (ACP) signatory countries. Negotiations for a successor to the present Convention are under way (Stevens 1984). This special relationship extends beyond the realm of trade to a wide range of economic and social ties including aid provisions.

Historically foreign aid has formed only a small part of the external resources of African states. However it now plays a key role in cushioning the low-income countries against a hostile external environment (Table 2.6). The official aid flow or Official Development Assistance (ODA) comes primarily from the Development Assistance Committee (DAC) of the Organisation for Economic Co-operation and Development (OECD) in the form of a complex array of bilateral and multilateral agreements (Arnold 1979). Arrangements have been made between recipients and such organisations as the United Nations agencies, the World Bank, the European Economic Community, regional banks including the African Development Bank and, of increasing importance, the Arab aid agencies. In addition to these aid provisions the International Monetary Fund (IMF), which is concerned with countries' balance of payments, provides loans to stabilise the export earnings of primary exporting countries where shortfalls in export earnings arise from conditions beyond their control. Tanzania, Zambia, Zaire, Kenya and Zimbabwe are among the countries which have negotiated IMF loans in the recent past.

While foreign aid may be seen as a form of support from the international

Table 2.6 External public debt of selected African countries. (Source: World Bank 1984: 248)

	DEBT OUTSTANDING AND DISBURSED			
	MILLIONS OF US DOLLARS		AS % OF GNP	
	1970	1982	1970	1982
Low-income economies				
Chad	32	189	11.9	59.0
Zaire	311	4087	17.6	78.4
Malawi	122	692	43.2	48.8
Tanzania	248	1659	19.4	32.7
Kenya	316	2359	20.5	39.2
Sierra Leone	59	370	14.3	29.8
Middle-income economies				
Sudan	319	5093	15.8	47.7
Liberia	158	641	49.6	68.1
Senegal	98	1329	11.6	55.0
Zambia	623	2381	37.0	66.3
Nigeria	480	6085	4.8	8.7

community for the developing countries, of central concern to development theorists is the extent to which such support inhibits the freedom of recipient countries and, by implication, intensifies international dependency. In the case of the IMF, for example, strong pressure has been placed on the African governments to alter those pricing policies which affect the value of their export commodities (Kanesa-Thasan 1981). Indeed as the level of foreign debt in countries like Zaire and Zambia has increased since independence so their vulnerability to external pressure has intensified and the debate over development or dependency comes into sharp focus (World Bank 1984).

But while external constraints inhibit the freedom of African states to achieve their economic and social goals, progress depends not only on a favourable external environment but also on positive internal conditions. In the case of Botswana despite burgeoning foreign exchange reserves Isaksen (1981) points out that conservatism at the centre has inhibited measures to redistribute income. Similarly in West Africa Ezenwe (1982: 305) indicates that due to a 'bunching' of unfortunate circumstances, both internal and external, during the 1970s trade expansion and growth were hampered. On the domestic front he cites 'political fragility, ill-suited institutions, a climate and topography hostile to development, an over-extended public sector vis-à-vis the available administrative capacity, neglect of export-orientated industries and biases against agriculture'. Thus while the power of external forces should not be underestimated, on the basis of evidence such as this doubts must also be expressed over the political will to undertake the types of reform which are necessary prerequisites for improvements in social and spatial terms. This issue is also important in relation to direct foreign investment.

Direct foreign investment

Similar doubts have been expressed over the relationship between direct foreign investment, national decision-makers and internal change. An extensive literature exists on the effects of foreign private investment on the economy and society within developing countries (cf. Streeten 1973; Killick 1973). Many studies of, for example, the technology transfer component of the multinationals maintain that social inequalities are intensified. Two particular social costs are widely emphasised; first, the adverse effects of production technology on employment expansion, and second, the skewed production patterns developed in the industrialised countries at the expense of necessities for the poor (Helleiner 1975; Stewart 1972; 1979). In the light of this literature any assessment of the indigenisation measures employed by the independent African states requires that we focus on their capacity to offset rather than remove any negative social effects. A similar qualification should be made in the economic sphere. For example, Kirkpatrick and Nixson (1981) emphasise the constraints imposed on the economic policies of the host countries by giant foreign corporations by virtue of their size, structure and, hence, superior bargaining position. Parson's (1980) study of Botswana provides a valuable illustration of the particular problems faced by land-locked states within this part of the continent. He outlines the 'limits' or constraints to autocentric development imposed on Botswana by, among other things, its geopolitical location within the southern African periphery and its historical constitution as a labour reserve economy for South Africa. As in the case of foreign trade reference should be made not only to the power of the State in implementing indigenisation measures, but also to the motivation of those who influence state policy. In effect it is the relationship between the so-called 'triple alliance' (Evans 1979) comprising international capital, domestic capital and the State which needs to be considered. Analysis of this kind forms part of a broad field of enquiry within the more radical development literature which focuses on the nature of capitalism and class formation in Africa. It is the theoretical base which provides a framework and essential logic for empirical study and it is to this base that we should return, notably to questions of class.

The African response to multinational investment must be placed within the total context of the local political economy and in particular the growing segmentation of society: in the words of Sunkel (1973), within the context of 'transnational integration and national disintegration' whereby a minority, including a well-paid stratum of industrial workers (Arrighi 1970), are integrated within the international community while the majority are excluded. A number of much-debated issues arise. (See, for example, *Review of African Political Economy* 1975 no. 2 and 1977 no. 8.) The status of capitalism in Africa and the extent to which independent capitalist development is possible under the control of an indigenous business group – a national bourgeoisie – is a key theme. (There is no general agreement on this point for developing countries as a whole. For example, Warren [1973] and Sunkel [1973; 1974] adopt opposing views.) Another theme is the power of the State in influencing the relationship between foreign and local capital and also in whose interests the state apparatus is employed.

Class and the postcolonial state

Issues such as these are central to radical development theory which seeks to explain the continued underdevelopment of the continent by linking internal inequalities with external control. Attention is focused directly on the structures within dependent territories, notably the state institutions and patterns of social stratification derived from the internal production relations which, in the words of Cohen and Daniel (1981: 75), are 'engendered by, linked to and [thereby] facilitate the international structures of dependency'. A new language has emerged in association with this approach dominated by terms like the bureaucratic bourgeoisie, the African 'ruling' and 'governing' class, the proletariat, exploitation and conflict. But what is the significance of this terminology? Are the class categories used purely descriptive or do they have a meaning in terms of the social relations of production in African society? It is with a brief discussion of these concepts and ideas that we conclude this section.

The analysis of inequality and stratification in the political economy of Africa has a long history and is an area of much controversy. The traditional approach associated with the theory of modernisation adopted an a-political non-Marxist stance using class as a descriptive category along with, and frequently subordinate to, other stratifying factors considered to be dominant in the sphere of social consciousness – notably ethnicity (Mafeje 1971). Some writers have preferred to use the concept of social differentiation rather than stratification, persuaded that the uncritical application of concepts designed to analyse social inequality in Western societies can be misleading in a non-Western context (Fallers 1973; Foster 1977). By contrast the appearance of a more radical use of class concepts in the early 1970s drawing on Marxist theory can be associated with the growing social and economic inequality within the continent, the failure of African regimes to deal with such problems, and a belief that classes were emerging in an economic sense accompanied by growing class consciousness. Conflicts of interests with serious political consequences were foreseen. Early works in this mould include studies by Arrighi and Saul (1973), Cohen (1972) and Kitching (1972) while the leading theoretical statements of the neo-Marxist tradition are those by Amin (1972a; 1973; 1974a), Kay (1975) and Wallerstein (1976; 1977). A wide range of case studies have followed applying Marxist concepts to selected areas of Africa including Ghana, Nigeria, Ivory Coast, Mali, Kenya and Tanzania. (See, for example, *Review of African Political Economy* nos. 3, 1975, 5, 1976, 8, 1977). A useful discussion and summary of social stratification in a Marxist context is provided by Cohen (1981: 75–111).

Fundamentally the more radical approach involves adapting the concepts and methods associated with the historical materialist model to the analysis of contemporary problems in Africa with a view to improving the quality of our explanation. Building on the early penetration of capitalism into the continent during the colonial period and the associated changes in the social relations of production, radical writers extend this analysis into the post-colonial period, arguing that the capitalist mode of production has become dominant and has intensified the process of social stratification polarising the population into three main groups – the bourgeoisie, the proletariat and the peasantry. This class formation in turn profoundly influences both ideology and politics. Analysis of the indigenous urban-based bourgeoisie and their links with international capital has become a major issue in studies of decision-making in government and must be borne in mind in our attempts to explain regional inequalities and projects which affect the poor.

A note of caution is needed. The literature on modes of production and class formation in Africa is complex and controversial (Harriss & Harriss 1979). There is no generally accepted class division (Cooperstock 1979). The relative importance of different groups within the bourgeoisie in controlling the State cannot be generalised between countries and is open to different interpretations within the same country. These points are effectively illustrated with reference to Kenya and Tanzania in the Editorial of *Review of African Political Economy* 1977, no. 8. Moreover, many writers continue to dispute the relevance of applying

Western class categories to fundamentally different cultures and societies (cf. Jackson 1973; Mazrui 1969). Indeed, as if to counterbalance the pessimists, there is an equally influential body of optimists among academics including geographers (O'Connor 1983), policy-makers and representatives of international agencies for whom a Marxist-style class analysis is unhelpful in the search for solutions to Africa's problems. The literature cannot, however, be ignored representing as it does an alternative and challenging approach to and interpretation of underdevelopment.

Conclusion

In seeking to explain changes in the political, economic and social organisation of space, a critical issue is the theoretical framework to be used. While there are differences in emphasis and in the language used between liberal and radical positions there are also common themes. Both approaches acknowledge the importance of so-called structural variables – the nature of the institutions and interest groups operating at national and international levels whose decisions and actions control patterns of change. It is recognised that during the colonial period international capitalism operating through the metropolitan powers played an important role in moulding the present economic and social structures in African countries. Moreover, through their control over patterns of trade, aid and direct foreign investment it is accepted that these foreign interests continue to influence politicians and the bureaucracy at the centre.

Some differences do occur, however, over the motivations ascribed to these leading decision-makers. While recognising that national governments may be unrepresentative of majority interests, liberals do not believe that it is either hopeless or naïve to work for change through existing government structures. For the more unorthodox, by contrast, problems of policy implementation are interpreted in terms of competition between classes. Spatial inequalities are seen as the inevitable outcome of social inequalities in which the influential and powerful seek to preserve their own interests.

It cannot be denied that the Western market economy has had its effects on traditional structures in a variety of clearly definable ways. The wage labour system, rural-urban migration, technological change, in certain areas rapid economic growth and, to some writers, the creation of a class structure, may be taken as evidence of this transition. But these effects are by no means uniform. The capitalist mode and its associated social relations of production are not everywhere predominant. Nor is there a simple rural-urban dichotomy between traditional and modern modes: the structure is more variable and complex. In view of this, is a theoretical framework which focuses on politico-economic institutions and agencies adequate in itself as we seek to explain changes in the organisation of space within African countries? Furthermore, how well does it account for the response of the African people to changes in their environment? It is to these questions that we now turn our attention.

Further reading

For a critical survey of alternative theories of development and underdevelopment and the contribution of geography to this see Forbes (1984).

The liberal 'developmentalist' position is reflected in the ILO (1972) report on Kenya while the basic needs approach is discussed in the *IDS Bulletin* (Brighton) 1978 vol. 9, no.4, 'Down to basics: reflections on the basic needs debate'. A less orthodox perspective is provided by Cohen and Daniel (1981) and in the *Review of African Political Economy* 1976, no.5 on 'The State in Africa', and 1977, no.8 on 'Capitalism in Africa'. Background on the economic structure of the African countries, including development planning, is contained in Livingstone and Ord (1980), Rimmer (1984) and Seidman (1980).

Chapter 3

THE CENTRALITY OF CULTURE

Introduction

The interaction between structure and culture forms an essential part of the broader discourse over development and underdevelopment as a whole and is therefore highly pertinent to the structural issues discussed in Chapter 2. How far is institutional behaviour as reflected in the decisions and actions of politicians and bureaucrats modified by culture? What is the outcome of the interaction between African and alien cultural forms where the latter are reflected in the values of the aid agency, the foreign consultant or the giant corporation? We must question the belief that in African countries, where power at the centre to resist outside forces is limited and where the tempo of change is therefore very rapid, no conflict of cultures has resulted. Issues such as these need to be discussed as we seek to make sense of the changing organisation and use of space.

Furthermore, in turning our attention to the African people, for both theoretical and practical reasons fundamental issues of culture are raised. What has been the response of the African people to the political and economic transformation of the continent? How far do changing patterns of demographic and social behaviour reflect this transformation? More particularly, what role do the African people play in the transformation process? How far have individuals and groups sought to achieve their aspirations? In what ways have they responded to the opportunities available and to the constraints imposed? In searching for answers doubts must be raised over the appropriateness of a structural framework alone. The assumption needs to be questioned that the State alone, by setting up the appropriate institutional machinery, can achieve improvements at local level. The interaction between structure and culture is of major importance.

Structure and culture

The concept 'culture' is at the centre of modern thought and practice. Williams (1981) points out that 'society', 'economy' and 'culture' as separate concepts are relatively recent historical developments. 'Culture' has undergone considerable changes of definition since the eighteenth century when it came to mean more than a noun of process – the culture of crops, animals and so on. It is used here in the sociological and anthropological sense to denote a process which shapes specific and distinct 'ways of life'. It therefore subsumes what we now call 'the arts' and all 'systems of meanings and values' associated with 'inner' development. Moreover, used in this sense it challenges the Marxist tendency to reduce culture to the superstructural – a realm of 'mere' ideas, beliefs, arts, customs – determined by basic material history (Johnston 1985).

Discussion in the *Bulletin* of the Institute of Development Studies (Brighton) for 1976 centres on the regrettable dichotomy which has emerged between the study of structures and cultures when in fact they are closely interlinked. The widely-held belief that 'culture, attitudes, value systems are somewhat improper concerns' (Editorial 1976:1) and hence the retreat from culture among many social scientists is an important area of general debate. It has been explained in part as a reaction to the modernisation school of the 1950s and 1960s which (from a sociological viewpoint) gave considerable importance to attitudes and values and (from a geographical viewpoint) interpreted development as a spatial diffusion process. Criticism followed, however, of the oversimplified assumptions on which these interpretations were based, notably the tendency to explain a lack of development in terms of a deficiency of certain cultural traits (achievement-motivation, future-orientation, universalistic norms) or institutional structures within developing countries (schools, hospitals, road and rail network) and the ethnocentric tendency to contrast 'desirable' modernity in the rich countries with 'backward' traditionalism in the poor countries. (For a discussion see Peil 1977; Hoogvelt 1982.) The reader will be familiar with the bases on which these interpretations were condemned, notably a failure to consider the external constraints on economic growth, that is, the 'structural factors' arising from global capitalism.

There is, however, extensive evidence to suggest that 'any analysis of social situations which does not look at both structural and cultural factors is liable to be partial and misleading' (Editorial, *IDS Bulletin* [Brighton] 1976, Vol.8 No.2: 2). Nor indeed should they be regarded as incompatible. A point which underlies this book is that analysis of beliefs, values and aspirations is in no way inconsistent with the distribution of resources and power. Structural and cultural features are in fact closely intertwined. Our framework must therefore be modified in order that explicit recognition be given to the role of social and cultural practices in reproducing and shaping the broader political economy. While structural interest group analysis is relevant to our understanding of social processes so too are the patterns of loyalties and cultural norms which influence on the one hand the direction of national and regional change and on the other hand the response of the African people to changing circumstances, and which in turn condition the means by which social change is achieved. Neither the African leadership nor the ordinary citizens are mere robots responding to 'external' inputs in an entirely predictable way.

In their study of the political economy of Africa, Cohen and Daniel (1981) acknowledge the importance of the cultural dimension in explaining patterns of change. It is interpreted, however, as a 'culture of dependency' adopted by those who assumed state power on independence and imposed by external control. It was transmitted through the various institutions (educational, religious, economic, the family) introduced with capitalist penetration and, according to them, comprises on the one hand 'submission to domination' and on the other hand 'emulation' of the attitudes, values and behaviour patterns of the international bourgeoisie. Indeed it is this cultural dimension which is used to account, at least in part, for the lack of any significant improvement in living standards for all within the African countries since independence. 'The imposition of a culture of dependency upon a dominated people is regarded, therefore, as being fundamental to the establishment and survival of an imperial relationship and, if one is to make any sense of contemporary African politics, then one must understand not just the political and economic dimensions of dependency but this vital cultural aspect too' (Daniel 1981: 164).

As if to counter this belief in the distortion of African culture, reference should also be made, however, to attempts to build upon and strengthen African traditional values and beliefs in the interests of national and supra-national progress. Pan-Africanism is an important example of the latter, a movement spearheaded by Kwame Nkrumah of Ghana which gained wide support within the continent during the colonial period and which has found expression in the Organisation of African Unity. In the early years of independence President Nyerere of Tanzania also expressed political ideals which were uniquely African (Ch. 6). His aim to create a new society compatible with traditional African culture reflected his belief in the continued power of the kinship system despite Western influence. It illustrates his commitment to the values implicit in traditional social and economic organisation and their power to influence the direction of the new African states. Development is indeed a culturally determined process. While it is an attempt to realise certain aspirations which may be regarded as universal – better living conditions, improved standards of health – Nyerere's writings emphasise how these must be set in the context of other values which the leaders of development wish to preserve.

Perspectives on demographic and social change

And what of the subjects of development? How can we make sense of the interaction between structure and culture as it relates to the African people? Let us begin by exploring the many different ways in which demographic and social change has been explored by social scientists at a variety of scales.

It is in historical and anthropological studies of selected African peoples that the cultural dimension has been most comprehensively explored hitherto. Historical studies of African populations continue to receive attention even though based in part on incomplete but fascinating secondary sources including reports of travellers and colonial administrators together with literary and artistic records. Among the themes explored are pre-colonial settlement, social organisation, material culture, racial composition, historical migrations and intermixtures (see Udo 1979a). As regards 'indigenous' African social structures, the pre-colonial regimes in Northern Nigeria, Ghana and among the Inter-lacustrine Bantu with their distinctive hierarchical organisation have been major focuses. Studies of the Nupe (Nadel 1942), the Hausa states (Hill 1977), the Ruanda (Maquet 1961) and the Buganda kingdom (Richards 1960; 1969) demonstrate this. Investigations such as these have been discussed by Goody (1971) in his critique of feudalism in Africa.

Detailed anthropological studies continue to be made of contemporary tribal structures. To take but one region of the continent which is discussed in detail later (Ch. 8), reference should be made to the outstanding work of Isaac Schapera among the Tswana people in Southern Africa. In 1928 he began his studies in what was then the Bechuanaland Protectorate in a programme of research which was to continue for over forty years. (See, for example, Schapera 1940; 1943; 1947; 1970.) Meyer Fortes (1975: 3 and 4), in an appreciation of Schapera, stresses that the quality of his work lies in the fact that it provides 'the most complete and comprehensive body of knowledge relating to the history, the social and political life and the contemporary situation of any single group of African peoples as yet assembled'. Equally important, 'his works are accepted as authoritative records of their customary laws and social history by the Tswana leaders'.

In contrast to these types of study perhaps more numerous today are investigations of contemporary demographic and social data by geographers and demographers including those which comment on the range of sources available and the problems which arise with their use. National demographic statistics classified by continent and covering such details as total population, birth and death rates, infant mortality, life expectancy and age distribution are available from a variety of sources including the United Nations, the Population Reference Bureau, Washington D.C. and the World Bank (see Table 3.1). Since the colonial period there has been a steady improvement in the quality and quantity of data available both at the macro-scale and the micro-scale. Kpedekpo (1979; 1982) discusses some of the techniques of demographic analysis and the main international and national sources of information including censuses, vital registration and sample surveys. Some lesser known documents are also outlined including school registers, tax registers, records of maternity clinics and child welfare services.

The quantity and quality of available statistics are thoroughly covered elsewhere. (See also Caldwell & Okonjo 1968; Ominde & Ejiogu 1972; Udo 1979a.) Brief reference will only therefore be made to census-taking. Even as late as 1971 twenty-five out of forty-one African member states of the Economic Commission for Africa had not conducted a total count of their populations. Various attempts have been made to identify phases in the development of census-taking in tropical Africa (cf. Kpedekpo 1982; Masser & Gould 1975). Phase one relates to the period before and immediately after the Second World War and is associated with the administrative requirements of the colonial regime. The 1950 round defines phase

Table 3.1 Demographic data for selected African countries (Source: World Bank 1984: 192, 256, 260)

	TOTAL POPULATION (MILLIONS)	CRUDE BIRTH RATE (PER 1000)	CRUDE DEATH RATE (PER 1000)	TOTAL FERTILITY RATE	RATE OF NATURAL INCREASE	URBAN POPULATION (% OF TOTAL) POPULATION)
	mid-1982	1982	1982	1982	2000	1982
Ethiopia	32.9	47	18	6.5	3.0	15
Mali	7.1	48	21	6.5	3.0	19
Zaire	30.7	46	16	6.3	3.1	38
Malawi	6.5	56	23	7.8	3.3	10
Burkino Faso (formerly Upper Volta)	6.5	48	21	6.5	2.9	11
Uganda	13.5	50	19	7.0	3.3	9
Tanzania	19.8	47	15	6.5	3.2	13
Guinea	5.7	49	27	6.5	2.4	20
Niger	5.9	52	20	7.0	3.1	14
Ghana	12.2	49	13	7.0	3.5	37
Kenya	18.1	55	12	8.0	4.1	15
Mozambique	12.9	49	16	6.5	3.1	9
Sudan	20.2	45	18	6.6	3.0	23
Senegal	6.0	48	21	6.5	2.8	34
Lesotho	1.4	42	15	5.8	2.7	13
Zambia	6.0	50	16	6.8	3.3	45
Zimbabwe	7.5	54	12	8.0	4.0	24
Nigeria	90.6	50	16	6.9	3.3	21
Cameroon	9.3	46	15	6.5	3.4	37
Ivory Coast	8.9	48	17	7.0	3.0	42
Angola	8.0	49	22	6.5	2.7	22

two during which time statistical agencies such as the East African Statistical Department were set up and initiated important improvements. Phase three coincides with the period of African independence and a recognition by newly independent governments of the need for sound demographic data as a basis for development planning. The 1970 round is associated with the establishment in 1971 of the African Census Programme on the initiative of the United Nations Population Commission, to standardise the types of question asked and to improve the effectiveness of the administrative procedures. From among its recommendations Table 3.2 summarises the range of questions proposed. Of the minimum requirements attention should be drawn to the place of birth question which represents a major source of information on population mobility at national level. (For more detailed discussion see Clarke & Kosinski 1983.) Questions of a socio-cultural nature are given second priority. A summary of the major censuses and surveys carried out is given in Table 3.3.

From the growing body of information a basic picture can be drawn of demographic patterns across the continent. While in total numbers the population of Africa is small in comparison to other continents it is nevertheless highly complex: 'no matter what the characteristic (absolute numbers, sex, age, fertility, mortality, mobility) or the scale (continental, regional, national, local)' (Thomas 1976: 55). This complexity has been discussed at different scales and explained by

43

Table 3.2 List of census questions for African countries defined by the African Census Programme (Source: Kpedekpo 1979: 14)

Minimum list of items recommended
    Name
    Place where found at the time of enumeration
    Place of birth
    Sex
    Age
    Children born alive
    Children living
    Live births in the past 12 months (by sex)
    Deaths in the past 12 months (by sex and age)

Additional list of items recommended
  (i) First priority
      Type of (economic) activity — Economic activity is the process of
      contribution to the supply of labour for the production of
      goods and services
      Occupation
      Educational attainment

  (ii) Second priority
      Relationship to head of household
      Ethnic group (or citizenship)
      Literacy
      School attendance
      Industry
      Status (employer, employee, etc.)
      Usual place of residence
      Duration of residence
      Previous place of residence
      Religion
      Number of wives
      Number of years since first marriage
      Children below school age
      Worked any time in the past 12 months

means of a range of variables. With regard to population distribution and density, for example, on the continental scale, density differentiation has been closely related to environmental conditions. Udo (1979b) recognises five population density zones on the demographic map of the continent. Among the most significant of these is the occurrence, frequency and distribution of towns – the striking visible expression of political, economic and social transformation within the continent. Bearing this in mind, as Bates (1983: 1) points out, 'Despite the rapid growth of towns and the concomitant growth in expectations of rapid social change, the vast preponderance of Africa's population has remained in the rural areas.' Only Zambia has a significant urban population recorded as 41 per cent in the 1980 census (Wood 1982).

    Spatial concentration at intra-national level has been related to a combination of history, culture and to contemporary economic forces (Agnew & Stubbs 1972;

Table 3.3 Censuses and surveys in selected countries of tropical Africa since 1960 (Source: United Nations Statistical Yearbook 1981; United Nations Demographic Yearbook 1982)

	PARTIAL CENSUS, SURVEY OR OFFICIAL ESTIMATE		COMPLETE CENSUS		
Angola		1981	1960		1970
Botswana			1972		1981
Burundi	1965			1979	
Cameroon	1960–1965 1981			1976	
Central African Republic	1960	1981		1975	
Chad	1964	1975		1974	
Congo	1960–1961	1980			
Equatorial Guinea	1973		1960		1970
Ethiopia	1980				
Gabon	1960–1961			1980	
Gambia	1980		1963		1973
Ghana	1966 1971	1980	1960		1970
Guinea	1980	1981			
Guinea Bissau (formerly Portuguese Guinea)			(1960,	1970)	1979
Ivory Coast	1979			1975	
Kenya			1961		1979
Lesotho		1980	1966		1976
Liberia	1969–1973	1981		1974	
Madagascar	1966	1981	1974–1975		
Malawi	1982		1966		1977
Mali	1960–1961	1981		1976	
Mauritania	1964–1965			1976	
Mozambique	1981		1960		1970
Namibia			1960	1970	1981
Niger	1960	1981		1977	
Nigeria	1975–1980		1963	1973	1978
Rwanda	1970–1971	1980		1978	
Senegal	1960 1970	1980		1976	
Sierra Leone	1981		1963	1964	1974
Somalia	1981				
Sudan	1981			1973	
Swaziland	1982		1966		1976
Tanzania	1981		1967		1978
Togo	1979			1970	
Uganda	1980			1969	
Burkina Faso (formerly Upper Volta)	1960–1961 1968–1969	1981		1975	
Zaire	1981				
Zambia	1963			1969	1980
Zimbabwe (formerly Rhodesia)	(1962,	1969)		1982	

Barbour 1982; Berry 1971; Clarke 1970; Davies 1971; Ebong 1982). Ojo (1968), for example, discusses the concept of 'critical density of population' in different parts of tropical Africa in relation to the prevailing economic system and, more particularly, to changing cultural practices. A similar issue is discussed by Allan (1965) and also more recently by Hance (1972: 36) who points out that by emphasising 'area not people' crude density figures are misleading and meaningless. they conceal regional differences of immense importance in understanding a country and take on a significance 'only when related to the

45

opportunities and limitations of the ecological and economic environments' (Hance 1972: 40).

Essential to the geographer's explanation of the social organisation of space is an understanding of the interaction between African cultural traditions and a range of environmental, economic and political forces. The importance of this interaction is indeed acknowledged in a number of contemporary geographical studies. Morgan's (1983) analysis of achieved landscapes in Nigeria highlights the diversity of outcomes arising from the interrelationship between different ethnic communities and their physical environment. Mabogunje (1980a) goes beyond this in pointing to the significance of cultural variety for development practice. In discussing ideology he emphasises that while the development process 'requires an articulated vision of the type of society it seeks to create, such a vision, in order to be realisable, must be grounded in the realities of the cultural and physical environment of each country' (Mabogunje 1980a: 31). However, while this concern for culture is vitally important it needs also to be incorporated into development theory. It is this issue which is of particular importance here.

Development theory and population

Underlying these discussions of population patterns and processes are important theoretical assumptions on which demographic study is based. Indeed the determinants of the African population profile and the welfare of the African people have become central issues of debate. The interrelations between demographic and social processes and the politico-economic transformation of Africa are not fully resolved despite the discussion and theorising which they have engendered. Changes in the mode of production and in the internal social relations under the influence of the State and external forces have been explored in detail. For example, the modernisation school of the 1960s based on orthodox theories of social change argued that through investment in human capital economically backward societies would modernise and develop (Peil 1973; Dore 1978). The spatial separation of the educated from their traditional rural environment, coupled with secure urban employment were assumed to consolidate a new pattern of social stratification based on educational qualification and income level (Foster 1977) while, in addition, reinforcing the process of acculturation into a Western value system (Foley 1977).

However, since the late 1960s the inadequacy of this formulation, arising among other things, from an increasingly complex range of problems associated with education and employment, has given rise to many reinterpretations. Liberal academics and practitioners emphasise the role of the State in the provision of basic needs – welfare, skills, job opportunities – as a means of tackling poverty and inequality. Within this context community participation is given particular attention in social policy as a mechanism by which to improve the conditions of the urban and rural poor.

46

In contrast the Marxian perspective has focused on the problems of poverty and social inequality in relation to class formation and the forces of exploitation and conflict within African society brought about by capitalist penetration. In the late 1960s Arrighi and Saul were discussing the relationship between class formation and economic development. They focused on the involvement of international capital in the area and developed the idea of a 'labour aristocracy' explored many years earlier by Elkan (1960) in Uganda. This they defined as 'the élites and sub-élites in bureaucratic employment in the civil service and expatriate concerns' together with the so-called 'proletariat proper of tropical Africa', that is, a small section of the labour force with 'incomes three of more times higher than those of unskilled labourers' who by virtue of their financial security had severed their ties with the traditional economy (Arrighi & Saul 1968: 149). These class inequalities, argued Arrighi and Saul, were responsible for the contemporary pattern of 'perverse growth' within the continent, 'that is, growth which undermines, rather than enhances, the potentialities of the economy for long-term growth' (Arrighi & Saul 1968: 150). a growth which encourages social polarisation and spatial concentration rather than redistribution.

In focusing on the demographic processes – fertility, mortality and migration – similar ideological differences in interpretation have emerged. With reference to natural population change, approaches derived from Malthus and Marx, though sharply contrasting, have both proved influential. Bondestam (1980a: 1) suggests that 'when unemployment, poverty, hunger, misery and famine spread and deepen, Malthus' theories offer a rescue'. His 'eternal law of nature', that the poverty of the working class was explained by its overgrowth, confirmed and reinforced establishment views regarding the causes of poverty in eighteenth-century England. By contrast, the views of Marx and Engels on surplus population were derived specifically from the laws which they themselves laid down concerning the relations between population and production in the capitalist system.

Both interpretations have been applied to the developing countries and to Africa in particular. The former, which defines over-population as an absolute occurring independent of the prevailing economic system, has proved a powerful tool for neo-Malthusian pessimists (Meadows et al. 1972) and provided a justification for ideologically motivated population control. The latter, which interprets over-population as a relative phenomenon caused by mechanisms inherent in the capitalist system, has equally well proved valuable to supporters of social revolution. (For a discussion of the ideological significance of these opposing views see Bondestam 1980a.)

With reference to labour migration, ideologically opposed views about its causes and effects can also be identified. Swindell (1979: 239), in a bibliographic survey of the major themes in labour migration research in Africa, points to the range of 'empirical descriptions, conceptual frameworks, typologies, models and theories' which have been put forward. In particular he questions whether workers are 'pushed' or 'pulled'. 'Should they be viewed as active decision-makers', a feature of liberal thinking among social scientists? Or, by contrast, are

47

they merely 'passive elements manipulated by external global forces' characteristic of Marxian analyses, in which labour migration is interpreted as being one of the most potent manifestations of underdevelopment? The debate proceeds as empirical studies continue to be carried out and concepts are redefined (Van Binsbergen & Meilink 1978).

Linking macro- and micro-scales

From this brief outline should be apparent the range of topics concerned with demographic and social processes, the alternative scales at which they can be investigated and, equally important, the different approaches and contrasting theoretical positions which have been adopted. Each one has a particular contribution to make. However, we should also ask ourselves how far these various themes and scales of analysis really contribute to our understanding of people as the recipients of development programmes and projects. Few allowances are made for the cultural dimension in established development theory.

The geographer's traditional concerns, namely, spatial variations in and changing patterns of fertility, mortality, migration, regional differences in school attendance, in employment, income levels and so on are all symptoms of Africa's political and economic transformation – the structural changes discussed in Chapter 2. But for the geographer concerned with the improvement of human welfare what matters is not merely spatial patterns, social structures and systems: it is people, their actions and interactions with which we should be concerned in space and over time within the constraints of a politico-economic environment beyond their complete control. Among the divisions of African society important to the African people is ethnicity. Although the nation state has engendered strong national feelings and its citizens are conscious of being Nigerian, Zambian or Zimbabwean, this national identity does not necessarily precede the loyalty attached to Yoruba, Bemba, or Shona. Ethnicity cuts across standard class categories. Harris (1975: 156) suggests that 'economic conflicts are more likely to be expressed in the language of tribalism'. And what of the role of the African people as active agents of change? Hyden (1980: 237) is highly critical of much current thinking which allows 'little room so far in development paradigms or models for the notion that small is powerful'.

While it may be argued that the inhabitants of a region, their lives, social relationships, occupations and family structure are more important than the political, legal, economic and social structures surrounding them, nevertheless problems arise with this focus. In studying people, their demographic behaviour, acceptance of innovations, social interactions and so on a complex combination of factors are involved operating at different scales. Not only are the personal characteristics of the individual important; so too are the local social and cultural practices. Beyond this the broader structure of the political economy governs key aspects of the locational structure – the distribution of schools, clinics, employment opportunities – within which actions take place. It is this broader structure which influences the opportunities available within communities and the social relations governing access to the scarce resources available. As Gugler (1982: 49) points out:

> Today rural populations raise the cash they need to settle taxes, to purchase manufactured goods, and to pay school fees, by selling some of the products they grow as independent producers, as tenant farmers, or as share croppers. Or they find employment with local landowners, in rural areas, or in the cities. Whether they sell produce on the market or their labour to an employer, they are part of a far-reaching economic system beyond their control. They experience the vagaries of the world economic system when they lose their jobs during recessions or when a sudden drop in world market prices depresses their earnings from export crops.

Our problem is therefore one of constructing a framework which combines human agency and structure. The approach outlined below provides a way forward (Fig. 3.1).

It is based on two premises. First, that explanations of demographic and social phenomena can proceed at two levels, namely, the macro and the micro. At the former level of continent, nation or region our concern is primarily with explaining gross features such as distribution, density, distance, direction, volume and rate. By contrast at the micro-scale our focus is upon features relating to community, family, household and individual. The second premise is that explanations offered at these two levels are empirically though not necessarily theoretically different. At the macro-scale the overt characteristics of the demographic and social phenomena observed represent the outcome of the political, economic, social and cultural processes (the latter reflected in, for example, ethnic differences) operating at that scale. These same processes defining the politico-economic system provide in turn the broad framework of supports and constraints – the setting – within which individuals and groups respond, over which they have relatively little control but which their individual and collective actions reproduce with or without some modification. At this micro-scale these same forces defining the setting are brought into sharp relief. They are manifest locally in the particular cultural practices, the social and economic environment and the demographic conditions peculiar to that community, family, household or individual within which decisions are taken and choices made.

Such a framework satisfies the geographer's concern to integrate both macro- and micro-processes. More particularly it stresses that people should not be seen merely as passive victims but rather as active agents in the processes of change. While similar settings may produce broadly similar spatial patterns if judged purely on the basis of their gross features, we cannot automatically assume that their causes are similar until the underlying processes and peculiar conditions at local level are explored.

THE SETTING

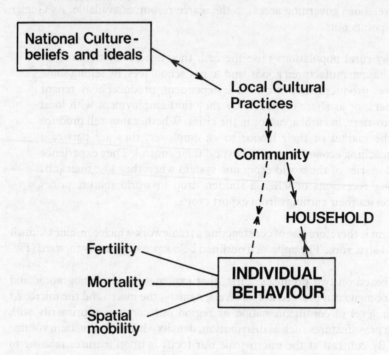

Figure 3.1 Links between macro- and micro-scales – the importance of culture

Before proceeding further a valuable illustration of the close integration between macro- and micro-processes can be found in Colin Murray's (1981) study of family change in Lesotho. Within the context of the Southern African political economy he demonstrates by means of detailed investigation the demographic and social consequences for one part of Lesotho of that country's incorporation into this regional system. His language is emotional and his feelings angry.

> In 1983 Lesotho was described as the 'granary of the Free State and part of the [Cape] Colony' (CB: 459). Today it is an impoverished labour reserve. A study of this transformation poses urgent and fundamental questions ... How is it possible to condone high unemployment, extreme poverty and social deprivation in the labour reserves of the rural periphery, while the coffers of the South African state are swelled by the gold boom of the 1970s? How can the systematic destruction of family life through mass labour migration be

reconciled with the principle of self-determination which is supposedly enshrined in the granting of political independence, both to the erstwhile British territories of Botswana, Lesotho and Swaziland and to the Bantustans within South Africa?

In this book I present empirical evidence relating to some aspects of the transformation of Lesotho from granary to labour reserve. I also analyse the impact of this transformation on the lives of migrants and their families ... But the way I have written it reflects two convictions in particular. One is that no aspect of contemporary village life can be understood without central reference to the dependence of villagers for their livelihood on earnings derived from the export of labour. The other is that this dependence must be understood in its proper historical context. (Murray 1981: xi)

These opening sentences of Murray's book highlight some of the major social problems of this impoverished state - unemployment, low incomes, family breakdown - which represent the symptoms of its politico-economic transformation and which are shared in common by many African peoples. They also demonstrate clearly on a macro-scale the unequal relationship between the two states, Lesotho and South Africa, and the resultant inequalities between them. But finally, moving down to the village level, they also stress that the decisions taken by families and individuals cannot be fully explained without reference to the constraints imposed by the broader setting, namely, Lesotho's role within the Southern African political economy.

Modes of production – interactions between cultural forms

In seeking to link macro- and micro-processes within a single framework and, by doing so, focus attention on the African people, culture is once again of central importance. Reference to work in anthropology illustrates the broad significance of culture in development and clarifies its role in binding together human agency and structure. In *Culture and Practical Reason* (1976) Marshall Sahlins criticises the two main types of anthropological theory – based on what he calls practical reason – which eliminate culture as the distinctive object of the discipline. The first he defines as the naturalistic or ecological type in which culture is seen merely as the 'human mode of adaptation' to the environment. The second type is utilitarian or economistic concerned with the purposeful activity of individuals in pursuit of their own interests: 'Culture is taken as an environment or means at the disposition of the 'manipulating individual', and also as a sedimented resultant of his self-interested machinations' (Sahlins 1976: 102). Neither in Western nor in non-capitalist societies does he claim that such interpretations are valid.

In developing his critique Sahlins discusses in some detail the problems inherent in the historical materialist idea that human cultures are formulated from practical activity and, underlying this, utilitarian interest. Besides an ideological resistance to it there are also serious substantive criticisms. For example, doubt must be expressed over the relevance of the Marxist analytic framework to societies in which there is no organisational distinction between economic base and political ideological superstructure; 'that is, where the two are formally the same structure' (Sahlins 1976: 3).

In contrast to the institutional diversity of Western capitalism with its distinctive and apparently independent economic, legal and political systems for which Marx achieved a materialist synthesis, within many non-capitalist or tribal societies an institutional unity has been found to exist already. There is no differentiation between base and superstructure as implied by the materialist conception.

> In the tribal cultures, economy, polity, ritual and ideology do not appear as distinct 'systems', nor can relationships be easily assigned to one or another of these functions. To put it positively, society is ordered by a single consistent system of relationships, having the properties we recognise as 'kinship', which is mapped on to various planes of social action. Tribal groups and relations are 'polyvalent' or 'multifunctional': they order all the activities which in western civilisation are the subject of special institutional developments. (Sahlins 1976: 6)

Although in the West kinship is merely one of these specialisations confined to the domestic sphere of social life, many studies in Africa and elsewhere have indicated that in the past kinship was the articulating principle of social organisation as a whole and the basis of social integration (Hill 1977; Schapera 1953). Kinship relations were the main relations of production. They were also the jural-political and ritual relations. In addition, they governed the way in which societies organised and used the resources of the environment – notably land – and the spatial interactions between members. Tswana society in Southern Africa, for example, has evolved a distinctive settlement pattern whereby most Batswana live in or close to a large tribal capital separated often by many miles from where crops, the primary responsibility of female members of Tswana families, are grown and where cattle, the responsibility of male members, are grazed. A circular seasonal migration has been characteristic of the Batswana for several centuries in which their main home in the village is supplemented by a second dwelling at the lands area and occasionally a third at the cattlepost. During the rainy season the village would be populated largely by the elderly and by children while crop production was at its peak. For periods of the year men and older boys would be occupied at the cattlepost. Such long-established mobility involving a clear division of labour in a closely integrated social and spatial system set the Batswana apart from many other groups in central and southern Africa (Kuper 1975).

Thus, while from the perspective of classic materialism kinship is a superstructure, it has been shown to form the base in the structure of many tribal societies. The discussion above is intended to illustrate three closely related points. First, that there are important differences in institutional design between Western capitalism and non-capitalist societies. Second, and leading on from this, in referring to non-capitalist structures in the past tense this is not intended to imply that traditional relations have disappeared. While the penetration of capitalism into Africa brought with it new political, economic and social institutions which have modified the traditional system, nevertheless, kinship is a well-tried institution. It is the basis on which Nyerere has built his distinctive form of African socialism. Moreover, it continues to play a significant role in the organisation of rural and urban life and in the interactions between countryside and town (Gulliver 1971; Mitchell 1959; 1969a&b). For example, within the kinship structure the household remains a major social and cultural institution which, although no longer the unit of production, remains the focus of distribution between members.

The third point is that in analysing the combination of continuity and change in the institutional structures of African societies today we must recognise the fundamental cultural significance of these different structures. A problem shared by all pragmatic interpretations of culture is their failure to appreciate that all economic systems, whether Western or non-Western, capitalist or non-capitalist, are a cultural specification. As Sahlins points out, the practical interest of men in production is not an intrinsic condition inherent in production; it is symbolically constituted. In opposing practical reason he

> poses a reason of another kind, the symbolic or meaningful. It takes as the distinctive quality of man not that he must live in a material world, a circumstance he shares with all organisms, but that he does so according to a meaningful scheme of his own devising, in which the capacity of man is unique. It therefore takes as the decisive quality of culture – as giving each mode of life the properties that characterise it – not that this culture must conform to material constraints but that it does so according to a definite symbolic scheme which is never the only one possible. (Sahlins 1976: viii)

Thus in any society it is the cultural system which organises and reproduces the material forces of production (labour, natural resources, technology) without which they are merely a set of physical possibilities and constraints lacking order or integration. It is the cultural system which determines the kinds of goods produced, the way in which the work period is organised and how labour is apportioned between men and women. Epstein (1975) emphasises how the sexual differentiation of reproductive tasks has provided the prototype of all division of labour. Differences in tasks performed by men and women have in turn led to a complementarity in their roles. In the case of Tswana society referred to above, women's prime responsibility has traditionally been subsistence foods while cattle have occupied the male sphere. From an early age through appropriate education and socialisation young girls would be trained in domestic duties such as collecting water and caring for their younger siblings while boys were introduced to herding.

Continuity and change

In the light of these comments it would appear that the debate over structures and cultures is inappropriate and irrelevant since the two are in fact inseparable. Rather, what needs to be explored is the combination of continuity and change within African society today with the penetration of capitalism and the values enshrined in its institutions. The existence of different institutional arrangements reflects a complex combination of cultural forms. It is the interactions between these forms with which we are concerned, as reflected in the response of different groups to changes in their environment, to the opportunities presented to them and to the constraints imposed.

We have already referred to Pan-Africanism and African socialism, both of which have sought to build upon traditional social and economic organisation in the modern world. On a more tangible level are the visible cultural forms – architecture, artistic traditions, forms of dress and language. Throughout Africa the range of styles adopted reflect much more than the wholesale adoption of Western material culture but rather in many cases an absorption of the former within the traditional.

It cannot be denied that there are also numerous illustrations of profound cultural and social changes within the continent under Western influence which find expression in, for example, a fall in mortality rates, rural-urban movement, wage and salary employment, rapid urban growth. To assume, however, that these patterns reflect the broad acceptance of a Western value system, or any other alien system for that matter, is to ignore the fact that within these general trends the attitudes, values and norms which govern the behaviour of individuals and groups vary widely. The effects of Western influence are by no means uniform. Nor is there a simple rural-urban dichotomy between traditional and modern modes. The essential feature is one of several modes of production existing side by side. In making sense of the observed spatial patterns what we need to explore is the interaction between traditional and alien modes, the way in which social relations have altered and their effects on different groups.

Some data problems and misleading assumptions

In conducting our investigations reference should finally be made to what is a major problem in achieving our aims – the practical difficulty of data availability including the widespread Western cultural bias implicit in the recording procedures.

Social scientists have come to rely heavily on statistics as a basis for describing, comparing and explaining the character of social and economic phenomena and the operation of national economies. The quantitative revolution in geography showed clearly how quantifiable variables could be manipulated in numerical models to produce plausible interpretations of demographic change, social differentiation and even of economic development itself (Berry 1960). This era has, of course, duly passed and its positivist scientific claims modified. Nevertheless, the influence of the data we use on our perception of both static conditions and dynamic phenomena remains significant. In the African context we should be particularly aware of this where culture mediates economic and social processes and where the categories which we associate with one particular mode of production cannot be automatically applied to those sectors of the economy where non-capitalist relations prevail.

Much has been written about the data problems associated with developing countries in general and Africa in particular (see *IDS Bulletin* [Brighton] 1975, Vol. 7 No.3; Dasgupta & Seers 1975). One major caveat concerns the detail and accuracy with which information can be acquired and recorded. There is much evidence to suggest that the information recorded is limited in quantity and poor in quality. It may be published only at the national level leaving the researcher to deduce regional variations in, for example, manpower available, employment structure, or economic output. Alternatively accurate information may be lacking below the regional or district levels thus inhibiting any detailed rural or urban comparisons. The current Botswana National Development Plan 1979–85 (Republic of Botswana 1980), for example, uses urban populations derived from projections based on the 1971 National Population Census (Central Statistics Office 1972) as a basis for formulating urban economic and social policies. In more recent studies, however, including the National Migration Study carried out in 1978–79 and the National Population Census of 1981 (preliminary figures) these calculations were shown to be significant underestimates.

The methods by which information is compiled also create difficulties. For example, gross national income can be calculated by different methods, notably by the product approach, the expenditure approach or the income approach. Frequently a combination must be used depending on the information available for the various sectors of the economy within a particular country. Furthermore, remittances from abroad may be treated in different ways in the process of national income accounting, leading to inconsistencies and problems of comparision. The problems of measuring standards of living are discussed in detail elsewhere (Livingstone & Ord 1980). A description of the outcomes of these problems does, however, usefully pinpoint the dangers of relying too heavily on statistical data.

Most national income data ... are based largely on hypotheses and guesses – about (e.g.) food production or the rental value of rural dwellings. The great majority of rural services, manufacturing and construction are usually not covered at all. Guesses are, moreover, added to relatively firm data from establishments which keep

55

accounts, the results being composite totals subject to substantial, but unknown, margins of error. In most countries any reasonably competent statistician could show a rate of economic growth 2% (say) higher or lower than that actually published. (Editorial, *IDS Bulletin* 1975 [Brighton] Vol. 7 No.3:2)

These comments lead to a second major issue connected with data, namely, the use of concepts and measurement techniques derived from the industrialised countries. African economies are not replicas of the Western model. They are a mixture of institutions derived from at least three major economic systems or modes of production – non-capitalist, capitalist and socialist. Elements of the capitalist and socialist systems combine to form the modern or formal sector of the economy, the characteristics of which resemble most closely the industrialised economies. The balance between capitalist enterprise owned by private local or foreign capital and the state sector varies between countries. So too does the combined size of this formal sector in terms of its contribution to GDP. Nevertheless, it is only this sector which is subject to official regulation and which is recorded statistically in official publications. Thus the recording of employment statistics tends to be biased in favour of wage and salary employment. With this, the assumption has prevailed that only activities in this modern sector can be equated with productive employment. Yet from the viewpoint of the African people it absorbs a relatively small proportion of the economically active and oversimplifies a highly complex structure of work and employment involving several sectors which closely interact (Bienefeld & Godfrey 1975).

As a statistical record of economic structure it excludes a wide range of activities both in rural and urban areas which conform most closely to the non-capitalist mode of production and which absorb either part-time or full-time the overwhelming majority of the labour force. These include elements of the subsistence economy, that is, a range of productive activities carried on within households for domestic consumption which do not enter the monetary economy such as food production, the building of huts, grain milling, the collection of firewood and water, many of which are carried out by women (Carr 1982) and remain unrecorded. Small-scale petty commodity production also forms part of this sector involving the exchange of household produce. Finally, reference should be made to a range of economic activities frequently in low-income urban areas associated with small-scale manufacturing, marketing and transport – the so-called informal sector of the economy – which, by virtue of the small size of the enterprises, their transient nature and/or their illegality, are not recorded in official statistics. National income accounts impute a monetary value to these various activities, nevertheless the accuracy and value of the estimates must be questioned. Only through protracted field investigation and personal observation can the content of both informal and non-monetary activities be assessed. Many detailed studies have been carried out for this purpose (Bray 1969; Browne 1981) although their coverage is of necessity limited.

Given the problems of defining these activities a further critical point

56

concerns the use of procedures from the industrialised countries to measure their significance and the income derived from them. By assigning a monetary value to such activities and in doing so deriving a measure of the value of output from the rural and urban non-formal sectors a major problem is raised concerning the relationship between income and welfare. Evidence suggests that the significance of the productive activities and services rendered outside the formal sector to the standard of living and the general welfare of the majority of the African people far outweighs the input monetary value which they are assigned in national statistics. One need only consider the famine, disease and death caused by crop failure or the lack of an adequate source of safe water in any one year to appreciate this point. Enough has been said at this stage to alert the reader to the cultural bias which frequently underlies both our approach to development problems and our tools of analysis.

In the light of these comments it can be argued that the micro-scale – the study of particular groups and localities – offers the most appropriate level at which to analyse in detail the relationships between cultural forms, their role in creating the broad patterns observed at macro-scale and in producing the variations within these patterns. In focusing on particular groups and localities it becomes clear that processes of conservation and change are at work simultaneously. On the one hand custom persists, on the other hand fundamental transformations are taking place in the pattern of social relations. How far does the macro-micro dichotomy outlined above help us to analyse this duality? It provides a partial solution by emphasising that social processes interact at a series of interlocking scales. What it does not indicate is the nature of these interactions. Does custom (reciprocal obligations, rituals, beliefs, traditional practices) persist in spite of or because of the broader transformations taking place? Furthermore, what kinds of custom persist – are maybe intensified – while others are breaking down? These questions can best be answered by detailed case study.

General issues and case studies

Changes in fertility and mortality are among the striking products of the interaction between structure and culture. As regards reductions in mortality, infant mortality in particular, improvements in environmental health through better water supply, sanitation and health education are among the most critical interventions which can be made. But within this context it is apparent that at the level of community and household, fundamental cultural practices and preferences linked with water supply and sanitation, and beliefs about disease must be understood and accommodated if improvements are to be realised. Turning to fertility, neither Malthusian nor Marxian perspectives give adequate attention to the significance of culture. What matters is the nature of the change in kinship and family structures under the influence of the market economy, rural-urban movement and diverse income earning opportunities. The effects of these factors upon decisions about family formation, family size and child rearing practices are critical. In explaining spatial variations in fertility and mortality, it is those elements of continuity and change in traditional social relations which we must explore within the context of a totally different national politico-economic environment from that of the past (Ch. 7).

Moreover, in studying demographic change, the links between culture and development are important not only from a theoretical viewpoint but also for their policy implications. Development projects depend for their success on the response of the recipients. It is now widely accepted that 'any system well used by people satisfies a need and is therefore a success. Any system not used by consumers is a failure.' A sensitivity to local social practices, to cultural values and preferences and to the potential or actual conflicts with external influence is therefore essential.

It is the significance of this externally induced change which is stressed by Goody (1971: 76) in his study of African social structures. In seeking to avoid crude materialistic determinism he emphasises that 'man's machinery is the product of his own inventiveness' and that changes in technology open up new possibilities which are among the factors in the process of social change. However, he goes on to emphasise that where new technology is introduced from outside there is frequently a failure on the part of politicians, planners and international experts to appreciate the character and significance of the technological base for the society within which they are working. Although the need is recognised to minimise the social disruption which frequently accompanies the implementation of development projects and the introduction of new technology, how to achieve this continues to be a major challenge when conditions and circumstances vary so widely in practice.

Social service provision, for example, may involve the conversion of a resource like water which has traditionally been freely available, to a commodity for purchase. Among the constraints on access, physical distance may therefore be compounded by social and economic distance. In addition, the response to innovations including schemes to improve environmental health and family planning programmes in many cases suggests that a cultural gulf between outside agency (represented by, for example, the engineer or the health worker) and clients (the local community) may further inhibit success. The gulf appears to be greatest for the poorest groups with least experience of and contact with government officials and/or modern medicine. As a means by which to overcome both types of problem, mention should be made of community participation, a strategy for development based on consultation and involvement of community members in schemes for the improvement of their own conditions (White 1981). It is an approach which above all builds upon traditional cultural practices and existing social organisational models at community level rather than seeking to replace them. The significance of such a strategy in influencing the social and spatial impact of development programmes needs to be explored (Ch. 6 & 7).

The significance of culture is also apparent when we focus on how people earn a living and the economic activities which sustain them. In seeking to explain the spatial distribution of economic opportunities by reference to the role of the State, an undue concentration on class categories and class analysis may fail to identify the particular set of values and beliefs which underlies decisions made at the centre. Moreover, a narrow class-based approach may ignore the cultural issues which lie behind the implementation of programmes such as rural development and the upgrading of spontaneous settlements (Ch. 6). In considering the means by which Africans cope with changes in their environment, with the problems of poverty and unequal access to scarce resources within and between rural and urban areas, it is also apparent that culture modifies standard class categories. Using as our starting point the changing nature of the family household, and the problems of women in particular, this can be clearly identified.

A concern with welfare and income distribution requires that we focus attention on traditional kinship relations and, within this, on the household which remains a fundamental cultural unit. While practical problems of definition do arise, the household may be regarded as synonymous with the basic family unit, a 'socially recognised group of people related by ties of blood or marriage who recognise mutual and explicit rights and duties towards each other, who contribute their labour, income and capital to each other and/or to the group, and who participate in decisions on familial, social or economic matters pertaining to the group' (Kerven 1980: 3). By adopting this focus the emphasis shifts from individuals and classes to the smallest cultural unit within which a range of decisions affecting social, economic and spatial behaviour is taken and upon which the effect of such decisions primarily falls.

It should not be assumed that family members are confined within a single dwelling unit or community. This was not traditionally the case in Tswana society (p.52) and indeed profound changes have taken place in the experience of household members under the influence of Africa's politico-economic trans- formation. Individual migration from rural to urban areas has promoted spatial separation. Wage employment provides a degree of financial independence, while urban life offers a greater range of social contacts than in the past. Under these conditions while the household is no longer the unit of production, and indeed individual members may be engaged in a range of economic activities both within and outside the formal sector in different localities, nevertheless in many cases it remains the primary income sharing unit (Bienefeld & Godfrey 1975). Thus in focusing on population mobility and rural-urban interactions a belief in the individual either as decision-maker or as passive victim of global forces does not adequately explain the processes involved. Of major importance in geographical study are the ways in which space is used to maintain the continuity of the household (through both physical movement and the remittance system), the reasons for this continuity under changed conditions and its importance to individual household members (Ch. 8).

Among the household members whose role and status have changed dramatically with the penetration of alien economic and social values, reference should be made to women. Any concern with the problems of poverty and inequality requires that of the various ways in which we may divide African society, gender be acknowledged as an important addition to class. Epstein (1975: 8) points out that 'The balance between sexual role specificity and the complementarity of male and female tasks worked reasonably well as long as there was little socio-economic change. The introduction of formal education and new economic opportunities upset this traditional balance by enabling men to raise their status while those of many women either remained static or even deteriorated.' Little valued activities as defined by the market economy such as child rearing and subsistence production are largely women's work with the result that the majority of women have become among the culturally-defined low status groups in much of Africa. Whether they are left behind in rural areas or migrants to the towns, as Bienefeld (1981: 8) points out, many women are both socially and economically oppressed. Facing social discrimination in the field of education they are 'forced into the labour market with relatively low levels of skill and formal qualification'. The impact of migration on women both as dependent wives left behind in rural areas and as women migrants forms an important focus of geographical study. Through detailed case study in selected areas of the continent the problems facing women may be placed not only in their geographical setting but also, and more particularly, in their politico-economic and cultural context (Ch. 8).

Conclusion

African countries comprise a combination of indigenous and alien cultural forms. In explaining institutional behaviour and the response of the ordinary African people to changes in their environment it is with the nature of these interactions that we should be concerned. Neither the African leaders nor their citizens are merely robots responding to external inputs in entirely predictable ways. Our framework for study must incorporate not only the so-called 'structural factors' arising from global capitalism but also the social and cultural practices which shape the broader political economy. Spatial outcomes can only be thoroughly explained by reference back to the cultural context and to the interactions between cultural forms. An exclusive reliance on material and physical factors, on the distribution of resources and power, fails to explain the direction of national and regional change and the range of responses by individuals and groups, both within and between African states, to the opportunities presented to them and to the constraints imposed.

African cultural traditions are diverse. Broad variations in ethnicity continue to be significant while at local level social and cultural practices relating to community, family and household influence the decisions and actions of particular groups. But at neither scale are these traditions static. In seeking to explain the contemporary geography of Africa our concern is with the elements of continuity and change in African social structures under the influence of external forces. The following chapters seek to explore these elements by means of case study: Chapters 4–6 consider the ways in which the interaction between cultural forms has shaped national and regional change while Chapters 7 and 8 focus on the level of community and household.

Further reading

For a discussion of the importance of culture in development theory and practice see *IDS Bulletin* (Brighton) 1976 vol.8, no.2, 'Culture revisited'. The significance of ethnicity in African countries is debated in Gutkind (1970). Peil (1977: Ch. 5) provides an introduction to the family and kinship. The importance of the household in studies of income distribution is stressed by Bienefeld and Godfrey (1975).

Chapter 4

AN HISTORICAL BACKGROUND

Introduction

An initial subdivision of African history into two broad time periods is offered in this chapter. First, the heritage of traditional society up to the fifteenth century and second, the impact of Europe from the fifteenth century to independence. Although this subdivision is based on political events perhaps of most immediate significance outside the continent, these are used because, as will become apparent, much of the history of the economy and society of Africa after the coming of the Europeans, together with the associated changes in the organisation of space, was shaped by events beyond the continent. This chapter seeks to emphasise, however, that in explaining the precise character of social and spatial change within different parts of Africa, of central importance was the interaction between colonial and indigenous cultures.

The pre-colonial period

The pre-colonial period is a major concern in much contemporary African literature. The tendency during the colonial era and within the 'modernisation' school of development study to dismiss as insignificant developments in African societies prior to European influence has elicited strong reaction both within the continent and outside. The belief in a distinctive 'African personality' gained strong support during the colonial period among African intellectuals such as Leopold Senghor who was frustrated by European attempts at cultural assimilation (Davidson 1961). More recently within the social sciences the old condescension has gradually been abandoned in favour of a lively interest in the African economy and society. As a result the rich variety of material and abstract culture which existed before the coming of the Europeans and which has hitherto been largely the preserve of anthropologists is well documented in a wide range of recent social science literature (Brain 1981; Curtin *et al.* 1979; Crumney & Stewart 1981).

The diverse social structures which existed in pre-colonial Africa gave rise to a varied organisation of space. While much of the contemporary urban structure of tropical Africa began to develop as recently as the late nineteenth and early twentieth century, many cities are long established particularly in West Africa. The Yoruba cities of south-west Nigeria are well documented (Mabogunje 1962; Lloyd 1973); so too the so-called 'Islamic cities' in the savannah belt, over 800 years old, which flourished as capitals of African empires, as religious centres and as terminals of trans-Saharan trade (Gugler & Flanagan 1978; O'Connor 1983). These cities formed part of a complex social organisation in which cultural continuity was maintained with the surrounding rural areas. Watts (1983) describes Hausaland in the semi-arid zone of West Africa where within the confines of the State and a subsistence economy a mutual support system operated at complementary spatial scales (household–community–region) to withstand the vagaries of the environment.

The migratory character of pastoral societies resulted in a less formal control over space. Seasonal migration between grazing lands was critical to survival. As a result rights of tribal ownership were more nebulous with access to, and control over land based not on continuous occupation. Regrettably it was a failure later by the colonial government to acknowledge the significance of apparently unoccupied land to pastoral communities which led in some cases to hostility within the colonial territories and threatened the security of pastoralism as a way of life. It is reported in East Africa, for example, that the reservation of tracts of land for European farming deprived the Masai of their 'best and most favoured grazing lands' (Harlow & Chilver 1965: 228).

Theoretical models relating mode of production to spatial organisation in the pre-colonial period have been developed by French anthropologists working in the Marxist tradition. Coquery-Vidrovitch (1976), for example, challenges the view of African traditional societies which prevailed among many Western social scientists during the first half of the twentieth century, that they were static motionless systems lacking the dynamism of the market economies. This Eurocentric myth she seeks to dispel by emphasising that their structure and evolution do not fit the standard models. She does acknowledge, however, the technological stagnation of the continent and demonstrates this with reference to the most vital resource essential for all life, namely, water supply (Coquery-Vidrovitch 1976: 100).

> The wheel was never adopted, even though it seems to have crossed the Sahara at the beginning of history, both in the West (by the caravan route of Tassili N'Ajjer) and the East (through Ethiopia and the eastern Sudan) and even though iron metallurgy had been known in Africa since the beginning of our era (Meroe in Nubia, Nok civilisation in Nigeria). They could therefore have neither animal nor human traction to harness wind or water power. While in the driest regions of the Eurasian continent the wheel played an important role in drawing water from wells, the black African limited himself to storing water

(cisterns dug in the laterite of Gonja, Northern Ghana, or in Salaga, 'the town of a thousand wells'). With certain exceptions, he never solved the enormous problem of the distribution of water, as his counterparts did in the Middle East or even in the oases of the Sahara.

Unlike certain writers (Goody 1971) she claims that this low level of technology is not sufficient to explain Africa's low productivity and economic stagnation. It is merely a symptom rather than a cause. Indeed, African peasants were aware of a range of agricultural techniques but their failure to exploit the potential for agricultural surpluses lay in what she defines as the peculiarly African mode of production which prevailed. In spatial terms this allowed for the creation of powerful state structures and for long-distance interaction across the continent based on trade and warfare.

Most crucial to the survival of the system was the dualistic socio-economic structure on which it was based. Exogenous circulation involved exploitation of neighbouring tribes such as cattle raids by the Masai of the Kikuyu in East Africa, the Nama against the Herero in South-west Africa or the warfare waged by the powerful Buganda kingdom in search of slaves and cattle in what is now Uganda. However, while wealth could be accumulated by élite groups in this way it was rarely used as an exploitable surplus. Moreover, alongside this system of interaction there existed a patriarchal agrarian economy in which the primary means of production – land – was allocated on an egalitarian basis. Economic change was hindered by the lack of any differentiation into classes through large-scale land acquisition and the social division of labour. Exchange at community level was based on reciprocity and redistribution rather than on supply and demand, its primary function being social rather than economic.

Coquery-Vidrovitch like many radical writers emphasises that the stimulus to change and with it the destruction of the traditional African mode came not from within but through the penetration into the continent of economic imperialism and colonial capitalism in the nineteenth century. The structure of rural life was no longer respected and with it there was a movement away from 'exploitation of (foreign) neighbours to the exploitation of individuals within their own communities' (Gutkind & Wallerstein 1976: 16). The concept of destruction and replacement is, however, misleading. Granted, traditional structures were profoundly altered by external influence, but they were hardly overthrown. Rather what matters is the form of interaction between indigenous and external forces as a stimulus to spatial change.

The distinctive and varied organisation of space which could be identified within the African continent before the coming of the Europeans – including powerful state structures, long-distance interactions between groups, the subdivision of land and agricultural land use – represented the outcome of particular forms of political, economic and social organisation (Mabogunje 1972). It was the nature of change in this organisation rather than replacement of it which informs our analysis of spatial change (Crush & Rogerson 1983).

European influence

The end of the fifteenth century is regarded as a significant landmark in African history. It initiated a slow process whereby the continent was incorporated into the international trading system. External contact in the form of Arab trade and Islamic culture had influenced the interior of West and North Africa and the East African coast from the seventh century onwards. However, the coming of the Europeans was to have a far more profound effect on the continent as a whole. From then onwards international events and crises initiated in Europe and elsewhere were to shape African political, economic and social evolution. Changes within the continent became inextricably linked with external change. Indeed, much of the contemporary academic debate concerning African development and underdevelopment centres around the part played by the imperial powers. In the present study by way of introduction to this debate focus is therefore placed upon the long period of European contact before the coming of independence.

It is impossible to review adequately this time period in a single chapter given the extensive literature available on the topic. Thus four key questions are posed as an initial basis for understanding the complex processes involved. First, which European powers were involved in Africa? Second, what were their spheres of influence across the continent? Third, within the territories which they dominated how did they exercise their political, social and economic influence? Finally, a broad question which cuts across the previous ones, how did the impact of Europe change over time?

A basic distinction in political terms can be made between European contact in the pre-colonial period (fifteenth century–1890) and Africa under colonialism (1890–1960). Several alternatives to this simple division have been suggested, however, and in particular the incorporation of the African political economy into the international capitalist system as a framework for division into periods. The various phases and modes of involvement form the basis for a system of classification which does not fit neatly within the political watersheds outlined above. Wallerstein (1976), for example, identifies three main periods of incorporation. From 1750 to 1900 he regards as the early stage of capitalist penetration, the phase of 'informal empire', when trading patterns expanded geographically and the coastal areas of Africa, through the provision of slave labour, made a major contribution to primary production in European industries. Phase 2 (1900–75), which ends with the independence of Portuguese Africa, is characterised as the era of intensive primary production within Africa itself, a process which gave rise to profound internal social and economic changes under the primary political influence of colonial rule. The contemporary period of Phase 3 (1975–present) Wallerstein suggests will complete Africa's integration into the world economy. Palloix (1973) presents a more sophisticated threefold classification using a somewhat different time scale: first, the period up to 1920 involving the penetration into Africa of international commodity capital in the form of goods produced in Europe; second, from 1920 to 1970 the domination of productive capital related to investment in agriculture and mining; and third, since 1970 the primacy of finance capital in the form of aid, grants and loans.

Clearly, precise specification of the various stages in the evolution of the African political economy is problematical. For this reason in the present discussion reference to the key changes which took place is made within the context of the undisputed political subdivisions defined above.

Trade with the continent – the regional impact

Long-distance trade across the continent together with the acquisition of slaves through warfare had been characteristic forms of interaction within Africa before the coming of the Europeans. During four centuries of European contact prior to colonial rule trade in both commodities and slaves was extended. The sphere of exchange expanded from continental to international scale. The slave trade grew into a highly directional inter-continental migration of large numbers of African people involved in a process which, like the refugee problems today, offered little or no prospects of return. European influence was more significant than any previous external contacts, however, not merely because of the increased scale of activities. Of greater long-term importance was that these initial links between Europe and Africa formed the early stages in the development of the capitalist mode of production, a system of economic organisation profoundly different from all previous systems in Africa and one which was to have far-reaching effects.

In the fifteenth century Portugal was the first European power to explore the African coast. By 1497 the Cape route to India had been discovered making possible the expansion of a Portuguese Empire across the Indian Ocean. Gold, ivory and slaves were obtained from coastal ports in West and East Africa, the slaves used as means of production, the gold and ivory as bases for exchange in the development of an international trading network from India and the Far East to Central and South America. Portuguese monopoly of goods and slaves from West Africa, the Congo region and the East African coast, lasted until the end of the sixteenth century when several European powers, notably the French, Dutch and British, became involved. The restriction of Portugal's influence to Portuguese Guinea and Angola in the west, and to Mozambique in the east, opened up a period of French and British rivalry in Africa which was to continue until the late nineteenth century (Fig. 4.1). The purchase of slaves for use in the plantations of the West Indies and the Americas reached a peak in the eighteenth century. In exchange, goods produced in Europe including firearms, textiles, spirits and metal products entered the coastal regions and ushered into the continent a period dominated by international commodity capital.

What were the effects of this external influence on Africa's development or underdevelopment at this time? European penetration involved the establishment of new overseas commercial relationships and transactions which exposed the continent to a wide range of goods from Europe and food crops such as maize,

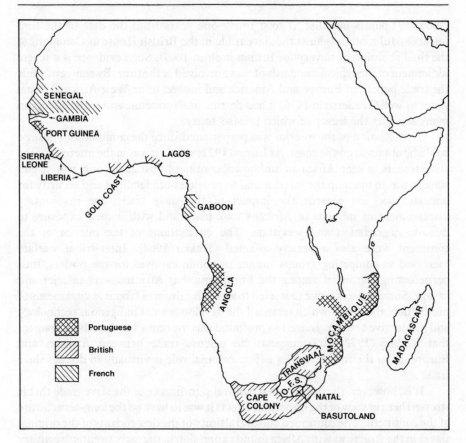

Figure 4.1 The pattern of alien rule in Africa south of the Sahara, 1880 (after Fage and Verity 1978)

sweet potato and cassava from South America. It could be suggested that these imports provided the potential for economic advance. However, in two respects it is apparent that Western imports had a negative effect. First, many of the commodities involved were consumer items which could not enter the production process. Second, the key factors determining the types and terms of trade were the patterns of production and consumption in Europe. Through an emphasis on external demand at the expense of local needs a distorted economic system emerged, regulated and controlled by exogenous forces.

As regards the trade in labour power, this trade reflects a feature which is characteristic of much of Europe's historical involvement in Africa. It was initiated by circumstances beyond the continent – in this instance the demands of a plantation economy in the Americas and the islands of the Indian Ocean – rather than by any intrinsic interest in the African economy *per se*. In assessing this trade it is clear that as with the subsequent colonial period the attitudes prevalent at the time differ significantly from the widely accepted contemporary view. Fordham

(1965: 59) points out that 'it took thirty-one years from the date of the first unsuccessful motion against the slave trade in the British House of Commons to the final abolition of slavery for Britain itself in 1807'. Such evidence is a severe indictment of the ethical standards of those involved at the time. By contrast, while the trade benefited Europe and America and indeed some West African coastal states as well (Wallerstein 1976) it had detrimental economic and social effects on many societies the legacy of which persists today.

The isolation of the interior was perpetuated since the commodities desired could be obtained on the coast. As Lucas (1922) states, it was in the interests of the slave traders to keep Africa an 'unknown' continent, just as the only way to end slavery was to open up the interior and to provide both facilities and security for honest trade. As regards the impact of the slave trade, the involuntary displacement of millions of Africans took place and with it their exposure to disease, degradation and servitude. The civilisations of the interior of the continent were also adversely affected (Daaku 1968). Inter-tribal warfare increased as competing groups sought to obtain captives for the traders, thus perpetuating the belief among the Europeans that Africans were inferior and savage. Some writers argue that it led to a massive drain of labour, a vital means of production, the loss of which retarded the development of indigenous technology and productive activity. Indeed so profound was the impact of this labour transfer that Rodney (1972: 103) suggests 'to discuss trade between Africans and Europeans in the four centuries before colonial rule is virtually to discuss slave trade'.

It is, however, the deep-rooted cultural significance of the slave trade that is stressed here in view of the important effects it was to have on the long-term future of the continent. The continued cultural affinity of the descendants of the original slaves in the Americas with Africa found expression in the early twentieth century in the Pan-African movement which held its first congress in 1900 and was later to become a powerful political force for African liberation.

Although Africa's resources were depleted the changes which took place were not entirely negative. Many societies continued to evolve and indeed in the case of such states as Yorubaland, Dahomey and the Interlacustrine Kingdoms of East Africa considerable political and cultural developments took place in spite of their involvement in slavery (Hopkins 1973). Advances such as these are not incompatible with the destructive social and economic forces already outlined when it is recalled the limited geographical extent of European penetration at this time. Contact was largely confined to the coast with the exception of the Portuguese in Angola and Mozambique, the French in Senegal and the Dutch in South Africa. Thus the degree and type of disruption and dislocation of traditional life within the continent varied considerably. In West Africa the loss of manpower in relation to total population was less severe than in Angola and East Africa where the indigenous economies depended upon their relatively sparse populations from which to draw a labour force.

Finally, in analysing this pre-colonial period reference should be made to the marked change in attitude towards Africa which was taking place in Europe by the beginning of the nineteenth century. The success of the anti-slavery movement in Britain and much of Europe during the two opening decades of the nineteenth century led to the penetration of the continent by missionaries and explorers for the first time. A new era of social contact had begun which had a profound effect on a greater number of ordinary people than hitherto. Trading patterns between certain parts of the continent, notably West Africa and Europe, were also modified with substitutes for labour purchase being found in items such as groundnuts, palm oil and timber (Fyfe 1974). Thus by the coming of the colonial period at the end of the nineteenth century international capital was beginning to penetrate the production process.

Political transformation

By the end of the nineteenth century the political map of tropical Africa had been dramatically transformed. Within the span of two decades from 1884 six Western powers, namely Belgium, Britain, France, Germany, Portugal and Spain, had established official political control over territories which had previously been merely informal spheres of influence (Fig. 4.2). Arbitrary territorial boundaries were defined cutting across tribal and linguistic groups and removing from traditional African leaders the political authority they had retained throughout the previous four centuries. The scramble for Africa is the object of controversy and debate in the historical literature (Chamberlain 1974; Hynes 1979). Before discussing the events surrounding it we need to clarify two processes, namely imperialism and colonialism. The former is an economic phenomenon. It describes the expansion of capitalism on a world-wide scale which followed the industrial revolution (Lenin 1916; 1964). By the late nineteenth century opportunities for growth within the national economies of Europe and North America had become limited. These countries turned to the less-developed world as a source of new raw materials, a market for Western products and as a profitable field for productive investment. Given the trade which had been evolving with Africa during the previous four centuries, clear possibilities existed for the further penetration of foreign capitalism. By contrast, colonialism essentially involves political control over a territory by a foreign power. The scramble for Africa which initiated political changes of this kind coincided with the process of economic transformation known as imperialism.

It is important to ask to what extent the rise of imperialism precipitated colonial expansion and leading on from this, how far political control directly or indirectly encouraged capitalist expansion within individual colonies and thereby became instrumental in the economic, social and spatial changes which took place. A largely discredited view expressed officially at the time and supported more recently by the modernisation school of development suggests that colonialism came about because of Africa's needs rather than those of Europe. Direct colonisation was a necessity: it would ensure the complete destruction of the slave trade and it would stimulate further progress within Africa. The radical alternative

69

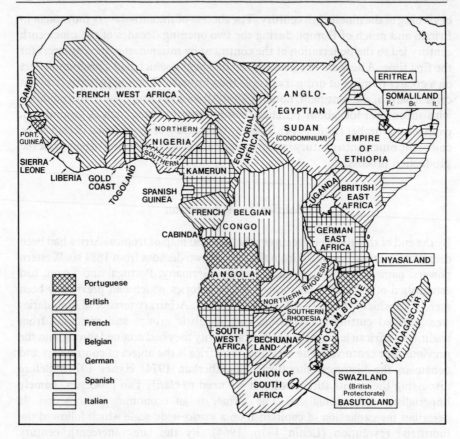

Figure 4.2 The pattern of alien rule in Africa south of the Sahara, 1914 (after Fage and Verity 1978)

to this view suggests that political and economic forces were manipulated by the imperial powers for their own benefit, that is, colonialism was a precondition for the expansion of capitalism. Rodney (1972: 151), for example, states that 'The common factor underlying the overthrow of African rulers in East, West, Central, North and South Africa was that they stood in the way of Europe's imperial needs. It was the only factor that mattered, with anti-slavery sentiments being at best superfluous and at worst calculated hypocrisy'.

This somewhat uncompromising view of partition tends, however, to oversimplify a period of complex international change which had serious ramifications not only in Africa but also, initially, more importantly in Europe. Indeed, as with many of the changes which took place in Africa under European influence, they were precipitated by events beyond the continent itself and must be interpreted within this wider context. Oliver and Fage (1966: 182) point out that 'So far as there was an economic motive for partition of the kind suggested by Marxist writers, it was a motive which appealed to those European powers which had no colonies and little commercial influence in Africa, rather than those whose influence was already established there'. The upsetting of the balance of power in Europe was fundamental to Africa's political transformation. During the first half of the nineteenth century Britain had controlled the capitalist world economy and monopolised African trade. By the mid-century this position was being challenged by France, Germany and the United States. The British share of West African trade was declining (Newbury 1969) as indeed was the value of export products from this region in the face of a world-wide expansion in commodity production. The world market for certain Western products was declining in relative terms and the competition for this market was therefore becoming more intense.

However, neither this international economic situation nor indeed the opening up of Africa during the previous decades were sufficient conditions for partition. It was political changes in Europe which precipitated the process (Hopkins 1973). The entry of Belgian interests into the Congo, and with it the founding of what was to prove the only European dictatorship in Africa, was followed by German annexation of territory in four widely separated parts of the continent, namely South-West Africa, Togoland, the Cameroons and East Africa. While neither Belgium nor Germany had maintained extensive interests in the continent hitherto, their actions upset the existing balance of power. Germany had achieved a major political triumph in Europe against France in 1870. Her industrial base was expanding and by securing African territory she could not only control a section of the world market but in addition revive the traditional rivalries between Britain and France, thereby preventing any Franco-British alliance in Europe. France responded to the German expansion and Britain retaliated. Thus, as Wallerstein (1970) suggests, colonisation did not merely reflect the economic importance of particular areas: it was primarily a pre-emptive process.

The impact of the scramble on the political geography of Africa was profound. The boundaries defined imposed a new uniformity on the political organisation of space which changed very little either during the colonial period or on independence. Discussed and delineated on maps in the European corridors of power following the Berlin Conference (1884–85), they are geographical curiosities which paid little regard to the pre-existing divisions of territory by cultural group. A reliance on lines of latitude and longitude in the absence of geographical detail resulted in tribal groups being politically divided, a particular feature in West Africa. For example, the Ewes were split between the Gold Coast (now Ghana) and Togoland, and the Yorubas between Nigeria and Dahomey (now Benin).

At the same time ethnic groups varying widely in custom, social and economic organisation were brought together within the same political unit for the first time, despite traditional rivalries, while in some cases powerful African kingdoms were combined with small minority groups to form the basis of new nation states. The Asante formed the core of the Gold Coast while in East Africa the formation of Uganda brought together the Bantu kingdom of Buganda with Nilotic and Nilo-Hamitic groups including the Bunyoro and Ankole states to the north and west. As Seidman (1980: 303) summarises with reference to West Africa

71

in particular, these new states 'reflect little more than the extent to which the colonising powers succeeded in carving empires out of coastal areas and extending them into the interior of the continent'. The consequences of this process of Balkanisation have been profound.[1] Besides the serious economic implications since political independence, in addition, much twentieth-century hostility within and between countries has reflected the power of ethnic over national identity.

Colonial rule

Much contemporary development literature focuses on the impact of colonialism in Africa. On one issue there is general agreement: that African political, economic and social structures were profoundly changed in a process of transformation which had begun during the previous four centuries. Within the new states socio-economic and political change was accompanied by changes in the administrative and economic organisation of space. A rational administrative network was created and an infrastructure laid out both of which emanated from the central focus of political and economic power – the capital city. In this way a certain uniformity emerged between countries. New spatial structures also emerged in relation to the economic activities associated with the capitalist mode of production. But there was also diversity.

The history of colonialism in the various parts of Africa is well-documented. (See, for example, Ajayi & Crowder 1974; Barber 1961; Birmingham & Martin 1983; Harlow & Chilver 1965; Ikime 1977; Isichei 1983; Rotberg 1966). From these studies it is clear that the types of political, administrative and economic structures established under colonialism and imposed upon the newly integrated African societies differed markedly between regions of the continent, between individual countries and within different parts of each country. For example, a dominant feature of West African colonial experience was that the principal factor in agricultural production, land, remained under African ownership while European capital concentrated on trading activities. By contrast much of East, Central and Southern Africa was dominated by European-owned estates or plantations while the distribution of foreign-owned mining concerns extended from Sierra Leone and Mauritania to the Congo and Northern and Southern Rhodesia. Just as the form and type of European penetration differed spatially so too did its economic and social impact. The nature and cause of these variations must be borne in mind as we turn now to consider three phases of colonial influence in Africa separated by the major political watersheds of the two World Wars.

[1]The term Balkanisation derives from the Balkan States of Eastern Europe which were arbitrarily divided into many small political units after the First World War.

1890–First World War: Control over territory

Throughout Africa colonial rule was established by a combination of persuasion and coercion. In parts of West Africa for example it arose from the military defeat of powerful states like the Asante and Ilorin while elsewhere European authority was accepted by treaty. Following this shift in political control a more integrated economic system was established based on the capitalist mode of production. The penetration of a market economy required a fiscal structure involving various forms of direct and indirect taxation. These developments, which were to have a profound long-term impact on the lives of the African people, depended initially on control over territory. A disciplined army, a co-ordinated district administration and a communications system were needed to integrate the various parts of each country, to collect taxes beyond the immediate core area and to facilitate the distribution and marketing of products. Political control by a foreign power was therefore reflected in the landscape – the colonial district town (McMaster 1968) directly responsible to the capital, and a road and rail network emanating from that centre. In Uganda direct taxation could not be introduced until the Uganda railway reached Lake Victoria in 1901 permitting the export of products like hides, skins and rubber. Even then direct political control was confined to the nucleus of the Protectorate until roads were constructed and the railway extended to the north of the country during the next two decades.

What was the early impact of these European institutions and this spatial reorganisation on the lives of the African people? A distinction must be made between the élite minority of indigenous rulers and the majority of the ordinary population. In the political sphere interaction between the colonial administration and indigenous rulers played an important role in determining the initial acceptance of external authority. Where the latter acknowledged the supremacy of the colonial government native institutions continued to retain certain powers and alien rule was reinforced from within the traditional setting. Thus, underlying the apparent uniformity of the imported colonial model traditional cultural diversity persisted, albeit in modified form. In the Gold Coast the colonial administration existed alongside the traditional system, the latter retaining some control over civil and criminal justice in local courts. Elsewhere the colonial administration sought to work through the traditional political structures so that ideally there was only one system of local government. This practice is most correctly termed Indirect Rule and was initiated by Lord Lugard in Northern Nigeria. The system spread to other parts of British Africa including Uganda in 1900 following the Uganda Agreement with the dominant tribal group, the Baganda. Here the existing native polity was made the instrument of British rule first in the southern kingdom of Buganda and subsequently throughout the Protectorate in such a way that although traditional structures were modified they were nevertheless conserved.

As regards the majority of the African population, changes in their social relations and use of space to engage in production were closely related to the types of economic structure which emerged under the influence of external forces. The introduction of direct taxation – a poll tax and hut tax – necessitated that Africans earned a cash income. But the opportunities available varied widely. Amin (1972a) and Wallerstein (1976) outline three major modes of agricultural activity which evolved to exploit rising world demand and to provide Africans with an essential monetary income. The African peasant farming model concentrated most intensely in West Africa though also in Uganda; the plantation system in Equatorial Africa, Tanganyika, Nyasaland and Angola, on concession land, owned by European companies and managed by expatriates who did not intend to settle; and the white settler system chiefly in Kenya and Southern Rhodesia where Europeans expropriated land from Africans for their own cultivation and settlement.

In discussing the reasons for these various types of organisation in different geographical locations Wallerstein (1976) suggests that two factors, the degree of previous involvement by Africans in market-orientated activities and the political influence of the Europeans interested in an alternative mode of activity, were of particular importance. In French and British West Africa pre-colonial economic activities and forms of exchange were well developed. Trading firms had also become firmly established during the nineteenth century with the result that peasant production was the most appropriate and least disruptive system of organisation for the colonial administration. In French and Belgian Equatorial Africa neither of these conditions existed and large concessionary companies were permitted to buy land and employ African labour in order to develop production for the world market. In East Africa a striking contrast emerged between the peasant production of Uganda and the emphasis on white settlers to provide cash crops in Kenya. In explaining this difference Wolff (1974) argues that in Kenya the social and economic disruption caused by the slave trade, coupled with the absence of a firm hierarchical tribal structure, obliged the colonial authorities to encourage white settlers using African labour. By contrast:

> The geographic position of Uganda in the interior of the continent greatly reduced the economically damaging effects of the slave trade and its abolition. Furthermore, the relatively strictly structured and 'stable' Buganda Kingdom offered the attractive possibility of organising African peasant agricultural production managed at middle and lower levels by Africans already accustomed to workable hierarchical relationships. (Wolff 1974: 177)

Thus, as with the administrative system so with economic activity: not only were external forces important in explaining geographical variations across the continent, so too was the nature of the existing socio-cultural system. The penetration of merchant and productive capital did not result in spatial uniformity or a linear pattern of economic change. In much of West Africa indigenous structures provided the foundation on which an export economy based on peasant commodity production could develop while elsewhere the means of production were taken out of African ownership. Labour became a commodity and large-scale wage labour migration became a significant result. Thus through the interaction between traditional and external modes a varied economic system emerged.

For Africans who participated in and reproduced this system the effects were profound. The financial and commercial institutions introduced, including banks, trading companies, mining and plantation organisations, and the agreements which these organisations made with the colonial government, significantly altered the terms on which Africans could engage in production and exchange. Although in certain areas land remained under African ownership commodity production shifted the orientation of communities from their internal needs to those of the towns and overseas markets. Labour migration altered the structure of population mobility (Gould & Prothero 1975) while the temporary loss of male labour to the mines, plantations and emerging towns altered the social relations at community level. The former cohesiveness of village life was eroded and replaced by a growing economic differentiation within and between peasant communities and within the towns. Patterns of social and regional inequality began to emerge which were to continue into independence. However the response of different groups within the African population to the opportunities presented and to the constraints imposed cannot be explained solely in structural terms. The variations which emerged in demographic behaviour and in the use of space to maintain social interactions and to engage in economic activities reflected once again the interplay of structural and cultural forces. (For a detailed discussion see Chs 7 & 8.)

Progress towards civil administration in many of the territories was slow with the result that it was some years after partition until the majority of local people became fully aware of and influenced by alien rule. In peripheral parts of East Africa, for example, tribes such as the Masai disdained European contact while in Uganda civil administration was only finally established in the North in 1919. A further striking feature is the apparent ambivalence of the imperial powers towards the economic exploitation of their newly acquired territories. Although economic change was a prerequisite for new fiscal structures both spread only gradually from the core areas and no immediate investment directed by the metropolitan centres took place. As regards the colonial governments, their primary responsibility at this stage was to maintain peace and a self-supporting administration. The provision of social facilities such as education and health lay with the missions while economic development depended on the initiative of individual producers and traders. While encouragement was given to foreign investors through the granting of concessions, through the lease or sale of land for plantations or settlement and by the issuing of mining rights, the primary motivation behind this colonial policy appeared to be the accumulation of revenue. Low (1965) points out that from 1900 onwards European farmers were encouraged to settle in Kenya and to grow cash crops primarily because the sale of their products would help to finance the Uganda Railway.

Although events beyond the continent established a colonial economic model in Africa based on the capitalist mode, access to the means of production, the organisation of production and changes in social relations, all of which influence the organisation and use of space, were conditioned by local circumstances. Among these the power of European private interests and the views of individual governors were, of course, important. But so too was the nature of the existing social and cultural system which in interacting with alien institutions played a central role in shaping Africa's transformation.

Inter-war period : Colonial cultures

The inter-war years in Africa were dominated by the influence of events in Europe and by the initiatives of Europeans. The establishment of the League of Nations following the end of the First World War stimulated significant changes in Western attitudes to colonialism and directly affected the degree of metropolitan involvement in the African territories. Under the Mandates system Britain, France and Belgium received responsibility for parts of the former German Empire in Africa. Togoland and the Cameroons were divided between France and Britain, German East Africa was partitioned between Britain and Belgium and South-West Africa was allocated to the Union of South Africa.

Acquisition of these territories coupled with the regulations for their control as laid down by the League prompted the need for the metropolitan powers to formulate more precisely than they had done hitherto a clear philosophy of colonialism. In Britain this found expression in the writings of the famous African administrator, Lord Lugard, notably in *The Dual Mandate in British Tropical Africa* (1922; 1965) and later in the Ormsby-Gore Reports of 1924 and 1926. French ideas at the time were reflected in the work of the colonial minister Albert Sarraut. Overall the approach advocated was one of enlightened self-interest. Colonial powers were under an obligation not only to ensure stability and peace but also to encourage the social and economic development of their territories through the promotion of education and health facilities and the expansion of capitalism. But these firm new directives from Europe did not result in a uniform pattern of change. During the inter-war years significant differences emerged between British attitudes towards the political and cultural evolution of her territories and the ideology of continental Europe. Any analysis of the colonial period and its legacy in Africa today is incomplete without reference to the regional experience derived from the ideals of the metropolitan powers and the contrasting systems they introduced. 'An understanding of the nature of these differences is not only essential to an understanding of colonial history in Africa but also to an appreciation of the differences between the two main language blocks in independent Africa today' (Crowder 1964: 205).

Indirect rule

The British philosophy has been described as paternalism and identity in contrast to the ideals of association and assimilation of continental Europe. When translated into the practice of native administration these different beliefs found expression in the systems of indirect and direct rule (Crowder 1964). Each approach derived its impetus from contrasting circumstances in Europe, it influenced the degree of colonial intervention in the economy and society of Africa and occasioned different responses from the African population.

British ideals found expression in a practice of decentralised administration. Colonial officials and district officers retained the authority to evolve a system of government suitable to local circumstances. The practice was therefore essentially empirical rather than uniform. Where possible indigenous political structures were incorporated into the administration in a system of indirect rule designed to reduce tensions and minimise financial costs (Lugard 1965). In view of the wide variety of native systems within and between countries this flexibility allowed for adaptation and modification where necessary of the political role of traditional rulers in their home areas. In West African Islamic societies, for example, Lloyd (1972) discusses the dependence of the colonial administrator on the influence of the Emir and the necessity to protect and preserve his traditional role in a complex native authority structure. Thus the sophisticated social and political systems which existed before the coming of the Europeans were used to satisfy colonial interests. Such an overt policy openly contradicts a fundamental principle of the modernisation school that African traditional society lacked formal organisation. Moreover, the contemporary significance of these traditional administrative structures can be seen in many parts of the continent through their use in district development and spatial planning (Chapter 6).

Behind this empirical and decentralising practice of the British were particular ideological beliefs regarding empire and cultural attitudes towards native societies. During the inter-war years there was no conception of a greater Britain overseas in which Africans should become British citizens. Although the idea of a Commonwealth was formulated in the Statute of Westminster in 1930 its form and content was not clearly defined. The principle upheld was that African territories should evolve in a way which was appropriate to their environment and society within the colonial government framework. In the long-term self-government would be granted when the indigenous population had achieved appropriate education levels and economic prosperity while in the meantime the colonial possessions would merely be held in trust (Hetherington 1978).

Given this philosophy of paternalism colonial governments were under an obligation to encourage the advancement of their people through the provision of educational facilities and outlets to the world market. The Great Britain Advisory Committee on Native Education in British Tropical African Dependencies (1925) indicated that the function of schools was to 'make the conscience sensitive to moral and intellectual truth' and to 'impart some power of discrimination between good and evil, between reality and superstition'. Following the policy of this Committee assistance was given to mission foundations through inspection and subsidy while a limited state system was established. In East Africa, following the early lead of Uganda, secondary schools were founded in Kenya and Tanganyika while in Kampala, Uganda, a 'higher college', later to become Makerere University, was begun in 1922 under government auspices.

Direct rule

The principles guiding the policies of continental Europe presented a sharp contrast to the British model. Direct, centralised control by European officials was the norm throughout French, Portuguese and Belgian territories. This centralised, somewhat inflexible, system led to a more uniform pattern of administration between territories and more direct control from the metropolitan centre than was apparent under the British. Furthermore, it occasioned much cruelty. The Portuguese, for example, were noted for ruthlessness in their dealings with the local inhabitants. While traditional chiefs were frequently used at local level the geographical units over which they were given control had already been defined by colonial administrators and frequently cut across ethnic and traditional political boundaries. This new administrative organisation of space did much to erode the status of the chief among the local population and with it an important cultural institution. Native systems of administration and justice were largely replaced by European institutions so much so that local leaders lost their traditional authority, were entirely subservient to alien officials and became dependent upon them for their status and influence. The long-term implications of this system for African culture and traditions can be seen, for example, in Guinea in 1957 on the eve of its political independence. Crowder (1964: 201) points out that when 'Sekou Touré (then Vice-President du Conseil) decided to do away with chiefs, the operation was effected with remarkably little protest from either the indigenous population or from the French administration that had made use of them'.

Behind the system of direct rule lay a very different philosophy from the British belief in paternalism and cultural identity. The doctrine of association and assimilation implied that the African people were not free to achieve their own political independence but rather that they would ultimately become citizens of the metropolitan power having first shown their loyalty to colonial authority and fully assimilated the alien culture. In France this doctrine stemmed from the revolutionary belief in the equality of man and, with it, the somewhat contradictory assumption that French culture was superior to African. During the early years of colonisation in the nineteenth century French enthusiasm for assimilation had resulted in many thousands of illiterate non-Christians from the coastal ports of Senegal being granted French citizenship (Crowder 1962). This was the only territory in French tropical Africa in which assimilation was fully applied. In the inter-war years, the process became more selective and French education policy became an important instrument of cultural assimilation through the establishment of schools with similar curricula to those of metropolitan France and the replacement of local languages by French as the medium of instruction. Through an appreciation of and loyalty to French culture it was implied that the African would be granted full social equality with his European counterpart.

Colonial practice

Although during the inter-war years the beliefs and values enshrined in colonial capitalism became more explicit, international events and crises, combined with changing circumstances in Europe and Africa, conspired to modify them somewhat. Thus, despite the apparent differences between French and British systems, Berman (1984: 176) points out that when we 'probe beneath the surface of formal structure and rhetoric, we find that the experiences and internal processes of French and British colonial administration were not only similar, but also in many instances practically identical'. The policies of centralisation and assimilation of continental Europe proved unrealistic and impracticable. In France they were in fact abandoned in favour of a *politique d'association*. Lewis (1962: 150) suggests that the relaxation of policy was an inevitable result of French unwillingness 'to undertake the massive work of social transformation which could alone make it a reality'. Educational provision in her territories was very limited owing to the meagre financial resources made available with the result that only a small African élite were eligible for citizenship. Lloyd (1972) points out that in 1936 there were merely 78,000 Africans in Senegal with French citizenship and only 2400 in the remaining French West African territories. In the Belgian and Portuguese territories a similar pattern emerged of limited educational facilities and restricted citizenship.

The closer integration of the colonial and metropolitan economies meant also that it was impossible for Africa to escape the detrimental effects of the Depression, notably the relative economic Stagnation and decline in the international demand for primary products (Brett 1973). Thus in British territories although under the Colonial Development Act of 1929 grants were made available to assist the financing of capital projects the onset of the Depression at the end of 1929 precluded much activity. When its worst effects were over in the mid-1930s certain countries did benefit from the Colonial Development Fund, such as Tanganyika which had suffered more than the other two East African territories. However, by 1938 the British dependencies overall had received a relatively small amount equivalent to the addition of only about one per cent of their combined revenue (Oliver & Page 1966).

But, although investment was limited its effects were not insignificant. Brett (1973) suggests that the foreign impact in the areas of European settlement was particularly marked since settlers necessarily demanded political control, special rights to land and social services, while the plantation and mining companies merely required security for their capital. Indeed, from the 1920s onwards, the

79

political rights of white settlers over Africans in East, Central and Southern Africa became an important constitutional issue.

In Kenya, for example, Low and Smith (1976: 479) suggest that the tensions and rivalries which persisted for much of the colonial period revolved in large part around the 'irreducible minimum demands' of the Europeans to maintain the paramountcy of their interests over both the African population and the growing Asian community. While the Devonshire Declaration of 1923 asserted the ultimate supremacy of African interests, nevertheless in relation to land, the most fundamental resource of the African population, the adoption by the colonial government of the principles of segregation and reservation failed to preserve these interests. Europeans were granted rights over what were to become known as the 'White Highlands' and parts of the rift valley while 'native occupation' was loosely interpreted and often openly violated (Harlow & Chilver 1965). In Southern Rhodesia also, colonial government policies regarding land had adverse effects on the prosperity of the dominant Shona and Ndebele peoples. The 'white agricultural policy' as it became known and which began in 1908 was designed specifically to promote European settlement and farming. In doing so, by restricting the access of Africans to the means of production it directly contributed to the decline of their agricultural economies and to the spread of poverty (Palmer 1977).

In addition to these particular problems in the white settled areas more generally within the African territories the pattern of European investment tended to intensify social and spatial inequalities. The expansion of the money economy and with it the provision of education facilities created new criteria for social stratification. As regards the location of these investments, development under capitalism favoured certain geographical areas. Spatial concentration led in turn to spatial inequalities in access to income earning opportunities and to social services.

In much of Central and Southern Africa these trends were particularly marked where the exploitation of industrial and agricultural resources by Europeans depended on stimulating and maintaining labour migration. Through various recruiting monopolies African labour was channelled into specific locations. The European farming areas and mines in South Africa were developed in this way. So too were the Northern Rhodesian Copper belt and the Katanga area of the Belgian Congo, the white farms around Salisbury and Bulawayo, the Nyasaland tea estates and the mines and sisal plantations in Tanganyika. By the 1930s the labour migration process had become firmly established. Arrighi (1970) points out with reference to Rhodesia that with the progressive weakening of the peasant agricultural sector the sale of labour time became a necessity for the African population.

The circular character of this labour migration is a well-researched theme among social scientists (Richards 1939; Wilson 1941). So too is the segregated urban social structure with which it was associated (Mitchell 1969). Derived from a stereotyped view of the African upheld by the European community in this part of the continent, it was a powerful visible symbol of the plural society which colonial urban policy reinforced. The colonists, operating through the government system, had an important influence on urban development and on the social organisation of urban space creating in the process what has been described as the distinctive 'European' city (O'Connor 1983).

1945–1960 : Decolonisation

The Second World War had a decisive effect upon African development and change. The wave of Asian independence during the 1940s together with the founding of the United Nations dedicated to equal rights and self-determination combined to enhance the position of the emergent groups in African society and to transform them into powerful political movements. Opposition to alien influence was not, of course, a new phenomenon in Africa. Indeed, protest groups had from time to time during the previous half century expressed resentment and resistance to Christianity, to Western education and to the disruption of traditional economic practices. One of the most widely documented examples is the rebellion in Nyasaland in 1915 (Rotberg 1966). However, such protests were sporadic and localised in their influence in comparison with developments after 1945. The initial impetus to political unrest derived from the contradictions and inequalities which had become apparent during the 1920s and 1930s, but the appeal of nationalism as a mass movement stemmed from the frustrations and disappointments of the post-war world. These were related to a change in colonial policy within Britain in particular towards her territories, to the growing frustration of the new élites in African society, and to the social and economic conditions within individual countries.

Policy changes

During the inter-war years the European philosophy of colonialism had been formulated in the belief that African territories had a long future under foreign rule. By contrast the post-war period was dominated by the realisation that independence and self-government would soon be realities. Against this background British paternalism took on a more active character. The Colonial Development and Welfare Acts (1940 and 1945) stated a principle which was to become widespread in post-war planning, namely the necessity for direct state involvement in social and economic development. Public investment was justified on the grounds that the African people must be fitted for self-government. Colonial territories were therefore instructed to draw up ten-year development plans. Funds were made available by both Britain and the colonial governments for their implementation and expatriate expertise was encouraged in what became described as the 'second colonial occupation' (Low & Smith 1976).

Thus an era of territorial self-sufficiency in finance was replaced by a period of intense government activity involving the entry of new forms of capital into the

African territories. The level of British aid for education and welfare services was greatly increased. Colonial government financial agencies made large-scale investments in African cash crop agriculture by extending loan capital to farmers and by providing technical expertise for agricultural and industrial projects. Furthermore, government policy became closely associated with international capital through its links with the multinational corporations. After 1945 the world economy became dominated by these large organisations and in many parts of Africa they became an important instrument of government policy by administering development schemes, influencing the quality and quantity of production and by acting as a medium of distribution for the world market (Swainson 1980).

This direct involvement of government brought with it new tensions. Expatriate officials, agents of improvement and instructors, penetrated down to community level where Africans had hitherto been allowed to retain a degree of autonomy. While this intervention was designed to improve the efficiency of African production, to protect African land from erosion and to increase standards of welfare, nevertheless indigenous authority was undermined and the cohesiveness of village life further threatened. As Low and Smith (1976) point out, only too often the complementary halves of colonial policy – to increase productivity while widening the incidence of popular participation in development – conflicted in practice. Among the many examples of the strains which resulted from this new interventionism, in East Africa two major tribal aggregations significant both in geographical size and social cohesion, Buganda in Uganda and Sukumaland in Tanganyika, became the scenes of serious political crises in the decade before independence. In common in both these examples was the frustration of local interests by an increasingly purposeful colonial government.

The organisation of local opposition into nationalist movements was undertaken by a small minority – the educated, independent traders and traditional leaders. These new social groups, the African 'middle class', were in the main products of the institutional structure established and regulated by the colonial state. They comprised the élite minority who had received the opportunity to acquire skills and to exploit the new economic resources introduced by colonial capital, but whose grievances stemmed from the limits which the colonial state sought to impose upon their aspirations notably their exclusion from access to decision-making and political influence beyond the local level.

Patterns of inequality

The new élites were assisted in rallying mass support for the nationalist cause by the contradictions and inequalities which had become a fundamental part of colonial society and which were clearly visible in the organisation of space. While a small minority had benefited from the resources provided by the State the majority of the African population were either exploited or marginal to the interests of the colonial economic system. Primary production, on which the

African countries had come to depend, was divided into three geographically discrete zones interrelated, according to Wallerstein (1976), in a pattern of dominance and dependency (Fig. 4.3). The first zone produced for the world market. The land was owned by white settlers, companies or African peasants and the manpower required was supplied by migrant labour. Capitalist relations prevailed. The size of this zone within individual countries fluctuated with the vagaries of world demand for the local primary products. Its variability in turn controlled the scale of activities and the relative productivity of the other two zones. The second zone produced food crops for workers in the export sector and related urban occupations. The land on which these cash crops were grown was frequently in peri-urban locations contiguous to the towns and export enclaves and was owned and run by Africans. This land was also used for subsistence production, the primary activity of the final zone.

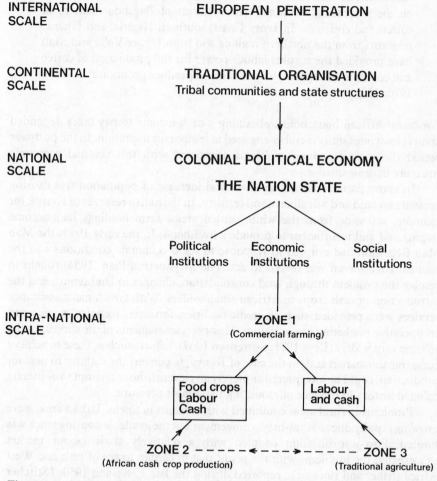

Figure 4.3 Africa's politico-economic transformation (adapted from Wallerstein 1976)

The third zone, which involved the vast majority of the indigenous population and covered the largest proportion of cultivable land, remained closest in character to the traditional African mode. Based on subsistence cultivation and pastoralism its primary link with the capitalist mode was as a source of the essential labour required for the expansion of export production. It produced and reproduced the wage labour force. While many writers (including Amin 1972a) in attempting to classify the continent into regions on the basis of their relationship with the capitalist mode have designated Central and Southern Africa as the 'labour reserves', if we reduce the scale from continent to nation then within most countries a labour reserve could also be identified. Peripheral areas lost labour not only to European-owned enterprises but also to those owned by Africans.

> Labourers from northern Uganda and from Rwanda, Burundi and northern Tanzania came not to work on settler plantations but to work on the increasingly commercialised farms of Baganda planters of cotton and coffee ... In Ivory Coast, southern Nigeria, and Ghana, migrants from the northern regions and from Upper Volta and Mali have provided the surplus labour power for the production of coffee and cocoa; in Senegal they have come to produce groundnuts. (Cliffe 1976: 117)

For many African households, obtaining a cash income to pay taxes depended upon at least one family member engaged in temporary migration. In the post-war period the socio-economic problems associated with this colonial economic structure became intense.

In many parts of Africa rapid natural increase of population was causing pressure on land and a decline in soil fertility. In the native reserves of Kenya, for example, set aside from the white settled areas, farm holdings had become fragmented and insufficient to provide a livelihood. In the early 1950s the Mau Mau Rebellion had erupted in response to socio-economic conditions and the colonial government was forced to act. The Swynnerton Plan (1954) sought to resolve the problem through land consolidation, changes in land tenure and the introduction of cash crops to African smallholders. With government assistance services were provided such as credit facilities, fertiliser, technical advice and co-operative marketing organisations. However, assessments of the success of the scheme vary widely (Leys 1971; Sorrenson 1967). Efforts such as these to achieve rural transformation and, in the case of Kenya, to convert the country to peasant production, could be interpreted as merely an eleventh-hour attempt to obliterate colonial history in the face of mounting nationalist pressure.

Problems in rural areas combined with tensions in towns. Urban areas were growing rapidly due to rural-urban movement but the available housing stock was limited. Post-war inflation coupled with a relatively static labour market exacerbated the problems with the result that in certain towns of East and West Africa strikes and riots were reported during the late 1940s and 1950s (Stitcher 1982; Waterman 1982). Thus for many groups in African society in both rural and urban areas of the continent it became apparent that their aspirations and grievances could be most effectively fulfilled and resolved by supporting the forces of nationalism.

Challenge of independence

Pressure for independence operated at different scales. At the international level representation was made by African politicians at the United Nations. At the continental scale, Pan-Africanism, and at the territorial level the forces of nationalism combined for the same purpose. These two latter movements had been in existence for much of the colonial period but it was only after the Second World War that they became firmly established political forces.

Pan-Africanism derived its initial impetus from a sense of African cultural identity, a unity of values and beliefs among people of African origin throughout the world (Bakpetu Thompson 1969). Founded among the black communities of the New World, the movement gradually received support from African intellectuals (obviously a minority) within the continent and in the French West African territories in particular as a reaction to the assimilationist tendencies of French colonial policy. This cultural dimension gave Pan-Africanism an important philosophical justification when after the Second World War its objectives became strongly political. It was at the Sixth Congress held in Manchester in 1945 and attended by young African nationalists including Kwame Nkrumah from the Gold Coast, Samuel Akintola from Nigeria and Jomo Kenyatta from Kenya that the Pan-African movement became committed through a wider unity of Africans to the overthrow of colonialism. It should be emphasised that this sense of African identity has continued to shape developments within the continent since independence. For example, the Organisation of African Unity was established in 1963 to work for the political and economic unity of independent Africa (Ch. 5).

The common purpose expressed in Pan-Africanism was converted into direct action at national level. Each country had within its boundaries nationalist movements dedicated to equality of status and of rights, to the pursuit of personal dignity, self-respect and social regeneration (Davidson 1967). However the tensions which built up varied in character and timing across the continent in response to local circumstances. West Africa became the initial focus of unrest. In contrast to East Africa, nationalist parties had not been banned from the area and indeed since before the Second World War the African élite had been permitted representation on legislative councils. However, such privileges failed to satisfy nationalist demands. In the Gold Coast by 1950 the Convention People's Party under the powerful leadership of Kwame Nkrumah had received mass support and was pressing for full self-government. In 1957 the country became independent Ghana.

An immediate consequence of this British action was for similar demands to be made both in the remaining British West African territories and also in French

West Africa. 1959–60 was the significant year of independence when both Nigeria and the Belgian Congo gained their freedom and when France withdrew political control from her eight West and four Equatorial African territories. Similar action then spread to British East Africa (Fig. 4.4). In Central and Southern Africa conditions were complicated by the position of Southern Rhodesia and South Africa both of which had gained self-government from the British in the early part of the century. The Central African Federation of Rhodesia and Nyasaland had been formed in 1953 to integrate the considerable resources of the three territories and thereby promote development. However it was the formation of this regional unit which in the case of Northern Rhodesia and Nyasaland promoted the desire for self-government. The federal constitution and with it the apparent subjugation of African interests to the ambitions of the white minority committed the nationalist movements to its destruction. The strength of African opposition was finally acknowledged by Britain in 1960 and in 1964 they were permitted to secede from the Federation forming the independent states of Zambia (1964) and Malawi (1964). In Southern Africa the geographical position of the three British Protectorates of Bechuanaland, Basutoland and Swaziland tied them economically

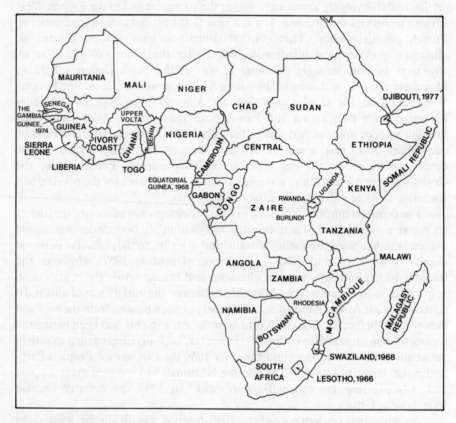

Figure 4.4 Independent Africa south of the Sahara, 1976 (after Fage and Verity 1978)

86

to the Republic of South Africa with the result that not until the latter tacitly accepted their demands for self-government in the mid-1960s did they attain political independence, as Botswana (1966), Lesotho (1966) and Swaziland (1968). Of the Portuguese territories Portuguese Guinea became the independent state of Guinea Bissau in 1974 with Angola and Mozambique following in 1975. The illegal declaration of UDI by the white minority leadership in Rhodesia in 1965 was finally brought to an end in 1980 with the creation of independent Zimbabwe under a democratically elected government.

Inherited spatial structures

The theoretical interest of the geographer in the colonial legacy in Africa forms part of a long-standing debate over the relationship between Europe and the continent. During the colonial era opposing views were expressed by those actively involved, namely, the colonising powers and the colonised peoples. At one extreme was the philanthropic paternalist approach of the colonial official and district officer who conducted their 'civilising mission' in the apparent interests of the indigenous population (Creech Jones 1951; Hetherington 1978). At the other extreme was a radical repudiation of European altruism by the African nationalist movements which propagated a belief in European exploitation and tyranny. There are many examples of leading Pan-Africanist intellectuals preaching on the evils of colonialism (Hunton 1959; Nkrumah 1963; 1965; Padmore 1936). Ranging between these two extremes was a continuum of impressions of the same set of measurable conditions and observable changes brought about under European influence. The views held by the protagonists at the time could be justified and substantiated by the light of personal experience. Illustrations of progress could be found – improvements in health and life expectancy – while allegations of ruthlessness and corruption could equally well be cited.

However, whatever the opinion held and the supporting material used, fundamental behind these irreconcilable views was an ethnocentric bias described by Bohannan (1964) as 'the working misunderstanding'. European officials assessed the political economy of their African territories in terms of Western culture while the same circumstances were evaluated by Africans in terms of their own cultural traditions. A barrier to complete and perfect communication existed. Neither side fully appreciated the codes used by the other to perceive and evaluate the conditions on which actions were taken. Thus suspicion and conflict could easily arise when aspirations appeared to be blocked and economic well-being was perceived to be maldistributed. As Bohannan (1964: 24) points out, 'Many a colonial official has been deeply hurt when after 30 years of selfless service to a colony, he has been charged with tyranny by a subject people who do not distinguish tyranny from paternalism but see only the disjunction between their own cultural views and those of the colonising power.'

This 'working misunderstanding' among the leading actors in the field can in turn be related to questions of space, development and underdevelopment. The 1960s modernisation school reflected strongly the colonial paternalist approach. Studies like those of Gould (1970), Riddell (1970) and Soja (1968) equated the advancement of African society with the spread of institutions and physical infrastructure imported from Europe. By means of sophisticated techniques indicative of this spatial analysis era in geography attempts were made to identify a modernisation surface which would define the spatial extent of socio-economic developments and would indicate key centres or 'islands of development' from which progress would diffuse. The inadequacies of this now discredited Eurocentric approach are well-documented, and it is apparent that debate surrounding the 'colonial balance sheet' now focuses on the organisation of space and patterns of inequality as structures created by society – an unequal social system produced by colonial capitalism.

Conclusion

Colonial space was organised in many different ways across the continent. In making sense of this diversity it is important to consider the interests of the colonisers – the administrators, the settlers and owners of capital – who dominated at the political, economic and spatial centre of power. But equally important was the interaction between colonial and indigenous structures mediated by their respective values and beliefs. It was through this interaction – in some cases conflict and subjugation, in others co-operation and adaptation – that colonial society with its inherent contradiction took shape and created the spatial structures inherited on independence.

The colonial interlude altered profoundly the political map of the continent. The new states were alien both in cultural and spatial terms. Yet the legacy is a long one. The boundaries proved remarkably resilient and were changed little by independence. A transformation also took place in the organisation of national space and certain common features emerged. The autonomy and cohesion of traditional communities was challenged as administrators, health workers, teachers, settlers and private capitalists gradually penetrated to village level. National space became formally controlled by a communications network oriented to the capital city and to the ports. New spatial forms emerged reflecting different levels of incorporation into the capitalist mode. Plantations, estates, mines and towns formed isolated islands where capitalist relations predominated but which ultimately influenced the entire national space. Peri-urban areas served the food needs of the towns and acted as a commuting zone for urban workers. Beyond these an extensive rural periphery including native reserves provided a source of wage labour.

Increased government activity after 1945 speeded up the process of spatial transformation. But it was a pattern of concentrated investment. Government development policies in the countryside favoured certain groups and areas while wage employment was confined to a limited range of activities and locations. Thus regional disparities in income earning opportunities and in welfare intensified. Frequently it was in peripheral locations that poverty was most widespread. Elsewhere differentiation within peasant communities between the wealthy with access to inputs and the poor became marked. It was in the towns, however, that social and, by implication, racial differences were brought into sharpest relief. Through policies of social segregation the urban poor lived spatially separated from the urban rich producing more striking visual contrasts than in rural areas.

But while the penetration of an alien polity, society and economic system created on one level a degree of uniformity, traditional society was not destroyed and indeed played an active role in the changes which took place. Granted traditional structures were greatly altered through interaction with external forces but the form, direction and speed with which changes took place were all products of the interplay between colonial and indigenous value systems. Thus in the administrative sphere the European origin of the new institutions coupled with the character of the indigenous structures influenced the form and functioning of the local government units and the degree of respect for traditional political boundaries and authority. In the economic sphere this same interaction influenced opportunity of access by both alien and indigenous communities to material and non-material resources and, by implication, influenced the degree of external control exercised over land and labour in rural areas. It influenced in turn the character of the urban system which expanded to serve the needs of economies oriented to export. Thus it was the interaction between traditional and alien structures which moulded the emerging regional disparities and social inequalities within and between rural and urban areas.

Further reading

New approaches in the historical geography of Africa are outlined by Crush and Rogerson (1983). Africa's incorporation into the international economic system is debated by Wallerstein (1976) and Rodney (1972) while a regional classification of the continent based on the organisation of economic activity to which it gave rise is discussed by Amin (1972a) and Wallerstein (1976).

Chapter 5

AFRICA AND THE INTERNATIONAL COMMUNITY

Introduction

The nation state should not be regarded as the only critical scale at which to explain the processes of post-independence change within the African continent. Despite political independence social and spatial inequalities within the states continue to be shaped by forces from beyond the continent through the external constraints placed upon national policy-making and practice. It is at times of world crisis that Africa's international involvement is brought into sharp relief. Seidman (1980) suggests that three major international economic crises have adversely affected the continent since independence: those associated with the monetary system, oil and the recession.

During the 1970s the international monetary crisis caused widespread inflation, balance of payments deficits and international debt, forcing the industrialised countries to seek ways of restructuring the international monetary system. Although most debts on the African continent are small on a world scale, in many countries, notably Zambia, important policy changes and rescheduling procedures including support from the International Monetary Fund (IMF) have been necessary (Table 2.6). A rise in demand for energy, particularly oil, and concomitant increases in oil prices brought about by the post-1945 technological revolution, have aggravated the monetary crisis. With the exception of a few oil-producing African states, notably Gabon and Nigeria, the majority have suffered from rising prices not only of oil but also of imported machinery and equipment upon which their economies have come to depend. Indeed, of the forty-five countries on the United Nations list of Most Seriously Affected (MSAs) as a result of the 1973 oil crisis, twenty-seven were in Africa. The third related economic crisis, international recession, has reduced the level of economic activity between Africa and the industrialised countries. Supply side difficulties and production problems within the African states have not been assisted by a new protectionism in the North which has narrowed the markets for certain raw material exports and produced a relative decline in world prices for the major exports of many African states. Among these are the unfavourable price movements for such mineral exporters as Zaire, Zambia and Liberia.

But Africa's international involvement is not merely at times of crisis. A long colonial history ensures that it is more deep-rooted and continuous and it is against this historical background that we should consider the post-colonial relationship between African countries and the international community.

Foreign presence and influence

African governments must interact with the international economic system through the mechanisms of foreign trade, aid and direct foreign investment. In focusing attention on these external links two questions arise. What has been the impact of foreign presence in Africa in the post-colonial period in terms of the spatial distribution of investment and how far has the colonial model changed? In explaining these spatial outcomes what has been the relationship between African states and these external forces?

During the colonial period a combination of foreign presence in Africa and foreign influence, notably through the trading mechanism, stimulated the spatial concentration of economic activities and population within the African states. Both foreign presence and influence remain significant today. Colonial authority has been replaced by bilateral and multilateral aid. Foreign private investment has intensified in the form of multinational or transnational corporations while trading links with countries beyond the continent remain significant. This foreign involvement has both sustained and modified the inherited spatial distribution of economic activities and social provision. In the field of production, mining development through transnational companies has added new towns to the urban system in, for example, Botswana and Liberia (O'Connor 1983). In the realm of public investment major infrastructure projects have been funded by the European Economic Community (Hewitt 1979) while World Bank attempts to address the problems of poverty have given a new importance to projects which are targeted directly on the urban and rural poor (Tendler 1982).

What matters, however, is not merely the type and location of foreign investment since political independence but, more particularly, the ways in which the nation state through the authority and influence of government has modified the international politico-economic structure in the interests of national values and aspirations. The following discussion is designed to challenge, as Wellings and McCarthy (1983: 342) have done, 'the popular but vulgar dependency model' that African states are 'simply spectators to the process of capitalist penetration, their policies dictated by the interests of international capitalism'. It does so by exploring two forms of foreign presence in Africa, one in the realm of private investment – transnational institutions – and the other in the public domain – the activities of the European Economic Community.

Foreign corporations are powerful agencies with their roots in the industrialised countries. They have sought to exploit the resource potential of the continent and in doing so have had a direct impact on the nature and distribution of economic opportunities through their control over the means of production and over investment decisions. Moving to a major political, economic and regional block within the industrialised world, the links forged by, and the impact of, the EEC in Africa are particularly appropriate bringing together as the EEC does the former colonising powers in a unique relationship with the continent which combines trade and aid. These two forms of institution – one public, one private – are chosen because they reflect a particular type of relationship between the African states and the international community. They represent the contemporary form of a long-standing external presence in Africa and are therefore particularly appropriate in informing debate over the extent to which patterns of investment within the African states instigated by external forces in the post-colonial period reflect an attempt by African governments to increase their degree of internal control. It is this commitment and effort on the part of national governments to influence the actions of external agencies which challenges the concept of a culture of dependency (Ch. 3) and which needs to be explored.

Investigation is made at two related scales. At the level of links between nations, strategies adopted by the leading agencies within the African states to alter their external relations are explored including efforts to indigenise economic operations and to promote decolonisation in the economic sphere, and at the intra-national level where the importance of these measures in changing the economic organisation of space is assessed (Fig. 5.1).

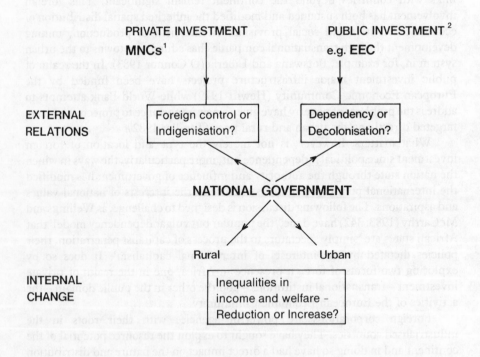

Figure 5.1 External relations and internal change

92

Direct foreign investment

Most direct foreign investment is conducted through the institution of the multinational or transnational corporation, an enterprise which has become increasingly important in the developing countries since the Second World War. It is the subject of discussion in Galbraith's book (1967) *The New Industrial State,* and its gradual penetration into the economies of different parts of Africa is the focus of much research (cf. Cooney 1980; Hopkins 1976; Mabogunje 1980b). By definition a multinational corporation is a firm which owns and/or controls income-generating assets such as plantations, mines and factories, in more than one country. In doing so it imports not only capital but a range of important factors including technology, and technical, managerial and organisational skills which many developing countries lack. Furthermore, in view of the size, structure and organisation of these firms they are essentially oligopolistic in character dominating in markets controlled by a few buyers and sellers. Thus their impact on developing economies extends far beyond mere ownership or control of specific enterprises.

Kirkpatrick and Nixson (1981) report that in 1972, 20.7 per cent of all direct foreign investment in the developing countries was concentrated in Africa (excluding South Africa which has for long been an important base) and of this some 61.5 per cent was concentrated in the petroleum, mining and smelting sectors. By comparison in 1973 Latin America accounted for 51.5 per cent of the total LDC stock of which 39.1 per cent was in the manufacturing sector. The comparable proportion for Africa was only 17.6 per cent reflecting its generally low level of industrialisation. Over the period 1967–78 the stock of investment increased substantially. For example, in thirty-nine African countries its nominal value rose by 72 per cent illustrating the intensification of this form of external influence since independence. However, as shown in Table 5.1 the extent of this influence varies considerably between states. In 1977 the major concentrations were in Nigeria, Liberia, Zaire, Gabon, Kenya and the Ivory Coast. Smaller concentrations were to be found in Zimbabwe, Zambia, Cameroon, Senegal and Ghana. For countries like Botswana, Gambia, Niger, Tanzania and Malawi foreign capital started from a very low base in 1967 and although it continues to be small in comparison to the above countries the rate of growth was very rapid over the decade.

While investment in manufacturing and services tends to be lower in Africa than in the developing countries as a whole, there are some notable exceptions and a movement into these sectors can be anticipated in the future. In Kenya, for example, Kaplinsky (1978) indicates that as early as 1967 32 per cent of direct foreign investment was in the manufacturing sector (in comparison to 18.8 per cent in Africa as a whole) and that by 1971/72 it dominated in a range of subsectors including footwear, leather, rubber, petroleum, industrial chemicals, paint, soap, cement and metal products. Furthermore there have been changes over time in the

93

Table 5.1 Stock of direct foreign investment in selected African countries (US $ million)
(Source: Kirkpatrick & Nixson 1981: 377; Lewis 1980: 165)

	End 1967	End 1975	End 1977	End 1978
Botswana	5	45	55	57
Cameroon	150	300	355	370
Gabon	270	620	740	780
Gambia	2	14	14	15
Ghana	260	300	275	280
Ivory Coast	200	420	500	530
Kenya	170	650	510	520
Liberia	300	800	1035	1230
Malawi	30	85	100	100
Niger	20	35	80	100
Nigeria	1100	2900	1040	1130
Senegal	150	300	350	340
Tanzania	50	140	160	170
Zaire	480	850	(1110)	(1250)
Zambia	420	200	305	330
Zimbabwe	250	(300)	(350)	—

value of the total stock of direct investment on the continent. In a few countries the
value declined, notably in Nigeria and Kenya (Table 5.1), reflecting the results of
localisation measures, an issue to which we shall return below. Changes recorded
over time are nevertheless influenced by the measurement criteria used and in this
context we need to distinguish between ownership and control. Ownership is
becoming an increasingly inadequate indicator of the extent of multinational
penetration in individual countries as the form of this influence changes and
diversifies under, among other things, the pressure of indigenisation measures. It
may range from 'relatively straightforward licensing, franchising, or management
agreements to highly complex combinations of a wide variety of provisions that are
collectively referred to as industrial co-operation. These include the supply or
leasing of plants, contract manufacturing and sub-contracting, joint research and
development; co-production, specialisation, co-marketing and provision of
after-sales services; joint tendering and joint projects.' (United Nations 1978:
68–9)

Indigenisation

Given the changing characteristics and varying penetration of foreign investment
on the continent over time, Adedeji (1981) identifies four types of indigenisation
measures which have been employed by African governments to secure greater
control over their economies. First a change from foreign to local ownership either
in the form of nationalisation or domestic private ownership or a combination of
the two. He points out that between 1960 and 1974 there were 340 cases of

nationalisation alone chiefly in sectors such as banking, insurance and petroleum distribution rather than in manufacturing. With the notable exceptions of Ivory Coast, Liberia and Gabon most African states took over at least one enterprise while in some cases like Tanzania with an overtly socialist ideology nationalisation was wide-ranging. Indigenisation of control represents the second major form identified, namely, the localisation of directorships and, by implication, local control over the management of enterprises. Indigenisation of manpower, that is, Africanisation, represents the third type, a process which was rapidly applied to the civil service in particular following independence. Finally, Adedeji refers to the indigenisation of technology, namely, a commitment to the development and use of technologies suited to local needs and domestic resources.

Several groupings of countries are subsequently identified based on their policy commitment to indigenisation (Adedeji 1981). In Nigeria and Ghana it is argued that a determined effort has been made with respect to key sectors of the economy. In Kenya, with a rapidly developing economy similar to that of Nigeria, by contrast a more cautious approach is identified in which the efforts made to strengthen indigenous enterprise have been promoted alongside continued foreign participation. Adedeji places Tanzania, Ethiopia, Uganda, Mozambique and Angola in another group by virtue of their revolutionary approach to nationalising the key economic sectors, stimulated in the case of Uganda by Asian economic domination and in the case of Mozambique and Angola by the fight against colonialism and neo-colonialism. The three Southern African countries of Botswana, Lesotho and Swaziland form a further group where, it is argued, in view of their exceptional position as enclaves of South Africa, policies of indigenisation are only in their infancy.

External constraints, national commitment and the culture of dependency

What has been the impact of indigenisation measures within and between countries on the distribution of investment and hence on patterns of social and spatial inequality? How far can these outcomes be related to the nature of the interactions between the key decision-makers involved? As regards the first point Ezeife's (1981) Nigerian study indicates that an already skewed income distribution and marked regional disparities have been perpetuated by indigenisation measures which have failed to include egalitarianism in their objectives. Ake (1981b) draws similar conclusions from Kenya suggesting that indigenisation policies have contributed to inequality and class formation. But how far can these similar outcomes be explained in terms of a common set of processes?

Important differences have emerged between countries in the policies adopted, the administrative machinery set up, the legislative measures and institutions established such as credit facilities, development banks, industrial estates and the like. These differences reflect in part differing internal conditions including the scale of foreign economic activity inherited on independence and the ideological bias of the political élite. Over and above this diversity there is the need to investigate the nature of the interaction between the triple alliance comprising international capital, domestic capital and the State; specifically the power of the State in relation to foreign capital and the motivation of those who influence state policy. In effect, to establish what evidence there is to challenge the concept of a culture of dependency.

In Nkrumah's (1965) famous book on neo-colonialism written in the early years of African political independence he argued that giant foreign interests continued to exert a dominant influence over individual states for their own benefit rather than in the interests of the less developed world. Much of the literature on private foreign investment in Africa since then has reiterated these sentiments. For example, a recent study of the impact of international mining companies in Africa concludes that:

> Foreign mining companies created Africa's dependent economic structure and incorporated the continent into the world economy ... today Africa's subordinate position in the world economy dominated by the advanced industrial nations is maintained by the giant international companies. The obstacles blocking the way are too great and the forces too powerful, for a poverty-stricken African state, however richly endowed with resources, to develop its potential as part of the world capitalist system. (Lanning & Mueller 1979: 495)

Scepticism over the ability of the State to control foreign influence is emphasised:

> Political independence has undoubtedly changed the operating environment for the mining companies. But it has remained very much an open question whether the increased state participation in the African mining industry will promote economic development. The governing élites, inheriting an underdeveloped economy and the overdeveloped state apparatus of the colonial era, are unable to tackle the structural imbalance in these economies. They are merely intermediaries between Africa's resources and the international mining companies. (Lanning & Mueller 1979: 495)

This intermediate position has been explained, at least in part, in terms of a culture of dependency. Daniel (1981:164) suggests that the norms, values, attitudes and behaviour transmitted by the colonising powers through their imported institutions – religious, educational, economic, the family – survived into the post-colonial era through those groups who assumed state power on independence and who had effectively assimilated European culture. 'It is this cultural factor which is seen as accounting in part for the minimal transformation effected to the metropole-satellite relationship since independence for these assimilated values harmonise with those of the metropolitan bourgeoisie and provide the compradors with the ideological means to justify their continued close alliance with the metropole.' Such an interpretation implies that there is an unwillingness on the part of indigenous groups representing the State and private capital to challenge the power of international capital.

From the findings of individual studies, it is apparent that not only do difficulties arise in generalising between countries with different conditions and circumstances but also that within the same country interpretations vary between different researchers. The following case studies illustrate these points. Von Freyhold (1977), in her assessment of Tanzania, argues that in view of the limited opportunities for private accumulation the metropolitan bourgeoisie represented by the multinationals and the international aid agencies remain unchallenged as the only ruling class while the bureaucracy fulfil a subordinate role as the local governing class. In Nigeria, where a powerful group of business people exists, Forrest (1977) suggests that the close alliance between national and international bourgeoisie in the highly profitable commercial sector rules out any large-scale domestic capitalist production. Despite the priority attached by planners to local manufacturing and to the development of intermediate and capital goods industries Forrest (1977: 46) points out that 'the strength of commercial relations and reliance on foreign management and technology supports the dominance of the commercial and managerial fractions of the bourgeoisie. Both the policies and the capacity to evolve a more productive national base for capital accumulation are weakened by these social relations.'

Contrasting conditions are reported by Kennedy (1977) in Ghana and Swainson (1977; 1980) in Kenya. Both draw attention to the emergence of a group of local business people engaged in productive investment who have the potential of becoming an 'independent' capitalist class able to control the industrial base and to challenge the power of the multinationals. Swainson's findings also conflict with the earlier work of Colin Leys (1975) in Kenya who asserts that the national bourgeoisie are mere 'auxiliaries' or 'intermediaries' to foreign capital. Such a claim Swainson (1977: 40) rejects as based on a 'static evaluation of classes, inherent in the dependency framework', one which fails to acknowledge 'the particularities of different social formations'.

Through her investigation of the expansion of local business interests Swainson also examines the use made of state powers to promote indigenous capital accumulation. She discusses the various legislative measures designed to increase the number and size of enterprises locally owned or managed and to assist in the transition of local business interests from the sphere of exchange into production. Pointing to the fact that many business people are also members of the bureaucracy or the political élite she strongly argues that the former in fact use the state apparatus in their own interests and in particular to assist in their transition from 'small-scale capitalists' into a national bourgeoisie. Swainson is careful to point out that the gradual conversion of indigenous merchant capital into industrial capital does not in the short term imply that an independent industrial base is emerging. Foreign finance capital and expertise will continue to be needed in large-scale industrial production. Rather what is important are the ways in which domestic links with international capital are changing.

The role of the Kenyan state in relation to both foreign and local capital is interpreted somewhat differently by Langdon (1977a;b; 1981). Using some of the same examples as Swainson he suggests that the State is not unambiguously supportive of either fraction of the bourgeoisie; rather it plays a very effective role in regulating, extending and defending 'a growing MNC–state–domestic bourgeoisie symbiosis in the country'. The local bourgeoisie, he argues, 'remains too state dependent to extend any opposition to MNC enterprise to destabilising lengths – while the strength of the state also guarantees that bourgeoisie a rising share in MNC profits, over time' (Langdon 1977a: 96). The State is therefore ascribed a central role in an indigenisation process which, according to Langdon, is producing a new form of dependency in Kenya on the lines of Sunkel's 'transnational integration, national disintegration model'.

Differences arise, therefore, both within and between states in the roles ascribed to the key actors (the 'triple alliance') in the indigenisation process. However, despite a lack of agreement on this level on one crucial underlying issue broad agreement does exist, namely, that the actions taken serve to intensify rather than to reduce internal inequalities. Thus the state fails to act in the interests of the majority but 'is an instrument furthering the exploitation of the working class and the peasantry' (Editorial, *Review of the African Political Economy,* 1977, No.8:3). In Langdon's study (1981) a similar emphasis is placed on the links between social and spatial inequalities arising from the symbiosis referred to above. The lower 50 per cent of families on the income scale – the small-scale peasant and rural labourer majority – suffer most dramatically while the relatively worse-off areas are those remote from the zones of concentrated multinational investment surrounding and extending north of Nairobi and around Mombasa.

These studies introduce a perspective which challenges two simplistic notions in relation to economic investment: on the one hand the culture of dependency argument that there is an unwillingness on the part of the State and local capital to operate independently of international capital; on the other, that conflict is primarily between the multinational and host government with the latter acting as a defender of 'national interest'. The relationships and interactions between the leading interest groups are clearly more complex but when explored in relation to their social and spatial outcomes differences in interpretation appear to make little difference.

The European Economic Community in Africa

Since 1975 economic assistance through aid and concessionary trade has gradually been extended by the EEC to a group of sixty-six African, Caribbean and Pacific countries (ACP) of which some forty-three are in Africa south of the Sahara (Fig. 5.2). This assistance is enshrined in the first Lomé Convention concluded in 1975 followed by a second in 1979 which runs until 1985 (EEC 1975; 1980a) both of which were signed in the capital of Togo. Preferential trading agreements and supplementary aid were originally available to a limited number of African countries (the seventeen colonial dependencies of member states) under Articles 131–136 of the Treaty of Rome (EEC 1958). Their initial status was as associated dependencies followed after their independence in 1960 by two Conventions of Association between the Community and the Association of African and Malagasy States, namely, Yaoundé I in 1963 and Yaoundé II in 1969. The Lomé Conventions therefore have important forerunners in Africa.

Stimulus to the latter came with British entry into the EEC in 1973 which necessitated arrangements for the Commonwealth countries' equivalent to

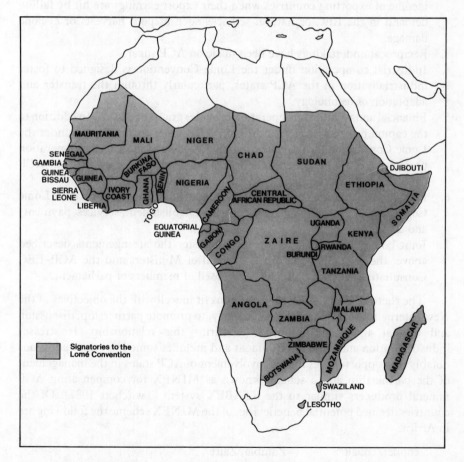

Figure 5.2 Signatories to the Lomé Convention (after *The Courier* 1984)

Yaoundé. Prior to Britain's entry, Kenya, Tanzania and Uganda had acquired limited association through the Arusha Convention (Twitchett 1978). However, following British entry a review took place of all association agreements the outcome of which was the first Lomé Convention signed on 28 February 1975. This covered a greater range of economic ties and a much wider geographical area than Yaoundé – forty-six states in all. Co-operation was established in seven major fields covering industrial restructuring, special arrangements on selected raw materials, preferential trading, financial and technical co-operation. These are detailed by the Commission of the European Communities (1977: 34–6) and summarised as follows:

1. Trade co-operation provides freedom of access to Community markets.
2. Stabilisation of the ACP countries' export earnings on thirty-six commodities is guaranteed by means of the STABEX system. STABEX can be regarded as a sort of social security arrangement at international level, making up the income of exporting countries when their export earnings are hit by falling demand in the EEC or natural setbacks such as poor harvests or cyclone damage.
3. Reciprocal undertakings have been made on ACP sugar.
4. Industrial co-operation under the Lomé Convention is designed to foster industrialisation in the ACP states, particularly through the transfer and adaptation of technology.
5. Financial and technical co-operation provides grants and loans. In addition to the capital projects put forward by the ACP states there is scope under the Lomé Convention for financing regional, trade and industrial co-operation projects, specific measures to help small and medium-sized firms in ACP countries and 'microprojects' at local level.
6. Equal treatment for companies and citizens of all states signatory to the Lomé Convention is ensured by clauses covering establishment, services, payments and capital.
7. Joint bodies have been set up to administer the arrangements described above: these include ACP–EEC Council of Ministers and the ACP–EEC Consultative Assembly which is composed of members of parliament.

The rhetoric is impressive and the aims fit in well with the objectives of the New International Economic Order, namely, to promote partnership, discussion and mutual agreement. Lomé II confirms this relationship. It stresses industrialisation and rural development and includes some important additions notably new opportunities for the involvement of ACP states in the management of the partnership and a scheme known as MINEX for compensating ACP mineral producers similar to the STABEX system (Twitchett 1981). Of the countries deemed potential beneficiaries of the MINEX scheme the following are in Africa:

copper/cobalt	–	Zambia, Zaire
phosphates	–	Togo, Senegal

iron ore	–	Liberia, Mauritania
tin	–	Rwanda

As regards community aid, this is available through the European Development Fund (EDF), the European Investment Bank (EIB) and the EEC budget. Of these the EDF is the most important source, financing among other things project aid and technical assistance. In reviewing the types of activity funded it should be emphasised that significant shifts have taken place over time both in the sectoral and in the spatial allocation process, shifts which reflect changes in development theory and in the reality of international politics (Rajana 1982). As regards sectoral priorities, initially (under EDF I, II, III) a strong emphasis was placed on infrastructure including road and rail transport, reinforcing, among other things, a widespread faith in the role of infrastructure as stimuli to development (Table 5.2). Then in the early 1970s and particularly following the Lomé Convention an important shift towards productive activities took place, notably towards basic needs in agriculture in order to improve the productivity of the small producer through appropriate technologies. Such a change in sectoral emphasis reflected development trends at the time and promoted also a spatial shift within countries from urban to rural areas. Lomé II reaffirms the need for rural development and food production both for domestic consumption and for export. In doing so it reinforces the concern of international agencies such as the World Bank to create 'a buoyant and productive agricultural sector [which] stimulates demand for industrial goods' (World Bank 1979: 61).

Table 5.2 European Development Fund sectoral commitments 1959–79 (Source: Rajana 1982: 204)

	EDF I	EDF II	EDF III	EDF I–III	EDF IV
	(%)	(%)	(%)	(%)	(%)
Transport	40.1	31.1	33.2	33.0	17.6
Communications	3.1	1.2	4.3	3.9	3.1
Rural production	16.5	37.2	29.6	30.0	23.4
Education	19.5	9.8	10.4	12.1	8.9
Housing/Urban infrastructure/ Water engineering	8.5	6.9	4.7	6.2	3.9
Industry	0.3	2.8	3.6	2.4	11.2
Manufacturing	0.4	2.7	3.6	2.8	4.3
Agro-industry	8.8	4.1	0.9	4.8	2.1
Emergency aid	—	0.1	4.7	1.6	5.1
Export promotion	—	—	0.3	0.1	1.0
Rural drainage and irrigation	—	0.2	1.0	0.1	1.4
Stabex	—	—	—	—	13.7

While sectoral shifts have influenced the spatial allocation of EEC aid within countries, it should also be recognised that independent of the types of activity funded a shift has also taken place between countries in the allocation process. Most notable is the decline in the concentration of aid on the Francophone states as the former British colonies have become members of what Jones (1973) has

101

called 'Europe's Chosen Few'. Since many of these countries fall within the EEC classification of least developed, their projects receive priority treatment and payment is in the form of grants or 'soft loans' (Hewitt 1982a).

Continuity and change

Some twenty years after independence it is apparent that Europe is still present and influential in the African continent. European-African relations combine elements of continuity and change. Fundamentally the point at issue is the extent to which the colonial economic and social structures have been transformed or conserved since independence (Galtung 1976; Green 1976). These can be explored once again at two related scales. First, at the level of links between nations, how far is a decolonisation process taking place based on a relationship of interdependence? Do Africa's links with Europe reflect a greater ability on the part of the former to control internal economic change? Conversely, does the relationship remain one of neo-colonialism and continued dependency? Second, at intranational level, how far does Africa's relationship with Europe promote or help to reduce social and spatial inequalities in income and welfare within countries?

Decolonisation or dependency?

Discussion of decolonisation and dependency rests upon a number of issues. These include the multilateral nature of the relationship between African countries and those beyond the continent, the arrangements for managing the partnership with Europe and how far the international division of labour is preserved.

On the first issue Zartman (1976) supports decolonisation theory suggesting that the established bilateral metropolitan influence is steadily being replaced by multilateral relations of which he cites Lomé I as an important example. Mention should also be made of the Arab aid agencies in view of their growing importance as major aid donors to the African ACPs. Focusing just on Community aid, co-financing has become an important trend for the support of projects ranging from small-scale rural development to large-scale schemes for regional co-operation. In West Africa, for example, a major regional industrial venture was initiated in 1975 when the governments of Ghana, Togo and Ivory Coast established Ciments de l'Afrique de l'Ouest (CIMAO), a company to produce clinker for the manufacture of cement in each of the three countries (Europe Information 10/1978). Financial assistance for the project was provided jointly by the EDF, the EIB, the World Bank, the African Development Bank, the Arab Bank for Economic Development in Africa and bilateral aid from France, Germany and Canada. Dependence by the African countries on a single donor was therefore removed. However, while joint aid may be interpreted as a trend towards decolonisation there is no universal agreement. Arnold (1979: 41) argues against the trend suggesting that it reduces the bargaining power of the recipient and 'in hard political terms this means less opportunity for African countries to play off one donor against another'.

A similar lack of consensus is apparent over arrangements for managing the partnership between Europe and Africa. Twitchett (1981: 1) outlines the ideals on which the relationship is based. 'Lomé II (like Lomé I) commits the ACP and EEC to work together as equal partners for their mutual benefit, compatible with the aspirations of the new international economic order.' She continues: 'Interdependence is the cornerstone of Lomé II, as in Lomé I before. Any assessment of the ACP–EEC partnership must therefore consider how far the treaty provisions create a viable structure for *mutual* interest and mutual dependence.' The primary body responsible for managing the partnership is the ACP–EEC Council. Under Lomé II new joint institutions were created to strengthen collaboration notably the ACP–EEC Committee on Financial and Technical Co-operation which shares responsibility for aid policy, project appraisal and evaluation. Overall, with respect to aid administration, the view is widely expressed that the ACP states have extensive powers of project determination and implementation. Nevertheless in one important respect the partnership is less than equal, namely, in the lack of effective representation by ACP states on the crucial EDF Committee. Responsibility for preparing financial conditions and for taking the final decision over projects and programmes lies with the EEC. Rajana (1982) does point out, however, that few projects are in fact rejected.

The view that Lomé aid reinforces the existing international division of labour is also open to debate. The World Bank, for example, in its 1978 report (World Bank 1978b: 50) considered that the preferential trading agreement enshrined in the conventions was highly significant. 'In the short run, it will be difficult for countries in sub-Saharan Africa to overcome the obstacles to expanding manufactured exports. Consequently, their preferential access to industrialised countries' markets, as made available under the Lomé Convention, is of particular importance.' Problems do, however, arise in the case of commodities such as beef, a leading export of Botswana, which are covered by the EEC Common Agricultural Policy (CAP) and which are therefore subject to rigid quotas.

Commodity Stabilisation Schemes have been hailed by the Commission as an important 'social security arrangement at international level' designed to buffer ACP states against harmful fluctuations in world market prices. In fact Arnold, writing in 1979, argued that of the various arrangements and concessions offered under Lomé I the establishment of STABEX was perhaps the most significant achievement and the only real innovation. A range of agricultural products was included, many of which provide a large proportion of Africa's export earnings and foreign exchange. As indicated above, Lomé II under the MINEX scheme offers somewhat similar assistance with mineral exports. But these schemes also have their critics. Ake (1981a) claims that despite the greater coverage of important commodities and the more flexible terms of the agreement under Lomé II such assistance can make little difference to the established economic order given the small size of the compensation payable. Perhaps 'most disturbing' of all, he claims, is the fact that such agreements 'are prone to freeze the ACP countries to their present role as primary producers in the international divisions of labour' (Ake 1981a: 166).

It should be recalled (Rajana 1982) that the Commodity Stabilisation schemes represent only part of the allocation to the ACP countries. In 1979 although funds to STABEX from the EDF comprised the largest single disbursement they nevertheless amounted to under one third of the total aid allocation (Hewitt 1982b) and indeed when the overall pattern is scrutinised 'the view that Lomé aid will reinforce the dependence and underdevelopment of the ACPs is [perhaps] tenuous' (Rajana 1982: 219). In the field of financial and technical co-operation, numerous country evaluations have been carried out. Hewitt (1982a: 12) suggests that such co-operation 'has been a factor enabling the Cameroon to experience substantial overall economic growth and remarkable political stability'. In Tanzania Sheck (1980) argues that Lomé aid has formed a substantial proportion of the government investment in non-export agriculture and has assisted in its basic-needs strategy. Similar conclusions are reached by Rita Cruise O'Brien (1980) in Senegal with respect to industrial investment.

Thus the evidence suggests that Africa's relations with Europe are equally controversial in terms of decolonisation and dependency as are her relations with the multinational corporations. This lack of agreement is in itself important in stressing the need to avoid simplistic interpretation at the level of links between nations. It cannot be denied that the African governments have achieved a measure of control over, and receive some benefits from, their association with the EEC. What matters is that the conditions and circumstances peculiar to each country be considered in any assessment made. For example, the degree and nature of dependency experienced by countries within the Southern African periphery are likely to be very different from those of Kenya or Nigeria.

Social and spatial outcomes

Bearing this point in mind, the critical next question is how far this interaction with Europe has influenced colonial patterns of regional development within countries. Does it assist the poorest groups in African society and in doing so shift the balance from urban to rural areas in general and from the urban rich to the urban poor in particular? Conversely, are the outcomes similar to those associated with private foreign investment where indigenisation with equality has proved to be a difficult combination?

It is through the strategy of rural development – which is both multi-sectoral and spatial in nature and which in 1979 received some 14 per cent of the EDF allocation – that direct assessment can be made. Detailed case studies suggest that intra-rural inequalities have not in fact been reduced. In a major evaluation conducted during 1976–77 of ten integrated rural development schemes covering nine countries in West and Central Africa financed by the first three EDF budgets it was concluded that the better-off farmers tended to benefit because of their easier access to the means of production and to commercial services (Dupriez 1978). These findings are not dissimilar from the results of projects funded by certain other aid donors, notably the World Bank (Binns & Funnell 1983). In explanation it is the attitudes, perceptions and interests of the major agencies involved which become important.

Wood and Smith (1984:5) point out with respect to Zambia that the European Economic Community, like the World Bank, believe 'Zambia cannot afford to wait for the slow returns that come from' an approach which focuses on less productive peripheral areas. Rather they 'should concentrate on increasing output within areas of high potential in order to generate increased production and revenue more rapidly'. For the recipient government there are also important priorities and interests at stake. Arnold (1979: 19) states that aid can be used as an instrument in the economic and political survival of a particular government by releasing that government from the obligation to and the responsibility for certain projects. Under such circumstances most projects may be accepted and hence in turn the policies and priorities of the donor agencies. Such is the case in Zambia where, in order to reduce the country's dependence on copper, government has sought to restructure the economy by, among other things, encouraging donor involvement in rural development. Aid from the European Economic Community has been included and, consistent with its priorities, has favoured the most developed agricultural regions along the line of rail.

Against this background it should nevertheless be recognised that unlike Africa's relations with the multinationals there are important dimensions of EEC involvement in Africa which are directly targeted on the poor. It is in the funding of micro-projects and in the provision of food aid that most significant efforts have been made in this direction. Micro-projects are small-scale grass-roots schemes, normally in rural areas, designed to respond to the needs of local communities. Although they absorb only a meagre proportion of the aid budget, by December 1978 the European Commission had approved the first twenty-eight annual programmes of which twenty-two were in sub-Saharan Africa extending through former British and French West Africa to the Sudan, Ethiopia, Kenya, Malawi, Zambia, Madagascar, Lesotho and Swaziland.

These programmes comprised over one thousand schemes, the majority of which sought to cater for 'basic needs' through the provision of social infrastructure such as schools, clinics and dispensaries (39 per cent of all schemes) concentrated in Malawi and Burkina Faso and rural water supply (23 per cent) chiefly in Liberia, Zambia and Burkina Faso (EEC 1980b). Micro-projects depend for their formulation and implementation on what has become a major development strategy for social improvement, namely, community participation which is sensitive to local social and economic organisation and cultural practices (see Chs 6 & 7). Initiatives already taken by a local community represent an important criterion in the selection of projects for support while active involvement is required of the beneficiaries in the implementation process through, among other things, the provision of labour. In this the timing of projects is crucial to avoid any conflict with busy agricultural seasons and traditional agricultural tasks.

Food aid

Lofchie and Commins (1982: 1) maintain that 'hunger is the most immediate, visible, and compelling symptom of a continent-wide agricultural breakdown in tropical Africa'. According to the Food and Agriculture Organisation (FAO) of the United Nations (UN), in 1981 some twenty-eight African countries faced critical food shortages and the possibility of imminent famine. These extended from the semi-arid zone across western and eastern Africa to the high rainfall regions of Zaire, Zambia and the West African coast. Against this background the EEC is an important food aid donor on which governments of the Sahel in particular and more especially their poor rural populations have come to depend to alleviate extensive starvation (Huddleston et al. 1982). The origins of an EEC food aid programme lie in the 1967 international Food Aid Convention since when the EEC has disbursed food in the form of a grant either directly to the developing countries or indirectly through multilateral and voluntary institutions including the World Food Programme which operates under the auspices of the UN and the FAO (Stevens 1979).

Like food aid in general EEC aid has been used in many different ways and in a multiplicity of projects. These include food for sale on the open market where the money value of the food aid is channelled into development projects which may not use food aid directly; food for nutrition where it is distributed to the most vulnerable groups including refugees, women and children; food for work projects where payment is in the form of a food ration. Stevens (1979) discusses these different types of aid in the context of Botswana, Lesotho, Burkina Faso and Tunisia and points to the benefits achieved. However EEC practices like those related to food aid in general have been the subject of close investigation and criticised on many grounds (Maxwell & Singer 1979; Tarrant 1980). These include structural issues such as the importance of food aid in sustaining inefficient agricultural policies in the industrialized countries. The EEC is, for example, the major source of dairy food aid which has been linked to the Community's butter mountains and milk lakes (Muller 1976).

However, both in explaining the causes of famine which food aid is designed to alleviate and in evaluating the effectiveness of food aid itself, it is with the interactions between the politico-economic structure and cultural practices that we should also be concerned. 'The crisis of food deficits has now become so perennial and so widespread that it can no longer be understood as the outcome of particular political or climatic occurrences such as wars, ethnic strife, or drought' (Lofchie & Commins 1982: 1). The decline in per capita food production in much of Africa is more deep-rooted and has given rise to a wide-ranging debate over the political economy of hunger, famine and environmental degradation. (See, for example, Anthony et al. 1979; Grigg 1981; Redclift 1984; Robinson 1978; *Review of African Political Economy* 1979 no.15/16). In this debate the penetration of the capitalist mode and relations of production during the colonial period is regarded as a major cause through its challenge to traditional systems of social and economic organisation adapted to the vagaries of the environment. A breakdown in traditional cropping patterns and in the mechanisms of social support characteristic of non-capitalist societies designed to protect the poor from seasonal underproduction have been particularly harmful. A detailed discussion of these issues in Southern Africa is provided in Chapter 8. At this point it is sufficient to emphasise that the contemporary food aid activities of the EEC represent an important palliative against earlier forms of foreign intervention which continue to threaten the social structures and cultural practices most adapted to Africa's delicate ecology.

Moreover, in evaluating the effects of food aid itself evidence points to the fact that it too may have harmful social and cultural consequences. At both national and local levels food aid has been observed to generate a mentality of dependency sufficient 'to postpone essential agricultural reforms, to give low priority to agricultural investment, and to maintain a pricing system which gives farmers inadequate incentives to increase local production required for greater self-reliance in basic foodstuffs' (Presidential Commission on World Hunger 1980: 140). By running counter to the needs and cultural preferences of African peasant communities its harmful effects on consumer behaviour and in turn on local food production have also been identified. Maxwell and Singer (1979: 235) point out that 'Food aid is never neutral ... its use is influenced by a constellation of interests in both donor and recipient countries, not all of which are concerned with true development for the poorest people in poor countries'. It has been seen to contribute towards an undesirable change in consumer tastes away from locally available foods towards imported varieties while disquiet has been expressed over the tendency of dried skimmed milk (DSM) used in feeding programmes to discourage breast feeding with adverse effects on nutrition and public health (Stevens 1979).

Consequences such as these, albeit controversial, tend to support the culture of dependency model. But the recipients should not be interpreted as merely passive victims of externally set priorities and goals. Consumer responses have indeed contributed to important policy changes, both internationally and within the EEC, towards the problems of hunger and malnutrition. Since 1979, in addition to the short-term expediency of food aid, the World Food Council has attached greater long-term importance to the promotion of national food strategies with the dual function of encouraging local food production in a manner appropriate to the particular circumstances of each country while also improving access of the poor to an adequate food supply. In 1982 the EEC agreed to support Mali, Kenya, Rwanda and Zambia in the implementation of their food strategies (Dossier 1984).

The ultimate success of food aid depends upon the clients' response and it is apparent that the recipients play an active role in shaping this contemporary form of Africa's long-standing relationship with Europe.

Regional co-operation within the continent

The ideology of Eurafrica, based on the two key concepts of 'complementarity' and 'interdependence', appears as a convenient justification for colonialism, and also helps to explain various contractual arrangements between Africa and Europe since independence, notably the Conventions of Yaoundé I (1964–69), Yaoundé II (1969–75), Lomé I (1975–80) and Lomé II (1980–85) ...

Ultimately ... it seems that continental economic and political integration offers the best prospects for extricating Africa from the neo-colonial predicaments in which it presently finds itself, and for the attainment of genuine and complete economic independence. (Martin 1982: 221)

This quotation provides a pessimistic view of the links between Europe and Africa but it also stresses the vital importance of a further initiative within the continent by which to reduce its foreign dependence – greater regional co-operation. As the world becomes increasingly interdependent through trade and aid so the political and economic significance of the nation state is being challenged and the need for a comparable linking of economic policies apparent. While this chapter has been concerned with the relations between the nation state in Africa and external forces it is fitting that we conclude with some discussion of activities within the continent at supra-national level.

The formation of distinct regional groupings is among the most tangible evidence of Africa's challenge to foreign domination and external dependence. Despite national political differences the debate over closer integration of adjacent political economies – in the spirit of the European Community – has a long history. Indeed the desirability and necessity for joint action to withstand international pressures has been a recurring theme since the nationalist drive for political independence (Ch. 4). As recently as 1980 at the annual conference of the Organisation of African Unity (founded in Addis Ababa in 1963) held in Lagos, African heads of state defined their primary goal as 'a more self-reliant, united Africa by 2000' (Organisation of African Unity 1981). In doing so they reinforced on the one hand the views expressed by many academics and policy-makers from beyond the continent and on the other the actions and efforts of individual groupings of states over time. Green and Seidman in their book *Unity or Poverty: The Economics of Pan-Africanism* published as long ago as 1968, present what remains a compelling argument for economic integration while within the international community the United Nations Economic Commission for Africa represents an influential and persistent sponsoring body (Gruhn 1979).

The case for regional co-operation is a powerful one. The Balkanisation process which brought many African states into existence produced political units, many of which, particularly in West Africa, were barely large enough to be economically viable. The constraints on the size of the market and on industrialisation are reflected in the fact that a large number of African countries are small in terms of total population and income per head with the result that purchasing power is limited. Statistics compiled by the World Bank (1984) indicate that according to the most recent (mid-1982) estimates of population in the developing countries of sub-Saharan Africa only nine have populations exceeding ten million. These are Ethiopia, Ghana, Nigeria, Tanzania, Kenya, Mozambique, Sudan, Uganda and Zaire.

To counteract this it is widely believed that 'Regional co-operation will help to mobilise more capital for development to operate certain projects on a scale which make them economic, to achieve product specialisation which is needed to increase inter-African trade and to improve efficiency in the use of human and natural resources' (Ake 1981a: 161). Economic co-operation, it is also argued, will strengthen Africa's bargaining position in relation to forces beyond the continent – the multinational corporations, foreign aid agencies, international and regional organisations such as the EEC. In short, her fight for economic independence will be assisted by greater unity.

Not only are the arguments in favour of closer co-operation old established, but also when we turn to the regional groupings themselves it is apparent that several of those formed after independence had their origins in the colonial period. The East African Common Services Organisation, the French West African and the French Equatorial African Customs Unions gave rise respectively to the East African Community (Kenya, Tanzania, Uganda), the West African Economic Community (Benin, Ivory Coast, Mali, Mauritania, Niger, Senegal, Burkina Faso) and the Central African Customs and Economic Union (Central African Republic, the Congo, Gabon, the United Republic of the Cameroon). While the East African Community finally collapsed in 1977 the second half of this decade saw the rise of two further groupings. The first of these, the Economic Community of West African States (ECOWAS), was formed in 1976 and comprises a combination of formerly French and British territories (Cape Verde, Benin, Gambia, Ghana, Guinea, Guinea-Bissau, Ivory Coast, Liberia, Mali, Mauritania, Niger, Nigeria, Senegal, Sierra Leone, Togo, Burkina Faso). The second, known as the Southern African Development Co-ordination Conference (SADCC), was established at a meeting in Arusha in 1979 by the five front-line states comprising Botswana, Zambia, Angola, Tanzania and Mozambique. At this meeting it was agreed to expand membership to Lesotho, Malawi and Swaziland and also to Zimbabwe and Namibia on their political independence. The group now comprises nine states (Hill 1983).

What has been the impact of these various groupings? Since independence the ability of African states to act collectively against foreign domination has proved problematic. Political immaturity and internal disunity have frustrated attempts at national integration let alone supra-national co-operation. Furthermore, geographical contiguity has proved an inadequate reason in itself for co-operation. Ideological differences between adjacent states have presented problems of maintaining a semblance of unity while even in the case of states with

109

similar ideologies national interests have frequently intervened. The difficulties faced by the East African Community (Hazlewood 1975) and, more recently, SADCC, provide apt illustrations. In the latter case Leys and Tostensen (1982) discuss the differing ideological and policy stances of the Nine in relation to South Africa – a particularly serious problem given that one of the four major objectives of SADCC is to reduce dependence on South Africa. For Botswana, Lesotho and Swaziland, it conflicts with their membership of a Customs Union with that country which dates back to 1910.

In West Africa a major feature acting against closer co-operation since independence has been the political and cultural division, and with it the economic competition between states, engendered by French and British colonial influence. Yansane (1977) discusses the numerous attempts made since the late 1950s to link contiguous and distant states within and across this divide. Among the most significant is ECOWAS, representing as it does a major attempt to re-establish the historic, ethnic and cultural links which underlie Anglophone and Francophone West Africa. It seeks to speed decolonisation by decreasing dependence on the former colonial metropolis and, in doing so, reduce economic inequalities between member states (Ezenwe 1982). However, obstacles to the achievement of these goals lie both in the colonial legacy and in contemporary politico-economic differences. French control over her former territories remains through the franc zone, an institution which inhibits financial and economic autonomy. National obstacles to integration arise through ideological differences between states including a tendency among the better-off to encourage overseas investors. Dakar, Abidjan, Accra and Lagos constitute the new urban centres of development (Yansane 1977). These enclaves provide profitable investment opportunities, they attract the major share of foreign capital investment and their governments can play a more active role in the international economic system than neighbouring more marginal economies.

Thus throughout the continent national ideological and economic differences weaken the collective resolve to fight long-distance dependence. Moreover, these constraints are compounded by the continued tight hold of external forces in the economic sphere. Horizontal economic links between African states do not combine easily with their long-established vertical integration with the metropolitan powers which continues to be reflected in trade statistics. The Economic Commission for Africa estimates that in 1975, for example, inter-African trade was a mere 4.3 per cent of total African trade and this represented a 1.2 per cent decline on the 1970 figure. The signing of the Lomé Convention in 1975 maintained this close vertical connection through the trade agreements with the EEC which followed and the financing of development projects by foreign private institutions.

As regards the future some writers remain pessimistic. Shaw (1982) predicts that the growing economic distinction between the Third and Fourth Worlds of Africa will adversely affect both national integration and the prospects for regional and continental unity. But achievements have already been made including a common defence of African interests as primary producers, improved communications between states and the provision of assistance to poorer regions. Moreover, despite the difficulties involved, as the Lagos Plan of Action clearly states, renewed efforts at integration at different scales and through as wide a range of approaches and projects as possible are among the key long-term solutions to the problems of African development and dependency (Organisation of African Unity 1981).

Conclusion

In summary the evidence suggests that at the level of links between nations the concept of a culture of dependency as reflected in the interaction between African states and external forces is too simple. In the examples discussed here it is apparent that indigenisation measures have increased domestic influence over foreign corporations while in Africa's relations with Europe a measure of decolonisation has been achieved. Moreover with reference to micro-projects and food aid the vital importance of the national and local cultural context in influencing project design and implementation has been emphasised. But the active participation of the African states in shaping their foreign relations cannot be linked automatically to improvements in social welfare and patterns of spatial development within these states. Explanations of the social and spatial outcomes require that we explore for each country the perceptions, the motivations and the nature of the interaction between the key agencies involved. Finally, the efforts made to transcend national political differences through greater regional co-operation within the continent provide further evidence to challenge the dependency notion. But at this level also the 'actors' involved, their motivations and priorities, need to be explored in our evaluation of the outcomes. We turn now to these issues and to demonstrate how since political independence African leaders have sought to define their own particular route to national development and that in doing so traditional structures have played a significant role.

Further reading

For a detailed summary of recent research on international industrial systems see Hamilton and Linge (1981), and Taylor and Thrift (1982). Case studies from selected African countries on the problems of, and the strategies associated with, indigenisation are provided by Adedeji (1981), Langdon (1981) and Swainson (1980). Foreign aid in Africa is discussed generally by Arnold (1981); food aid in particular by Stevens (1979). The aid activities of the EEC are outlined in *The Courier* published every two months by the Commission of the European

Communities. Discussion of the EEC–ACP relationship is provided by Twitchett (1981) and Rajana (1982). The case for regional co-operation has been clearly made by Green and Seidman (1968).

Chapter 6

IDEOLOGIES, POLICIES AND REGIONAL CHANGE

Introduction

National differences as defined by a range of socio-economic statistics (Table 2.1) fail to portray the marked contrasts in social and economic conditions experienced by particular groups within African countries since independence. Nor do they record the political differences at national level which influence the character of intra-national change. Patterns of regional development, of rural and urban growth or decline have been studied in detail by social scientists including geographers in particular African states since independence.

In these studies due consideration has been given to the role of government in influencing regional disparities in social welfare and economic activity. Both Ebong (1982) and Mabogunje (1970; 1978; 1980a) working in Nigeria, for example, have emphasised the need for policies relating to decentralisation and migration to overcome the problems of spatial disparities and rural–urban inequalities in particular. Regional differences are frequently reduced to a simple rural–urban dichotomy. However, the dangers implicit in this simplistic dualism have been acknowledged and differences between social groups within both rural and urban areas also recognised: in the countryside the existence of a powerful landowning or cattleowning élite; in towns the underemployment, low incomes, poor housing and lack of access to social services which are the lot of the urban poor.

A proper concern with issues such as these prompts us to investigate what kinds of government intervention are relevant to explanations of social and spatial change; what are the dominant influences and constraints upon government agencies which affect policy formulation and implementation and what are the outcomes in practice?

The nature of government intervention

In most African countries state intervention in social and economic development combines spatial and non-spatial policy and planning. Hinderink and Sterkenburg (1978) point out that spatial policy, which may focus on particular regions, on rural

113

or on urban areas, is based on the assumption that physical space and the built environment are variables which explain inequality and that without government intervention convergence between core and periphery will not take place. Indeed, Gilbert (1982: 162) points out that a common feature in developing countries

is the frequency with which politicians and planners have averred that something must be done about the growth of cities and the increasing levels of regional inequality. The city is devouring national resources at the expense of the countryside and the farmer; centralisation is destroying the dynamism of the provincial city; there is urban bias, metropolitan bias, rural underdevelopment; development is required in the poorest regions.

He goes on to point out that the degree of regional and urban imbalance in any country can be difficult to measure and the terminology loosely applied. Nevertheless, in African countries with, in the majority of cases, a short history of very rapid urban growth and a highly primate urban structure, imbalance between countryside and town and distortion in the settlement system have some validity. Attempts at regional development since independence reflect this concern.

In addition to spatial measures many social and economic policies and plans do not have an explicitly spatial dimension, for example, social service provision, employment, wages and prices policies which have become major government responsibilities. Despite their apparently non-spatial character and, in consequence, the relatively little attention paid to them by geographers hitherto, the effects of these measures on social and spatial disparities in welfare and income can be significant. This point is crucial in our attempts to explain the social organisation of space. While variations may occur in the orientation of and the assumptions behind government policy, interpreting the effects of government intervention is not solely a question of identifying the physical-spatial framework as the ultimate cause of inequality. What matters is the politico-economic context 'which determines the nature, form and functioning of [the] physical-spatial unit' (Hinderink & Sterkenburg 1978: 10) and, by implication, patterns of inequality.

Two complementary approaches are adopted here in order to assess the influence of government on social groups and areas: by focusing directly on the policy documents and development plans which outline government objectives and how they are to be achieved; and by scrutinising selected case studies concerned with the relationship between policy and practice. Underlying each approach are important assumptions: in the first, ideological and practical considerations of government; in the second the value biases and theoretical position of the writers. In the discussion an important link is provided between each approach by concentrating on the relationship between traditional structures and the State in the formulation and implementation of government policies and plans.

African socialism

Since independence the African states have been further drawn into the orbit of alien influences through their adoption of political ideals from beyond the continent. But 'capitalism' and 'socialism' are general and variable labels. While African states have adopted a particular orientation, the precise characteristics of each model have varied according to the social, economic and political conditions within particular countries and also over time in response to changing internal and external pressures. Young (1982: 10–11) points out that

> The texture of the policy thinking of a Houphouet-Boigny is simply not the same as that of a Nyerere; nor does Samora Machel of Mozambique view the world through the same prism as Daniel arap Moi of Kenya ... More than rhetoric separates Brazzaville and Kinshasa, Dar es Salaam and Nairobi, Cotonou and Lagos. Even the most casual visitor to these contrasting capitals will sense the divergence. Nor is this mere illusion or intuition; over time, these various polities have come to differ from each other in quite significant ways, and these differences can be imputed in good measure to the variation in ideological persuasion.

What I wish to emphasise here is an important cultural dimension which has underlain the characterisation of many regimes by their own leadership. On independence the most vocal African leaders, many of whom were also traditional tribal leaders in their own countries, shared a rhetorical commitment to a new, peculiarly African ideology which was to cut across the 'capitalist-socialist' divide. This was African socialism. Alien cultural influences had already established a significant impact on the landscape of both rural and urban Africa through the spread of 'institutions of modernisation' (Riddell 1970) such as schools, health facilities, an infrastructure of transport routes and a local government administration. With these has come a change in the values, aspirations and behaviour patterns expected of Africans. African socialism represented an attempt to assert independence in the sphere of political thought by charting a new route to internal social and economic change, one which would leave a distinctive mark both on the cultural landscape and on the values of its citizens.

The legacy of colonialism based as it was on Western capitalism encouraged the view among many that a form of socialist option following independence would be the most appropriate strategy by which to achieve national regeneration. The strength of this socialist commitment in the early years was clearly emphasised by Davidson when (1967: 113, 116) he indicated that

115

Between the proffered alternatives of capitalism and socialism ... the ideologists who have made the running have all opted for socialism ... By 1961 ... all those leaders whose governments were based on broad mass movements, as distinct from minority groups of one sort or another, had opted for the socialist alternative. Notable among these were the leaders of Ghana, Guinea and Mali in West Africa, and of Tanganyika in East Africa.

But this enthusiasm for a socialist route did not entail becoming a satellite of either the Soviet Union or China. Indeed, non-alignment in the arena of international politics was strongly supported (Ottaway 1978). Socialism in Africa was to be a distinctive ideology based on the continent's unique social and cultural traditions and it was these particular features of the doctrine which were to provide the justification for a peculiarly African form of socialism.

At the time of independence economic and cultural conditions within the continent justified the widespread acceptance of African socialist principles. As regards economic circumstances, certain basic questions had to be answered concerning the role of the State and the nature of its intervention in the economy. Should government influence be limited to indicative planning or should investment be organised and directed from the centre? Should public control be confined to social infrastructure or extended to productive activity? Should the State focus attention on certain key sectors of the economy or be concerned with all aspects of development? Should the State encourage public or private institutions to mobilise the financial resources? Overall, these questions could be resolved into a fundamental issue of an ideological and practical nature – should the market or the State control activities?

At the time of independence there was active support for the latter as a matter of preference and necessity. It seemed among many to be the most appropriate sector through which to obtain and control the capital needed for investment and growth and, with these, economic independence. For private enterprise to achieve the desired results a group of indigenous businessmen was needed to make the required investment. But in many African states it appeared that few local citizens existed with sufficient capital and experience to fulfil this role. Nkrumah claimed with respect to Ghana, one of Africa's richest states on independence, that although local businessmen did exist they did not invest their resources in a way which would compete with overseas firms. In Tanzania, which was much poorer, it is widely assumed that there were no African capitalists who could develop the private sector (Von Freyhold 1977). Thus if the State, which represented the only indigenous organisation with the means of raising capital, did not become involved the only alternative source would be foreign enterprise. But encouragement to outside investment would merely perpetuate the economic dependence from which African states sought to achieve freedom. Direct state involvement seemed essential, therefore, if the much-needed radical changes in the socio-economic structures of the continent were to be realised.

Cultural justification

Within the context of this book more important in the attraction of African socialism, however, was a belief in the African personality, a conviction expressed cogently in the speeches and writings of President Nyerere (1962; 1968). He claimed that the traditional African economy and social organisation were based on socialist principles of communal ownership of the means of production in which kinship and family groups participated in economic activity and were jointly responsible for welfare and security. The socialist system of co-operative production appeared to be more compatible with African culture than the individualism of capitalism and on the basis of these cultural roots Nyerere sought to emphasise the distinctive characteristics of African socialism. It was not to be a socialism imported from outside based on Soviet, Chinese or East European models where internal class struggle leading to a socialist society had been paramount. As Nyerere wrote in 1962

> The foundation and the objective of African socialism is the extended family. The true African Socialist does not look on one class of men as his brethren and another as his natural enemies ... He regards *all* men as his brethren – as members of his ever extending family. That is why the first article of TANU's creed is: 'Binadamu wote ni ndugu zangu, na Afrika ni moja.' If this had been originally put in English, it could have been: 'I believe in Human Brotherhood and the Unity of Africa'. 'Ujamma', then, or 'Familyhood' describes our Socialism. It is opposed to Capitalism, which seeks to build a happy society on the basis of the exploitation of man by man; and it is equally opposed to doctrinaire socialism which seeks to build its happy society on a philosophy of inevitable conflict between man and man ... (quoted in Davidson 1967 pp 118–119).

Essentially African socialism was seen as an ideology of development arising from the unique circumstances of oppressive colonial rule and incorporating within it the essential qualities of traditional society. It was a banner which appealed to the African leadership. But how to translate its goals of freedom and progress into practice was another matter. In contrast to the Afro-Marxist model which was to be adopted later by many states including Angola, Benin, Congo, Ethiopia and Mozambique, there were no policies, programmes or projects made explicit. It was for the politicians and the bureaucrats to decide. It is at this point that we see important contrasts emerging between the African leaders in their interpretation of the same ideals and beliefs and thus in the ways in which they have sought to shape post-colonial development.

The rhetoric – policy documents

From the wealth of literature which exists – the speeches and writings of leading statesmen, official policy statements and development plans – it is clear that African socialism has become a useful omnibus label for systems of political and economic organisation which vary widely in policy and practice. Metz (1982), for example, discusses the contrasting ideas of the two founding fathers of African socialism, Kwame Nkrumah and Julius Nyerere, in Ghana and Tanzania respectively. These contrasts are also well illustrated in two widely quoted policy documents relating to Kenya and Tanzania respectively. Sessional Paper no. 10 – 'African Socialism and its Application to Planning in Kenya' (Republic of Kenya 1965) – was one of the first major policy statements to be published in independent Kenya by the political party in government, the Kenya African National Union (KANU). In Tanzania a document of comparable significance is the Arusha Declaration issued by the ruling party the Tanzania African National Union (TANU – now the Chama Cha Mapinduzi or CCM) in 1967 (Republic of Tanzania 1967). Interest in these statements lies in their significance both at the time of publication and today as important blueprints for newly independent Africa and also because of the markedly different interpretations of the African socialist ideology to which they subscribe (Mohiddin 1981). Contrasting relationships sought at international level combine with somewhat different approaches to internal regional development. Discussion of the two documents is central to our understanding of the particular social and spatial patterns of development which have evolved within the two countries. In recognising the diversity between them it will nevertheless be stressed that central to both strategies has been an avoidance of models formulated outside Africa without modification to local circumstances.

Both documents display a commitment to equality and social justice, and to reducing international and internal inequalities. For example, the Kenyan document stresses at the outset that 'In African socialism every member of society is important and equal ... The State has an obligation to ensure equal opportunities to all its citizens, eliminate exploitation and discrimination, and provide needed social services such as education, medical care and social security' (Republic of Kenya 1965: 4). Similarly in Tanzania the TANU Constitution, acknowledging as the first socialist principle 'that all human beings are equal', pledges that the government should give 'equal opportunity to all men and women', and should eradicate 'all types of exploitation' so as to 'prevent the accumulation of wealth which is inconsistent with the existence of a classless society' (Republic of Tanzania 1967: 1).

However, the prescriptions offered and the mechanisms set out for achieving these objectives are somewhat different. In Tanzania a determination to reconstruct the economy and society on non-capitalist principles has been paramount since 1967, and is reflected in the emphasis placed on state control and self-reliance. By contrast in Kenya the capitalist principles of individualism and private enterprise in partnership with foreign capital have prevailed. Such differences can be seen in these early policy documents.

The Kenyan approach

Kenya's approach as defined in 1965 stresses the need for flexibility and adaptability in the implementation of African socialism 'because the problems it will confront and the incomes and desires of the people will change over time, often quickly and substantially. A rigid, doctrinaire system will have little chance for survival' (Republic of Kenya 1965: 5). In emphasising this point the Kenya document supports an eclectic rather than doctrinaire approach borrowing the procedures which have proved successful elsewhere. 'Unlike many countries that have eliminated many successful economic mechanisms on narrow, ideological grounds, Kenya is free to pick and choose those methods that have been proven in practice and are adaptable to Kenya conditions regardless of the ideologies that others may attach to them' (Republic of Kenya 1965: 8). In doing so it favours adopting production techniques which combine scale economies with various forms of ownership. State, co-operative, corporate and individual ownership are all favoured so long as they are efficient and promote the government's overall objectives. In accepting the need for control by the State over resource allocation and use, ownership is not therefore the major mechanism used. Flexibility is favoured through a range of controls which can be modified over time and can permit various forms of private participation where appropriate. These controls may extend from 'influence, guidance and the control of a few variables such as prices, or quantities, to absolute control represented by state ownership and operation. Price, wage, rent and output controls, import duties, income taxes and subsidies can be used selectively and in combinations to direct the users to private property, limit profits, and influence the distribution of gains' (Republic of Kenya 1965: 11).

In Kenya's external relations a flexible approach is also apparent. While recognising the need to avoid a satellite relationship with any country or group of countries it nevertheless recognises the benefits to be gained from borrowing 'technological knowledge and proven economic methods from any country – without commitment'; accepting 'technical and financial assistance from any source – without strings', and participating 'fully in world trade – without political domination' (Republic of Kenya 1965: 8). Thus, far from prescribing a policy of isolation, foreign trade, aid and investment are encouraged where they fulfil the obligations to Kenyan society defined by the state.

The Tanzanian approach

Tanzania's approach offers the possibilities of an alternative system. In the TANU Creed the State is awarded a central role in the control and allocation of resources between sectors and regions and in the distribution of rewards. It is stated that 'wherever possible the government directly participates in the economic development of this country', that it should exercise 'effective control over the principal means of production and pursue policies which facilitate the way to collective ownership of the [internal] resources' (Republic of Tanzania 1967: 2).

TANU commitment to self-reliant development reflects a determination to end the foreign exploitation and dependency of the colonial and early post-colonial years.

> How can we depend upon gifts, loans and investments from foreign countries and foreign companies without endangering our independence? ... How can we depend upon foreign governments and companies for the major part of our development without giving to those governments and countries a great part of our freedom to act as we please? The truth is that we cannot.
>
> Let us repeat. We made a mistake in choosing money – something we do not have – to be the big instrument of our development. We are making a mistake to think that we shall get sufficient money for our economic development; and secondly, because even if we could get all that we need, such dependence upon others would endanger our independence and our ability to choose our own political policies. (Republic of Tanzania 1967: 10–11.)

Following logically from this resolve to achieve economic independence the TANU Creed stresses the use of Tanzania's own internal resources to attain development, notably its 'people' and 'land'. In doing so it seeks to avoid the social and spatial inequalities which arise from the exploitation of rural by urban groups:

> our emphasis on money and industries [from external sources] has made us concentrate on urban development ... [But] the foreign currency we shall use to pay back the loans used in the development of the urban areas will not come from the towns or the industries ... The largest proportion of the repayment will be made through the efforts of the farmers ... [Thus] if we are not careful we might get into a position where the real exploitation in Tanzania is that of the town dwellers exploiting the peasants. (Republic of Tanzania 1967: 12.)

With some 85 per cent of Tanzania's population in rural areas this desire to avoid the social ills of exploitation coupled with a deliberate restructuring at the centre find expression in a specifically spatial strategy of development with agriculture at its base.

> A great part of Tanzania's land is fertile, and gets sufficient rain. Our country can produce various crops for home consumption and for export.

We can produce food crops ... And we can produce such cash crops as sisal, cotton, coffee, etc. .... All our farmers are in areas which can produce two or three or even more of the food and cash crops enumerated above, and each farmer could increase his production so as to get more food or more money. And because the main aim of development is to get more food, and more money for our needs, our purpose must be to increase production of these agricultural crops. This is in fact the only road through which we can develop our country – in other words, only by increasing our production of these things can we get more food and more money for every Tanzanian. (Republic of Tanzania 1967: 14.)

Thus while the Kenya document supports the flexible approach which has been characteristic of that country since independence and described by many as closer to capitalist than socialist principles – investment in both the countryside and the towns, public and private, large-scale and small-scale – Tanzania's strategy is narrow and specific. These differences should not, however, be allowed to obscure the fact that both documents display a contempt for ideas and policies imported from outside Africa without modification and share in common the search for approaches appropriate to their own circumstances. The cultural context as perceived by the African leadership is therefore respected and provides the common African socialist base on which contrasting – but nevertheless uniquely African – policy statements have been formulated. Thus while Kenya appears to follow a capitalist route it is a distinctly African form of capitalism (Iliffe 1983). The socialism of President Nyerere is equally striking in its desire to uphold and strengthen what he interprets as the values of African traditional society.

Spatial planning

The Arusha Declaration launched Tanzania on what was at the time a pioneering and revolutionary approach to national development. Based on the resources of rural areas and communal ownership of the means of production it was designed to influence directly regional change and community life. This early emphasis on rural development is not now peculiar to Tanzania. Indeed since the early 1970s broad-based rural development targeted on the poor and involving not only the improvement of agricultural production but also the extension of public services into the countryside from the towns has been encouraged by international aid agencies and formed part of the rhetoric of most African development plans. In countries where the majority of people are rural and agricultural products are among the key export commodities the urban–industrial model has proved inappropriate.

Rural development forms one of three major specifically spatial strategies by which African governments have sought to influence directly the social and economic organisation of space. In addition reference should be made to decentralisation of power and decision-making from the capital city including growth centre strategies to reduce employment concentration and finally more efficient metropolitan expansion through urban planning.

Both Kenya and Tanzania have sought to decentralise future urban expansion through growth centre strategies. The Kenya Development Plan, 1970–74 (Republic of Kenya 1969), for example, designated seven towns other than Nairobi and Mombasa as 'major growth centres'. The Plan for 1979–83 (Republic of Kenya 1979: 47) reiterates government policy to 'spread urbanisation around the country rather than permit excessive concentration in Nairobi and Mombasa' and in doing so reinforces an established concern for the whole urban hierarchy down to small centres (Richardson 1980). Tanzania's Second Five-Year Plan, 1969–74 (Republic of Tanzania 1969) similarly laid down measures to decentralise industry and some government functions from Dar-es-Salaam and in doing so identified eight towns for 'concentrated urban development'. An announcement by President Nyerere in 1973 extended this regional development policy to the resiting of the capital city from Dar-es-Salaam to Dodoma some 300 miles (483 km) to the west. Similar action had been taken by Malawi during the 1970s when Lilongwe took over certain functions from the administrative capital of Zomba and from the primate city and commercial capital of Blantyre. Nigeria represents a further example where the shift has begun from congested Lagos to the new town of Abuja (O'Connor 1983).

Establishing a better balanced urban hierarchy has been seen in some countries both as a means of developing the economic capacities of the regions and also as an essential tool in integrating rural and urban economies. The importance of these links has been discussed (Funnell 1976; Rondinelli 1983a) and with it the need to decentralise development planning and to strengthen regional administration (Rondinelli 1983b): although, as O'Connor (1983: Ch. 8) points out, neither is discussion nor action widespread. Nigeria with its federal structure represents an important example of a country where regional planning has become well developed. Its first National Development Plan 1962–68 did in fact comprise four plans, one for each Regional Government (Northern, Eastern, Western) and one for the Federation (Nigeria Ministry of Economic Development 1962). The system was subsequently extended when in 1967 twelve states were established followed in 1976 by further subdivisions to create nineteen, each with its own state capital.

Elsewhere during the early years of independence most African states transformed their system of local government inherited from the colonial period into an elected body responsible for the provision of major public services. While this initial commitment has been replaced in many cases by a return to central authority in the capital city nevertheless the rhetoric persists. In Zambia President Kaunda's writings on his philosophy of humanism or 'participatory democracy' have assigned a key role to local government in the implementation process as a channel of popular participation (Kaunda 1967; 1974). In Kenya similar views have prevailed. Bewayo (1979: 3) reports the Minister for Local Government in the mid-1970s restating the official position as follows:

Politically our local government system provides the foundation for the expression of our democratic ideals. [Local government] is also critically important for the success of development projects [which] cannot succeed without the effective support of the people for whom they are intended ... local authorities ... provide a suitable forum for discussion and for generating new ideas ... In the great task of nation building, the government requires to mobilize all the manpower resources available. Local authorities form a vital medium through which continuous appraisal of the success of the government's development plans can be realised.

Tanzania and Botswana provide further examples of countries which have sought to promote popular participation in development through active local government (Belshaw 1979; Maro & Mlay 1979; Picard 1979a; b).

As an essential complement to decentralisation most countries have developed urban planning policies to cope with metropolitan expansion. Rapid urban growth and the skewed urban hierarchy characteristic of many African countries (O'Connor 1983: Ch. 2) reflect the persistence into independence of the export-oriented economic model established during the colonial period. The spatial concentration of perceived wage labour opportunities, lack of access to rural land and inadequate income earning opportunities in the countryside have combined to promote rural–urban movement and with it intense pressure on urban land and services. In response to these circumstances land use policies have determined among other things the area designated to shelter provision in towns while laws and regulations have influenced the process of land allocation to different owners, housing standards and the tenurial pattern. Thus the State has played an important role in the operation of the land and housing markets and, by implication, the opportunity of access to both by particular sections of the population including the urban poor.

To the authorities in towns and cities housing the urban poor has become a central concern. Kabagambe and Moughtin (1983) point to the growth of Nairobi from a population of 100,000 in 1948 to 830,000 in 1979 and the inability of some 60–70 per cent of the city's present population to afford the housing erected by the State or city council. Ageni (1981) outlines similar problems in Lagos, Africa's major urban agglomeration, which through in-migration and the corresponding expansion of the built-up area has grown at rates of over 11 per cent/annum in recent years. The creation of spontaneous settlements has been one inevitable result. Early official responses to these illegal settlements – evict, bulldoze, rehouse in low-cost housing – have largely failed to cope with the symptoms of the 'informal housing' problem and since the early 1970s site and service schemes and squatter upgrading have represented the minimum and most characteristic form of central government or local authority intervention to meet the demand.

The State and traditional structures

Within the context of this book interest in these various strategies is twofold: first, these strategies reflect complementary efforts to overcome the problems of spatially biased development inherited from the colonial period; second, and more particularly, in formulating and implementing these strategies the State has been faced with fundamental questions concerning its relationship with traditional social structures and values. In the design and implementation of rural development, for example, these structures have been confronted *in situ* and the nature of the interaction to be encouraged between traditional and external modes of production has been a central issue. In regional development and urban planning the promotion of popular participation has posed questions concerning its form and organisation and in particular the application of traditional social organisational models to these new spatial forms.

Rural development

Tanzania is an important example of a country where rural development has sought to build on traditional structures. It aimed to shift the centre of power from the towns, the politicians and the rural élite to the peasants and in so doing reduce both spatial and social inequalities. To achieve these ends the concept of ujamaa (familyhood), apparently familiar to peasant communities, was invoked. It specifically rejected the rural capitalist approach and with it the individualistic social attitudes which Nyerere claimed had been fostered by colonialism. Rather, responsibility was placed on every rural worker to found or encourage communal village production units, that is, ujamaa or socialist villages based on his perception of the norms of behaviour and the customary rules characteristic of traditional village life. 'We shall achieve the goals we in this country have set ourselves if the basis of Tanzanian life consists of rural *economic and social communities where people live together for the good of all,* and which are interlocked so that all of the different communities also work together in co-operation for the common good of the nation as a whole' (Nyerere 1967: 347–8).

Many studies chart the progress of and the changes in Nyerere's policy of rural development after 1967. These are considered later. The point to be emphasised here is that the reorganisation of the rural environment sought through State intervention – a change in settlement pattern and access to land and the reorganisation of production – derived from Nyerere's interpretation of the principles governing traditional society and his use of these principles to create a national ideology.

In Tanzania rural development has also become closely linked with attempts at administrative decentralisation and the development of an integrated settlement system which incorporates the rural spheres of influence. 'The more comprehensively and systematically rural development is planned and assisted by the state and its regional agencies the more certain it is that local points of concentration will assume a tiered structure in two and eventually three levels ... ' (Maro & Mlay 1979: 291), from village, through district and regional headquarters to the capital city at the apex.

Administrative decentralisation

Like rural development much of the rhetoric behind administrative decentralisation has derived from a commitment to promoting economic and social initiatives beyond the centre of power and decision-making, the capital city. Indeed, at the time of independence local government was seen as an important instrument for local democracy. It was also seen as a further means by which to break away from the imported colonial model based on district commissioners and district officers. Reform of local government was regarded as a major institutional change by which to give credibility at grass-roots level to Africa's political independence and in turn to assist in the maintenance of stability during the early years. As a result new structures were widely introduced with control exercised by the appropriate government ministry (Bewayo 1979). In this process of reorganisation a sensitivity to the actual variety within countries was essential. Nigeria's federal system was designed to nourish and harness the diversities of ethnic origin, language and religion within the country as a means of enriching the Federal Republic while also fostering national unity (Phillips 1980).

In the process of decentralisation it should not be assumed, however, that a search for independence from the colonial image has heralded a simple return to traditional structures. Throughout independence an important contradiction has emerged between on the one hand a respect for cultural diversity and, on the other, the association between political instability and ethnic rivalries which have been both a fear and a reality in several countries. It was this fear which prompted the Federal Military Government in Nigeria during the transition to civilian rule in the mid-1970s to insist that every political party, at least in its organisational structure and officers, must demonstrate a national base with support which exceeded the boundaries of any local group. Its title was to be national without any attachment to ethnic or religious labels (Phillips 1980).

Thus in the bureaucratic structures of local government an acceptance by the central State of the important role to be played by traditional leadership has in some cases conflicted with a fear of its threat to national unity. The experience of Botswana provides a further illustration. Picard (1979a: 287) points out that on independence the system of district councils established as the basic unit of local government was designed to replace tribal councils and act as 'a countervailing force to the still very powerful traditional leadership'. Traditional structures and the leadership in particular were interpreted in this case as a threat to the newly independent governments rather than as a mechanism for expressing popular views and promoting national goals.

Urban planning

In urban planning we see yet another pattern of interaction between the State and traditional structures. As a context for this interaction two points should be emphasised: the marked contrasts in social character of towns across the continent with which it has been the responsibility of urban authorities to deal; and an important change in approach to urban housing problems with a more general change in attitudes at international level towards the problems of poverty.

Marked differences in the cultural origins of urbanisation between West Africa and the rest of the continent have been associated with variations in land tenure and control over access to land. Peil (1976: 163) points out that in many West African cities in particular, which are old-established and pre-date the colonial period, illegal squatting 'in the sense of taking over land without the owner's permission' and the growth of spontaneous settlements are less common than elsewhere. Among the reasons given is official tolerance in both British and French colonial territories of substandard housing in towns during the colonial period and in British territories in particular a respect for customary law and control by traditional chiefs over land allocation which permitted those Africans who sought housing to acquire a plot. With reference to two case studies in Ghana Peil (1976) discusses the persistence of these traditional norms regarding land tenure into independence and their continued influence upon government attitudes to and actions over 'unauthorised settlement'.

In the European towns of eastern and central Africa by contrast, land tenure was largely under state control and colonial government powers were strong enough to determine the urban social and ethnic structure. However, in the post-independence period, during which time large-scale rural–urban movement has led to very rapid urban growth, one inevitable result of this less flexible attitude to land, coupled with the inability of urban authorities to meet the housing demand, has been officially defined illegal squatting and the growth of spontaneous settlements around such cities as Dar es Salaam, Lusaka and Nairobi (O'Connor 1983).

Not only has the interaction between structure and culture influenced the growth of spontaneous settlements, but it is also apparent that a re-evaluation of the cultural practices of traditional society has underlain recent approaches adopted by governments to alleviate the housing problems of which these settlements are a symptom. A change in official policy in the developing countries towards spontaneous settlements from bulldoze to upgrade reflects not only the failure of low cost housing programmes to meet the demand but also, and more particularly, a change in attitude towards the urban poor. The exposure by Mangin (1967) and Turner (1967; 1969) of erroneous concepts like the 'culture of poverty' (Lewis 1970) has played a central role in this change. Characteristics of rationality and mutual support found in traditional society have been widely identified and with these a recognition of the important contribution to be made by traditional social organisational models in the implementation of urban housing policies.

In Botswana community action has formed the basis on which Gaborone's spontaneous settlement, Old Naledi, has been upgraded involving the provision of improved housing, a standpost water supply and household latrines (Bell 1981a). In Kenya similar principles have been widely advocated. Kabagambe and Moughtin (1983) point to the constraints imposed by bye-laws – the colonial legacy of unrealistic building standards – on achieving low cost solutions to Nairobi's housing problems. Yet in Korokocho, a recent extension of Mathare Valley the city's largest concentration of unapproved housing, all is not bleak:

> activity abounds, from commerce to industry, farming to building and individual to group action. The Muslim community is one such active group. It is organised by a religious/social worker and has built a mosque, installed piped water to it for public use and is busy building a school with funds from the Arab world. Christian groups are strongly in evidence making the area attractive to others of the same persuasion ... Individuals, too, assist with community works and are members of community organisations, while the baraza held by the chief to launch our project was a well attended and lively event.
> (Kabagambe & Moughtin 1983: 241)

This strong spirit of community which is a characteristic feature of African rural society and finds its roots in the communal mode of production has become widely recognised as an important instrument for local development in the urban context.

From these case studies we can identify different attitudes to and uses of traditional structures in the process of spatial planning. The relationship between structure and culture has been varied and not always harmonious. Tanzania's experiment in rural development represents perhaps the most radical attempt to transform the geographical and social environment of rural areas by altering the basis on which production is organised and sustained in a manner intended to be sympathetic to traditional values. Urban planning authorities have similarly drawn upon the characteristics of traditional society in the formulation and implementation of programmes for housing the urban poor. Local initiative has also been encouraged through decentralisation strategies but in this case, where some redistribution of power from the centre has been an important issue, strengthening the authority of an already powerful and potentially threatening traditional leadership has not always been encouraged.

Evaluations in practice

What of the results in practice? How far has the interaction between institutions of government and traditional structures influenced opportunity of access to scarce resources in rural and urban areas and hence those who gain and those who lose from state intervention? A major indictment of the post-colonial state in Africa is its failure to tackle effectively the social and economic problems of rural areas and in particular the ecological crises in African agriculture (Cliffe 1976). Spontaneous settlements continue to grow while the enthusiasm for local democracy on independence has in many cases given way to recentralisation. What issues lie at the root of these problems? Our evaluations must take into account both the content of the plans and the difficulties of implementation. In doing so we should bear in mind that the theoretical framework used influences our interpretations.

The forces involved, both supports and constraints, can be seen to operate at a series of interlocking scales. Change in rural and urban communities must be related back to state intervention at the centre, the capital city. The priorities, defined at this level, should in turn be linked to the international arena. Below this national/international scale the degree and nature of change within particular communities must in turn be related to the interpretation placed upon, and the ability to implement, government objectives in the light of local circumstances, notably the interaction between social organisation, technology and the environment. Thus the problems of inappropriate technological choice in agricultural production and housing or the administrative inefficiencies and financial constraints which inhibit the effectiveness of field workers cannot be separated from the broader political economy in African countries while their significance locally depends upon the circumstances at this level. Who then are the key groups involved at these various scales whose actions and reactions influence the formulation and effectiveness of particular programmes and projects? Tendler (1982: ii) suggests the following: 'included and excluded beneficiaries, participating and non-participating agencies, supplier and other private interest groups, local and central government élites, and other political actors with something to gain or lose'. Fig. 6.1 provides a framework within which to proceed.

The formulation of priorities

At the stage of plan formulation let us concentrate on the key groups operating at the centre since priorities in spatial planning should be seen in the context of national and international goals. Powerful influences on the bureaucracy come internally from the politicians and externally through the medium of international aid. Green (1965: 252) emphasises with reference to development planning as a whole that to be effective it must gain political backing and in order to do so 'must be, and be seen to be, a quantitative programme designed to create conditions in which national socio-political objectives can be attained'. He goes on to stress that 'if a close relationship is to exist between national goals as expressed by politicians and economic programmes as expressed in the plans, close interaction is essential between political leaders and planners (whether expatriate or national)'.

Evidence of this close interaction can be found in Kenya and Tanzania. Following publication of the Kenya Sessional Paper no. 10 in 1965, a revised

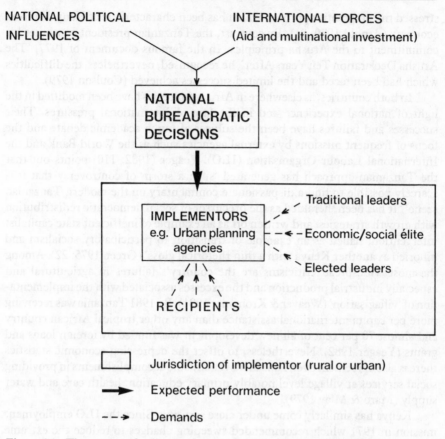

NATIONAL POLITICAL
INFLUENCES

INTERNATIONAL FORCES
(Aid and multinational investment)

NATIONAL
BUREAUCRATIC
DECISIONS

IMPLEMENTORS
e.g. Urban planning
agencies

Traditional leaders

Economic/social élite

Elected leaders

RECIPIENTS

Jurisdiction of implementor (rural or urban)

Expected performance

Demands

Figure 6.1 The context of policy implementation (after Grindle 1977: 205)

Development Plan 1966–70 (Republic of Kenya 1966) was produced, a document which unlike its predecessor (Development Plan 1964–70) derived its basic objectives directly from this important policy statement. In the case of Tanzania the Arusha Declaration (Republic of Tanzania 1967) went far beyond the objectives of the first Five-Year Plan 1964–69 with the result that in its successor (the Tanzania Second Five-Year Plan for Economic and Social Development 1969–74) a new strategy was set out to fulfil more explicitly the Arusha philosophy.

However, these two key policy documents of Kenya and Tanzania, to which much reference has been made above, and which have profoundly influenced the direction of development planning, are only among the earlier ones in a series of pronouncements which have defined the development paths of each country. Despite their significance both internally and within the continent as a whole the rhetoric has been modified over time and so, in turn, specific programmes and projects. By the mid-1970s Kenya's adherence to African socialism was less explicit than formerly. A member of former President Kenyatta's Cabinet has stressed the pragmatic approach which has been characteristic of Kenya's mixed economy (Arnold 1979: 94). By contrast, the Tanzanian president continues his commitment to the Arusha principles. In the famous document of 1977, 'The Arusha Declaration Ten Years After', he recognised, nevertheless, the difficulties which had been faced and the limited successes achieved (Coulson 1979).

In both countries, as elsewhere in Africa, strategies have been modified in the light of national experience and in the face of international pressures. Their successes and failures have been the subject of much academic debate and the focus of frequent missions by external agencies such as the World Bank and the International Labour Organisation (ILO). Yeager (1982: 110) points out that the Tanzanian approach has generated 'such a storm of controversy that it is scarcely possible to find a dispassionate commentary on the modern Tanzanian scene'. It has been 'heralded as the precursor of social democratic redistribution with growth strategies, and written off as an example of inefficient state capitalist intervention; hailed as an example of transition to participatory socialism and pilloried as another Kenya with a thin rhetorical gloss' (Green 1975: 22). Among the most widespread criticisms are the country's failures in agricultural and especially industrial production and the excesses associated with the implementation of 'villagisation' (Weaver & Kronemer 1981). By 1981 Tanzania was receiving more per capita international assistance than any other tropical African country and almost 70 per cent of all new development was funded by foreign loans and grants (Yeager 1982). Nevertheless, to offset the depressing economic statistics there is also agreement over Tanzania's remarkable accomplishments in providing social services at village level notably primary education, health care and water supply (Maro & Mlay 1979).

Kenya has similarly come under close scrutiny. Since the ILO employment mission in 1971 which recommended sweeping changes to reduce the extreme economic and social imbalances within the country (ILO 1972), its findings and recommendations have been criticised by some as politically naïve (Leys 1975; 1978) and supported by others (World Bank 1975). Indeed, in liberal circles the country has been acclaimed as 'among the few countries to adopt explicitly the basic needs approach to development as an operational strategy' (Ghai *et al.* 1979). Nevertheless, recent figures point to the slow growth in national income between 1962 and 1979, to a fall in GDP in real terms between 1979 and 1980 and, more particularly, to a continued extremely unequal income distribution, 'one of the worst ... in the world' (Anker & Knowles 1983: 13).

Constraints on implementation – structural explanations

Assessments of the development performance of individual countries are clearly influenced by the theoretical position adopted and the focus of study. So too are interpretations of the causes. However some common ground exists in the importance attached to structural issues at international, national and local levels.

With finance and skilled manpower still limited in the African countries many writers suggest that their reliance on international aid for resources and advice makes the implementation of programmes and projects an uncertain and unpredictable exercise (Pinfold & Anderson 1981). Indeed, it is this foreign involvement in development planning which has been much attacked by radical writers. Cohen and Daniel (1981: 221) discuss the wide publicity given to 'details of the currently favoured strategy, or an analysis of the latest failed "development" project or a prescription for the road ahead, one which will avoid the pitfalls of previous efforts'. Combined with this publicity they refer to the apparent help received from outside in the form of 'a veritable invasion of Africa by an "army" of expatriate specialists from either the development agencies of the donor nations, or the myriad of international organisations that have mushroomed in the so-called field of development'. In charting the lack of any significant economic and social progress they offer their explanation: 'failure is as much a legacy of Africa's exploitation by colonial capitalism as it is an indicator of how development programmes formulated within the framework of international capitalism exacerbate Africa's conditions of dependency rather than reduce it'.

Leys' (1975) analysis of 'underdevelopment in Kenya' adopts this historical structural approach. Contemporary income inequalities within the country are related to the specific social relations of production which evolved during the colonial period and which continue to 'militate against the productive investment of the surplus at the periphery' (Leys 1978: 245). A similar approach has been adopted for Tanzania by one of the country's most outspoken citizens (Shivji 1973; 1976). The importance of the politico-economic 'structure and struggle' in Tanzania is also stressed by Samoff (1981). He cites the hostile external environment towards the socialist transition reflected in petroleum price increases and the strength of international pressure on Tanzania through the International Monetary Fund to participate in the world economic system. But he also stresses the 'supportive trends', namely, the socialist commitment in Angola, Mozambique and Zimbabwe and the pressure which this places on Western nations to provide capital and technical assistance.

Convergences between national and international interests at the expense of the majority of African people are discussed in a range of African countries. An analysis of political decision-making in Botswana (Isaksen 1981) indicates how the current rhetorical commitment to job creation and rural development is unlikely to succeed owing to the inherent financial conservatism of the leading groups involved, notably the political élite, the bureaucracy and professionals from outside in the form of foreign consultants and representatives of donor agencies. Isaksen demonstrates how, in the absence of appropriate institutions and organisations at grass-roots level in the countryside to challenge the status quo, a set of élite interests is preserved at the centre which for significantly different reasons favour broadly similar risk-averting policies of accumulation.

At sub-national level an important relationship has been identified between political ideology and the constraints on implementation. In the case of urban planning, for example, while both Kenya and Tanzania share a commitment to improving access to adequate shelter in towns, Stren (1975) explains their very different approaches to spontaneous settlements and the urban poor in terms of contrasting political structures and ideologies. These contrasting approaches are linked in turn to somewhat different implementation problems.

In the case of Kenya where no radical policy changes have taken place since independence and where bureaucratic capacity is well developed he suggests that a major problem has been to cope with the demands of all sections of urban society. Thus through residential segregation spontaneous settlements are screened from those with upper and middle incomes in the same way that during the colonial period in Zambia, for example, legislation preserved ethnic segregation (Tipple 1976). Coupled with this zoning the upgrading of spontaneous settlements and the introduction of site-and-service projects does not threaten the existing social and economic order. Indeed, private capital may profit through the provision of building materials. A case is described in Nairobi where through the adoption of unnecessarily high standards the cost of materials exceeded the budget of the poorest groups with the result that heavy government subsidy was necessary (Stren 1975).

Through approaches such as these urban planning authorities seek to legitimise state policies to assist the urban poor before the various income groups in towns. In the case of Tanzania, however, where policies have been more innovative and urban authorities are politically constrained to focus on lower-income groups, the pressure of opposing interests is less significant than the problem of inadequate resources. Innovative programmes are costly to carry out in terms of bureaucratic resources and as Stren (1975: 293) argues 'to put too much pressure on administrators to effect changes is in the end to invite stagnation, and a situation whereby only those with access to the bureaucracy and its agencies will get what they need'.

In pointing to the structural roots of Africa's development problems, explanations such as these remind us of the inequalities which development planning in general and spatial planning in particular seek to redress. Gilbert (1982: 196) stresses that 'It has been the importation of development models on national and international space which has created so many of the problems of urban and rural development', and that in searching for solutions through spatial planning an important distinction needs to be made between 'place and personal welfare'. While rural and urban planning together with an encouragement of local democracy are all important, spatial inequality is a structure created by society and spatial planning should be seen above all as a means by which resources can be more equitably distributed and biases against the poor redressed.

Cultural issues and the importance of the recipients

In explaining the gulf between planning and practice it is not merely with structural issues that we should be concerned, however, but also their interactions with culture. On the negative side it is ethnicity which has frequently served to sharpen the distinction between ideology and politics. Regrettably, in many African states since independence power struggles exacerbated by ethnic rivalries have led to much political instability which has in turn frustrated genuine attempts at progress (Akintoye 1980; Gutkind & Waterman 1977; Harris 1975). Perhaps the most striking and tragic example is that of Uganda. Within the context of the modern nation state interactions between cultures have all too frequently been a destructive force. But cultural practices may also be a progressive influence when acknowledged and supported. Reference to those whom development planning is designed to serve illustrates this point.

In the case of programmes and projects with distributive and redistributive goals the intended beneficiaries are frequently low status groups – peasants, villagers, urban squatters. But they should not be regarded as powerless in the face of pressure from political or economic élites: they are not merely 'passive victims' in the process of change. Undoubtedly the social structures in Africa have been profoundly modified by the penetration of an alien mode of production. Those with political and economic power now strongly influence the allocation of resources between groups and areas and hence the speed and direction of change. But our analysis of the success or otherwise of policy implementation cannot be reduced merely to a discussion of controlling élites or emerging social classes. Africa's social structures are a product of the interaction between traditional and alien modes and from national to local level the influence of this interaction is apparent in the values, the beliefs and the pattern of loyalties which lie behind the response to particular policies and spatial plans. Here we have an important common thread linking the various scales of our analysis.

At national level in both Kenya and Tanzania, as elsewhere in Africa, culture is now given more prominence in the policies and practices of government than in the 1960s when national ideologies were first formulated. It reflects a recognition that insensitivity to cultural variety can produce only limited progress. Some of the negative effects of past approaches can be illustrated in relation to the three forms of spatial planning discussed above. In the case of rural development a failure to understand the peasant mode of production by the political élite at national level and by field workers at local level is central to our explanation of the lack of improvement in agricultural productivity. In the case of popular participation an important inconsistency exists between on the one hand attitudes to the involvement of traditional leadership in formal structures and the involvement of communities in their own development. At village level it has become clear that traditional authority is often vital to the success of particular projects. In the case of self-help housing strategies for the urban poor, while strengthening traditional social organisational models has become an important expedient, success depends upon the willingness and ability of the State to facilitate such bottom-up development through the concessions made. Some examples will illustrate these points.

In parts of rural Africa traditional structures have not yielded to the pressures of either capitalism or socialism but continue to exist in a controversial relationship with these alien modes. This is particularly the case in areas where land is not a scarce resource and peasants are the owners of the means of production. Under such circumstances a major constraint on development programmes and projects concerned with rural production is, in the words of Hyden (1980: 229), 'the irrelevance of such efforts to the vast majority of the producers'. Government officials have difficulty in exercising real economic power since peasants can 'seek security in withdrawal'.

Since 1967 Tanzania's major thrust has been rural development but a key reason given for the limited success achieved by state intervention in the rural environment is a misinterpretation of the peasant mode by the political leadership at the centre (Hyden 1980; Lofchie 1978; Weaver & Kronemer 1981). Hyden points out that Nyerere sought through the ujamaa ideology to apply the rules governing production within rural households to larger social and economic forms of organisation within the modern world – what Mushi (1971) describes as 'modernisation by traditionalisation'. In doing so Nyerere combined his perception of domestic circumstances with a knowledge of the Chinese experience under Mao Tse-tung. But in practice the system failed to distinguish between communal activity in the sense of reciprocity and mutual aid, and communal ownership: 'it asked the peasant farmers to accept a social relation that they did not conceive as necessary for their own reproduction'. (Hyden 1980 p. 105.) Hence, considerable regional variations occurred in the extent to which the existing rural settlement pattern was altered and communal production as a complement to individual production adopted (Von Freyhold 1979).

Policy approaches until 1976 including, from 1973, the compulsory movement of rural people into villages, reflected a somewhat blind adherence to ideology and a desire for quick results with the apparent resistance of the recipients to respond explained in terms of slow cultural adjustment. In the light of experience, however, a change in official policy became necessary (Coulson 1977; 1979; Mushi 1981). The inappropriateness of agricultural extension to serve the needs of peasant communities was apparent (De Vries 1978) together with the environmental problems associated with 'villagisation' which militated 'against a number of time-tested peasant answers to advantageous man–land relationships' (Kjekshus 1977: 282). In consequence Yeager (1982: 86) identifies a new flexibility in the Tanzanian policy process, 'a kind of ideologically disciplined pragmatism' which, among other things, allows each village to set its own pace in creating socialist institutions and processes.

Although the experience of Tanzania cannot easily be generalised, arising from it and other studies relating to the peasant farmer is an important common theme – the need for a proper understanding of existing practices in relation to agricultural production. Richards (1979; 1983) describes the emergence of a new paradigm for understanding the African environment in which the resistance of the peasant farmer to new agricultural technologies or cropping patterns is no longer explained in terms of ignorance, apathy or intransigence. Rather, the rationality of peasant producers in their agricultural practices in relation to technology and the environment is acknowledged and with it the existence of a rich 'village science' tradition to be utilised in improving the use of environmental resources. (See also *IDS Bulletin* (Brighton) 1979, Vol 10 No 2.)

What may be interpreted as the power of the peasant farmer in relation to productive activity at local level may be linked in turn with the continued power of traditional political structures and modes of leadership in collective decision-making at this level. In the case of Botswana while the authority of traditional leaders has been reduced in local government, nevertheless at village level they continue to represent a powerful force between implementing agency and beneficiary. Tribal leaders control the kgotla, the tribal assembly, which has a major local judicial function and also 'remains the only legitimate means of government communication with the populace. All meetings, except political rallies, must be held in the kgotla and sanctioned by the appropriate chief or headman' (Vengroff 1977: 59). Information from central government or district councils reaches the community through the kgotla and in view of the control by traditional leaders over this institution they can strongly influence the success of government projects by translating, interpreting and mediating government goals. Vengroff (1977: 60) argues that

> The main importance of the kgotla lies in the fact that it represents the point of intersection of the traditional political system and the organisations of the central government and district council. It acts as the means of providing traditional legitimacy to the introduction of new ideas, ways of doing things, and regulations issued by the new élites at the central and local level.

It is through these traditional channels that community participation in development projects is sanctioned. At their base is the most fundamental social and cultural unit, the family, on which traditional leadership depends for its legitimacy and which plays a key role in sustaining development projects and community activities based on self help. The threat to this unit from externally induced change is now the object of some concern. The Kenya National Development Plan for the period 1979 to 1983 (Republic of Kenya 1979: 2), for example, acknowledges that 'progress itself may create problems which did not exist before ... The impact of modernisation on cultural and family traditions is but one example.' A determination to overcome 'second generational problems' such as these is clearly expressed:

> The family is the pivotal social unit. It has the main responsibility for determining family size, improving the quality of life of its members and inculcating in children the values which will guide their social and economic conduct when they mature. It is Government policy to strengthen the family as a social unit through its several community activities, its functional literacy programmes and its support for family-oriented activities of voluntary agencies. (Republic of Kenya 1979: 25.)

The difficulties involved in reconciling traditional leadership structures and the family with the modern world are particularly marked in towns. It is in towns we receive the sharpest reminder that communal activity and self help, although traditional characteristics of African communities and a cost saving to government, are being encouraged not only in a changed politico-economic environment but also in an alien geographical environment. As a result, although community participation is regarded as an essential strategy by which to improve the housing conditions of the urban poor, building on traditional social organisational models is problematic. In spontaneous settlements government seeks to mobilise collective enterprise among those who are, in the main, unable to compete in the urban housing market and who in the modern world are regarded as of low status. It is not therefore surprising that the initial response may be apathy, even resistance or hostility to urban officials and planning authorities.

Success in projects to improve the conditions of the urban poor depends primarily on the willingness and ability of the State to facilitate community involvement by providing the conditions within which such enterprise can operate. For low-income groups three crucial policy areas are land allocation, security of tenure and realistic bye-law standards for self-built housing. It is only when these conditions are satisfied that the incentives will exist for 'the untapped energies of the squatters' to be released in order that they may 'improve their homes and so invest incrementally in property' (Kabagambe & Moughtin 1983: 245). An effective interrelationship between the State and the community is critical to long-term success.

Conclusion

This chapter has emphasised that since independence African leadership has sought freedom from beyond the continent in the realm of political thought and ideals. A distinctly African form of socialism has not precluded ideological differences between states as reflected in contrasting political and social attitudes to national development and internal inequality. Nevertheless, despite this diversity, there has been shared in common a political commitment to state involvement in social and economic development through the planning mechanism. With reference to alternative forms of spatial planning the importance of interaction between state structures and traditional systems has been highlighted both in the formulation and implementation process. But while traditional structures are critical they have also been modified and remain under threat. Among these is the most basic social and cultural unit, the family, to which more detailed attention will now be given.

Further reading

Young (1982) provides a detailed analysis of contrasting political regimes in Africa while African socialism in Kenya and Tanzania is explored in detail by Mohiddin (1981). As regards spatial policy and planning in selected African countries, for a discussion of administrative decentralisation see Belshaw (1979), Maro and Mlay (1979) and Picard (1979a; b); rural development with particular reference to the recipients is provided by Hyden (1980) and, in the case of urban planning, Kabagambe and Moughtin (1983) and Peil (1976).

Chapter 7

CULTURE, THE STATE AND NATURAL POPULATION CHANGE

Introduction

Over the last sixty years African societies have undergone considerable change under the influence of forces from beyond the continent (Chs 4 & 5). Within the confines of an alien politico-economic system and the boundaries of the independent nation states each with its own particular ideology (Ch. 6) the loyalties and behaviour patterns expected of individuals have proved to be significantly different from those characteristic of tribal society. When social change is examined within the continent it is apparent that the penetration of new institutions – political, economic, religious, educational, the nuclear family – has brought with it new role relationships within which the interactions between people are organised. A new set of values, norms of behaviour and sanctions has been introduced by which these interactions are controlled. Among the major symptoms of this social and cultural transformation are the demographic processes – fertility, mortality, spatial mobility – which have altered significantly in character during this century. (Population mobility is considered in Ch. 8.)

At the macro-scale of continent, nation and region certain broad trends can be identified including, most notably, a rapidly growing population – the rates are among the highest in the world (Table 3.1). Below this level it is apparent that the penetration and impact of external forces have varied socially and spatially within African countries. Detailed investigation at the level of community and household helps us to identify the form of these external pressures and the particular social and cultural practices which influence the demographic response. Central to the discussion is the role of the State in influencing fertility and mortality and, by implication, the extent to which the new political structures imposed on African society have responsibility for behavioural change.

Natural population change

Although the statistical analysis of population dynamics is now an essential part of social and economic development planning, both individually and in combination the component parts are extremely complex and difficult to explain. There are two

138

issues with which we should be concerned. Using Woods' (1982: 2) description, 'what causes population to ... and what influence population has on ... , population as effect and cause'. What are the factors which bring about changes in fertility and mortality, and what are the effects of changes in fertility and mortality on the social and economic organisation of space? In the first case population dynamics are the visible symptoms of Africa's transformation; in the second, they are active agents in the process of change. In view of the complexity of the issues involved, for those concerned with the study of population, models and theories have provided a useful aid to explanation. Fig. 7.1 outlines six groups of factors which interact to influence fertility, mortality, migration and, by implication, population growth. As Woods (1982: 14) points out, they represent 'the first and most easily completed stage in the construction of theoretical statements in population geography'. The second stage requires more precise specification of the variables and their interactions in particular instances.

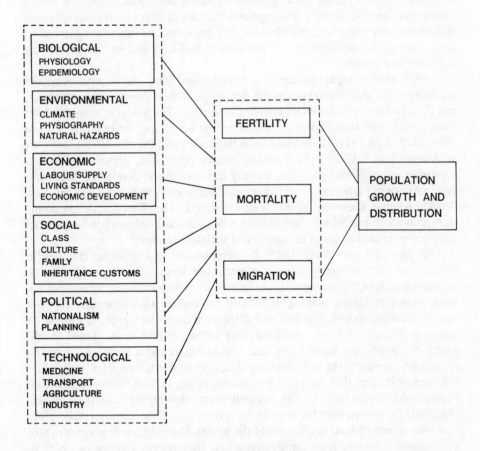

Figure 7.1 Demographic relationships (after Woods 1982: 15)

It is the relevance of theoretical formulations as descriptions and/or explanations of the patterns and changes in the present-day African population with which we are concerned. The two perhaps most widely discussed are associated with Malthus (see Flew 1970) and Marx (1867; 1976: 781–94), both of whom 'have shaped seemingly irreconcilable views on the nature of the relationship between population and socio-economic development' (Woods 1982: 45). Added to these is the so-called demographic transition model which can be traced back to Thompson (1929) and which describes the actual demographic transition which took place in Europe and North America over a period of two centuries from high fertility–high mortality to a state of low fertility–low mortality. In effect, though not explicitly stated, it deals with the demographic changes which accompanied the shift to a capitalist, technologically advanced economy and the new social formation associated with it. Details of these formulations, their supporters and their critics, can be found elsewhere. (Woods [1982] provides an excellent introduction, particularly Chs 1 & 5). The point to be emphasised here is that besides the many questions and doubts which have been raised over some of the basic assumptions, they are in effect both geographically and historically specific. Nevertheless, they have had an important impact on discussion of the development of population in Africa and in the developing countries as a whole.

After 1945 a rapid decrease in mortality in many developing countries encouraged the view that this was the first stage in their demographic transition and that it would be followed by a decline in fertility. The model appeared to have some predictive value. (For a discussion of the issues see, for example, Cassen 1976; 1978; Kirk 1971; 1979; Mauldin & Berelson 1978; Preston 1976.) However as Monsted and Walji (1978) among others point out, present-day social, economic and political conditions are very different in the developing countries, and in Africa in particular, from those found historically in Europe and the New World. Among these we should emphasise that the Western demographic transition accompanied a period of industrialisation and urbanisation associated with widespread changes in economic and social structures.

As Monsted and Walji (1978: 27) demonstrate, the resulting changes 'in relation to the previously dominant rural life were towards fixed salaries, increasing costs of children and lack of benefit from their labour, limited housing, work away from home making it difficult for women simultaneously to work outside the home as well as to take care of their children'. However, they go on: 'A complete change of living conditions has not occurred for the Third World countries, where the majority of the population remains rural and with no immediate increase in the cost of raising children'. In short, if we refer back to Fig. 7.1, then it is clear that the precise character of the various factors influencing demographic behaviour in the contemporary developing countries differs materially from those over the last two centuries in the West. Caution is therefore necessary in any general application of the model. Moreover, as it is a descriptive generalisation derived from trends over a long time period, fluctuations both in space and time which deviate from the overall pattern are obscured.

140

So in summary as we turn to the demographic position within Africa difficulties arise for two reasons. First, just as in the West birth and death rates changed at different rates in different places at different times, so too within the continent important temporal and spatial variations can be identified within and between countries. For example, some studies record higher fertility in urban than in rural areas (e.g. Adegbola *et al.* 1977). Others point to important variations in mortality by region or district (Thomas 1972). Findings such as these, perhaps inconveniently, cloud any overall picture. Nevertheless they need to be explained.

The second point concerns our approach to explanation. The broad thesis, which appears so persuasive, that a relationship exists between demographic regime and mode of production poses problems when we try to determine the characteristics of the latter within the African context. It raises many fundamental and controversial questions concerning modes of production in Africa. To take but one example, in view of the complexity of traditions and cultural backgrounds within the continent, difficulties arise in presenting any general definition of non-capitalist systems. By the same token no simple characterisation of the accompanying demographic regime is possible. Indeed, if we accept that there are demographic implications of material relations what is clear is that the transformation towards a market economy in Africa has been accompanied by marked variations both within and between rural and urban areas in fertility, mortality and migration. Furthermore, we should recall that the origins of the forces which have stimulated population change lie beyond the continent. These points alone imply that no direct parallel with Western experience can be predicted and that models based on this experience are questionable in their value.

Modernisation and culture

There is a growing body of literature which suggests that the independent status of culture has been underestimated in much Western thinking on population and development (Caldwell 1982). For example, in the neo-Marxist writings derived from the historical materialist model of Marx there is a tendency to regard social organisation, culture and the demographic regime itself as dependent upon the economic system, that is, as merely a dependent part of the superstructure. Criticisms may also be made of the ideologically very different demographic transition model. In its traditional form the composite term 'modernisation' is used to explain changes in fertility and mortality. This comprises both economic growth and 'social modernisation'. Indeed, Jones (1981: 88) suggests that it has three components: 'sociological, economic and psychological arguments'. Woods (1982: 158) goes so far as to suggest that 'The theory is in a sense revolutionary; it deals with the collapse of old relationships and foretells the creation of new ones'.

However, two limitations may be identified in the use of the term modernisation to account for this revolutionary change. The first relates to the

Eurocentricity of the assumptions on which the term is based. Economic growth is defined in Western terms as a rise in per capita real income with little regard for the critical distributional component. Social modernisation is associated with the economic rationality and the individualism of so-called modern society. The second limiting factor concerns the composite nature of the term 'modernisation' itself. Although the role of social organisation and culture is acknowledged in the model the need has been expressed to go beyond this, in particular to see the economic and socio-cultural components as two separate forces for change. Woods (1982: 166) outlines the argument and reasons that of the two, social modernisation is perhaps the most important in initiating a demographic revolution.

However, the vexed question remains: how can we characterise this complex process of social modernisation and, in doing so, avoid the dangers of Eurocentric bias? Careful study is needed of the social and cultural traditions in Africa which influence demographic behaviour, how and why they are changing and their effects upon spatial variations in fertility and mortality. Cultural traditions and practices play a crucial role in mediating the material relations, the social processes and the institutional interventions which affect demographic behaviour and in doing so they make an important contribution to explaining spatial variations in demographic change. This will be demonstrated not only with reference to fertility which is now more widely acknowledged than in the past, but also in relation to mortality.

Broad theories relating to population and development depend for their verification upon the identification of aggregate trends over time. However, in seeking to identify the influence of cultural beliefs, attitudes and preferences one must in the first instance move the focus of enquiry from the statistical analysis of macro-scale data to the level of particular cases. As indicated in Chapter 3, this is not to imply that culture has a significance only at the micro-scale, but is merely to illustrate that more thorough research can be carried out and more penetrating conclusions reached by initial investigation at this level. In geographical terms it is important in encouraging a shift away from the interpretation of space as a formal unit for data purposes. Such an approach based on pre-defined macro-units (regions, districts, towns) constrains interpretation since geographical comparison is the basis on which spatial variation is identified and explained. The approach adopted here focuses attention on the social processes which give rise to differences in fertility and mortality within and between rural and urban areas.

Mortality

It has already been suggested that perhaps the most important demographic change in Africa in the recent past has been a marked increase in the population growth rate of the area. While the usual explanation for this trend is a decrease in death rates due to improvements in medical facilities, hygiene and nutrition, such an interpretation must be applied with caution. By international standards mortality rates in Africa remain high and some investigations suggest that within parts of the continent they are as high as ever they were (cf. Condé 1973a). While the average life expectancy at birth is about 72 years in the more developed countries, it is about 57 years in the less developed countries and a mere 47 years in Africa south of the Sahara excluding South Africa (Table 3.1). Focusing just on infant and early childhood deaths, which are the leading cause of low life expectancy, a similar pattern arises. Data on the former indicate that while the infant mortality rate is about 20 per 1000 live births in the most developed countries, many African countries have rates of over 150 and in some instances it exceeds 200 per 1000 live births. World Health Organisation (1981) information on the death rate of children between 1 and 5 years confirms this pattern.

Given the high rates for Africa as a whole, if we look more closely at the situation within the continent then both over space and through time further important differences can be identified. Adegbola (1977), for example, has demonstrated that during the 1960s infant mortality ranged from 150 per 1000 in Kenya to a high 332 per 1000 in Burkina Faso. By the late 1970s the figures had fallen to 83 and 182 per 1000 respectively. Accepting that over time improvements have been made at national level, if we concentrate on conditions within each country, then further important spatial and social differences in life expectancy emerge. For example, in Kenya Anker and Knowles (1977) and Faruqee (1980) have identified variations by region, tribe, education, sex and age. Evidence of this kind can be found in all countries (cf. Condé 1971; Makinwa 1976). It emphasises the need for caution in interpreting national statistics, and more broadly, in assessing demographic trends within the continent as a whole.

Fig. 7.1 shows the wide range of factors which interact in many complex ways. It is the relative importance of these various factors and the nature of the interrelationships in particular instances which offer the major challenge. Many studies emphasise the critical role of access to modern medical services in explaining mortality differentials. For example, Orubuloye and Caldwell (1975) found this to be the case in two Nigerian villages with similar culture and socio-economic conditions but with markedly different mortality rates. (See also Faulkingham & Thorbahn 1975). These findings are confirmed in many developing countries. But significantly in the now industrialised countries improvements in medicine were not the initial cause of mortality decline. It was better housing, sanitation and hygiene which led the way to the Western demographic transition. In this discussion the role of improvements in environmental health in influencing morbidity and mortality in Africa is stressed. Their critical importance in reducing both social and spatial inequalities in life expectancy has been acknowledged only relatively recently at international level and in the development strategies of particular countries. In discussing the state action needed, particular attention is given to the vital importance of cultural appraisal in determining the success of programme efforts.

Environmental health

The prevalence of endemic diseases and epidemics are among the key biological factors directly responsible for continued high mortality in much of Africa. Among the former, infectious and parasitic diseases, reduced to minor nuisances in the industrialised countries, remain widespread. Cassen (1978: 335) points out that 'Any analysis of the causes of Africa's population trends must begin with health conditions which explain the almost universal low life expectancy'. Equally clearly these direct determinants of mortality are influenced by environmental and socio-economic variables. For example, drought combined with crop failure has been particularly serious in the Sahel region since 1973 (Caldwell 1975; Sène 1982) while internal and international migration brought on by these conditions has increased the risks of spreading communicable diseases.

Often sudden and devastating forces such as these in selected areas should be set against trends which over the last thirty years have created or exacerbated health problems in all countries. They include rapid population growth which has hampered the ability of governments to improve access to both curative and preventive medicine. Mott and Mott (1980) emphasise this with respect to Kenya. Movement to towns and with it the growth of spontaneous settlements and urban slums lacking essential services have further encouraged the spread of disease. Reference should also be made to capital projects in rural areas such as dams and irrigation schemes which although designed to increase national wealth and rural incomes have often created health problems (Bradley 1977a). Some three million Kenyans, for example, are estimated to have schistosomiasis, a debilitating disease carried by snails which thrive in slow-moving water (Ministry of Health undated).

From the above evidence it is apparent that not all population groups have been equally threatened. Income levels, influencing as they do diet, standard of housing and access to essential social services, play an important role in explaining variations in the incidence and impact of disease especially since these social disparities have an important spatial dimension. The threat has indeed been greatest where low income groups are concentrated, namely, in high density urban slums, in spontaneous settlements and among the rural poor. It should also be stressed that among poor people, infant and child mortality in particular account for a large proportion of the total death rate. Infant and early childhood mortality is widely regarded as the most doleful indicator of the state of public health in developing countries today and high rates are reported for many parts of Africa (Table 3.1). Indeed, Agarwal et al. (1981: 20) report that 'Fifty five per cent of all deaths in West Africa in 1978 were of children under five.' At intra-national level Thomas (1972; 1976) in a detailed study of regional variations in infant mortality in Tanzania found that although there were marked differences between rural areas most striking overall were the higher rates recorded for the countryside than for the towns.

Malnourishment and the 'diseases of poverty' which affect all age groups are particularly harmful to infants and young children. These include diarrhoeas and malaria both of which are classified as water-related diseases (Bradley 1977b). Sickness and disease reduce the work potential of the present and future economically active population, they affect life expectancy and the fecundity of women. Within the modern politico-economic system the State therefore has an important role to play in improving the conditions which influence environmental health and, by implication, morbidity, mortality and demographic change. Indirect measures include those which raise the incomes of the poorest groups. Discussed here are the direct measures, namely, a commitment to appropriate social planning as part of national development planning. As many studies have shown this must include improving access to such basic needs as clean water supply, better sanitation and preventive medical care (cf. Anker & Knowles 1977; Harrington 1979). Cassen (1978: 339) summarises the priorities as follows: 'The most urgent requirement is for improved health which many countries could achieve fairly quickly through widely diffused health services and better living conditions.' Social priorities of this kind are essentially directed to the poor and in this way move out from the capital city to the countryside and from the urban rich to the urban poor. They are therefore best able to reduce social and spatial disparities in access to services and, in turn, in standards of health.

Social service provision – water supply and sanitation

The public provision of basic social services in African countries has formed part of national planning since before independence. However, as Okediji (1975) reports with respect to Western State Nigeria, resources allocated to public health and medical facilities have tended to be inadequate in relation to the needs of a growing population and small in comparison to other social services like education. Moreover, of the funds allocated to health an emphasis on curative rather than preventive medicine has prevailed and with it a concentration on sophisticated medical technology accessible to the urban educated élite. These emphases correlate with the 'wrong priorities in health' which have been widely reported in the developing countries as a whole (de Kadt 1976).

Appropriate technology in the field of water supply and sanitation together with non-physician centred primary health care are relatively recent priorities in social service provision. They are the outcome of changes in development thinking during the 1970s towards satisfying basic needs and with this a new status attached to the 'human' factor in development planning (Conyers 1982). Above all they stress low cost, socially acceptable solutions to development problems which will meet the needs of the most vulnerable groups. The priority attached to these has been recognised at international level, in the case of primary health care following the International Conference on Primary Health Care held in Alma-Ata in 1978 (Golladay 1980), and in the field of water supply and sanitation through the designation by the United Nations of the period 1981–1990 as the International

Drinking Water Supply and Sanitation Decade. Water is fundamental to human survival and to economic activity in both rural and urban areas. It is needed for drinking and washing, for agriculture and cattle and in a range of industrial processes. It therefore lies at the base of all rural development designed to improve welfare and incomes and is an essential service in towns. A concern with reducing social and spatial inequalities in health must therefore focus on improving access to a better water supply. For this reason water together with improvements in sanitation, from which it should not be separated, are the objects of discussion here.

The World Health Organisation estimates that 80 per cent of all sickness and disease in the world is attributable to inadequate water or sanitation (Agarwal *et al.* 1981) and, as indicated above, water-related diseases are a primary cause of infant mortality. Table 7.1 shows the vast numbers of people in urban and more particularly in rural Africa to be reached with clean water and safer excreta disposal systems by 1990. It is reported that in East Africa women use some 12 per cent of their daily energy in fetching water, a figure which rises to 27 per cent in hilly districts while in some African cities workers may spend as much as 10 per cent of their wages on buying water (Sebina 1980). In seeking to fulfil the aims of the Water Decade country targets have been set (World Water 1978/1979) and government strategies reported in national development plans. For the African region as a whole the objectives include providing 45 per cent of the 1980 urban population with house connections and an additional 35 per cent with public standposts, while rural targets seek to provide accessible and safe water to 35 per cent of the 1980 rural population.

In seeking to achieve these targets many theoretical and practical issues arise. The needs of the African people in relation to water and sanitation can be related to three dimensions of accessibility: physical – improvements in geographical access to reduce the time and effort involved in carrying water and to increase the convenience of latrines; economic – low cost schemes affordable by poor people; cultural – the selection of water and sanitation systems which are compatible with existing beliefs and practices. The importance of these factors is stressed by Bwibo

Table 7.1 Numbers of people in developing countries (in millions) to be reached with clean water and improved sanitation in 1981–90 if the targets of the International Water Decade are to be achieved. (Source: Agarwal *et al.* 1981: 12)

	WATER			SANITATION		
	URBAN	RURAL	TOTAL	URBAN	RURAL	TOTAL
Africa (includes North Africa)	104	310	414	130	342	472
Asia and the Pacific	203	925	1128	355	1136	1491
Latin America (including Caribbean)	108	110	218	212	120	332
West Asia (Arab world excluding Africa)	16	22	38	20	25	45
Europe	14	21	35	30	30	60

(1981) with respect to the utilisation of health services in Kenya. Their achievement, however, depends upon overcoming many constraints. Politics cannot be ignored, notably interest group pressures to influence priorities within and between rural and urban areas. Bureaucratic structures are also important including the difficulties of co-ordinating between the various international, national and local agencies involved in plan formulation and implementation. (These practical and bureaucratic issues are discussed more fully later in relation to family planning programmes.)

Two aspects of culture have become an integral part of development theory and both, in practical terms, influence the success of water and sanitation projects. They also help to explain the cultural gulf which frequently emerges between agency and client when new technology is introduced from outside. The first relates to the traditional beliefs and customs associated with water use and excreta disposal which, if ignored at the design stage of a project, may lead to a lack of use or misuse of the facilities provided. The second is concerned with traditional social organisation at local level which through community participation can play a vital role in the installation and management of new projects which conversely, if by-passed or ignored, may result in only limited commitment to the new services.

The State and the community

Water use habits, excreta disposal systems and attitudes to sickness and health are culture bound as indeed are all patterns of human behaviour and beliefs. White *et al.* (1972) in a pioneering study in East Africa demonstrated the underlying importance of local customs associated with water collection and use among households who must draw their daily supply from outside the home. Traditional methods of water purification based on simple technologies are discussed by Jahn (1981) together with the beliefs surrounding such treatment and the choice of materials and practices used. As regards attitudes to health and environmental conditions these have been studied in Western State Nigeria by Okediji (1975). Through detailed analysis of two Yoruba communities in Ibadan, a low income group in the congested central core of the city and an élite residential area, he found the use of modern health services markedly lower in the former. This he explained not only as a result of a bias in health planning towards the educated élite but also and more particularly because of fundamental differences in knowledge of and attitudes to health problems.

Among the low-income group traditional systems of medicine and care for the sick prevailed which Okediji (1975: 292) emphasised should not be seen as 'a haphazard agglomeration of customs without tangible meaning but as institution-alised patterns of social relationships and cultural patterns of behaviour and thought'. This, he claimed, operated in three ways to help solve and explain ill health. The social structure based on household and kin provided the mutual dependence of individuals in sickness. It also legitimised community respect for

147

traditional healers. Well-tried methods of treatment were invoked while within the Yoruba system of beliefs, sickness and health were explained in terms of natural and supernatural forces rather than poor environmental conditions. It was through this institutionalised system of beliefs and practices that the cultural gulf between low income groups and modern health service personnel could be explained.

In the light of this evidence what approach should the State adopt in seeking to improve environmental health among low income groups in rural and urban areas? Caldwell (1979: 408) among others (Janes 1974) emphasises the vital role of maternal education, not 'as a proxy for general social and economic change but ... as an important force in its own right'. It is the education of the mother, which changes the family reaction to illness, the decisions taken during illness and the child care practices used. But beliefs and practices relating to health and general environmental conditions change only slowly. Besides the physical constraints upon access to education which affect poor people in particular these are compounded in many societies by the social constraints upon female access. Moreover, the status attached to and the resources allocated to preventive medicine and primary health care are as yet inadequate (Akpovi *et al.* 1981; Pisharoti 1975).

In the short term, therefore, equally important is the role of the State in improving the environmental conditions notably water supply and sanitation, which are the source of much infection and high infant mortality. In doing so it is now acknowledged that a strategy is required which above all reflects an awareness of and sensitivity to the cultural context within which low income rural and urban communities operate. The delicate process of technological adaptation of the facilities to achieve a socially acceptable design is needed as is the use of existing cultural institutions at local level in the installation and maintenance of the facilities – the leadership structure, the communications pattern by which decisions are taken, and community actions carried out. It is through these that community support is harnessed, an awareness of the need for change acknowledged and active participation in environmental improvements sustained (White 1981).

Programmes of squatter upgrading illustrate a strong sense of community which frequently exists within apparently disorganised spontaneous settlements. Ross (1973: 171–2), for example, describes Kiboro, the highly successful chairman of a Mathare Valley settlement in Nairobi, a charismatic figure able to galvanise the community into action.

> His abilities as a leader and organiser are extraordinary, and he is responsible for almost all of the important decisions the village committees make. He chairs all meetings whenever he is present, talks more than anyone else, and continually oversees the work of others in the village. Of tremendous importance to his success as leader is the wide range of contacts he has with politicians, administrators and businessmen in Nairobi and Kiambu. When problems arise that he is

148

not able to solve, he knows whom to go to for assistance, and how to approach him. His contacts have been tremendously important in gaining informal promises from the government that the community will not be bulldozed, in getting school fees remitted for many villagers (i.e. residents) and in obtaining government encouragement for many village development projects.

Community action has similarly formed the basis on which Gaborone's spontaneous settlement, Old Naledi, in Botswana has been upgraded involving the provision of improved housing, a standpost water supply and household latrines (Bell 1982). Such activities challenge the basis on which the concept, a 'culture of poverty', has been defined and used (Lloyd 1976; 1979). Equally important is community participation in rural areas. An outstanding example is the remarkable progress made by the Malawi government in providing potable water to some 50 per cent of its rural population by 1980 through the principle of self-help (Glennie 1983). Similar examples can be cited in Kenya (Kabuage 1983) and in Lesotho (Feachem et al. 1978).

Within the modern nation state it is apparent that the demographic behaviour of individuals is slow to change. A complex relationship exists between technology, the bureaucracy and culture in which a sensitivity to local beliefs and social organisation is critical as changes in behaviour which affect morbidity, mortality and life expectancy are initiated from outside. Ironically, it is these cultural practices – treated with contempt by the modernisation school – which have become a central issue in contemporary development theory and which on pragmatic grounds are now respected in development projects. Principles of self help and community participation are old-established in African societies. It is only now that they are being harnessed by the State as part of an acceptable development strategy (Dore & Mars 1981). Popular participation is not only desirable in the design of socially acceptable water supply and sanitation systems and as a means by which to employ local skills, expertise and labour, but it is also necessary if national targets for the International Water Decade are to be approached.

Fertility

From the evidence above it is apparent that changes in mortality are highly complex. They involve the interaction of environmental, biological and socio-economic factors which operate within the context of national political values regarding desirable standards of health and welfare and which are in turn mediated by particular cultural practices in rural and urban areas. The evidence also suggests that a decline in mortality is not solely responsible for Africa's increasing population. An examination of changes in fertility indicates that it too is a highly complex process. The need is therefore underlined for caution in

149

accepting any superficial explanations. As Jones (1981: 88) points out with respect to the demographic transition model, despite the obvious appeal and the apparent simplicity of its core idea, namely, 'that fertility declines appreciably and probably irreversibly as traditional, non-industrial, usually agrarian societies are trans-formed by modernisation or development into bureaucratic urban societies', it is probably the most actively debated topic in demography. The evidence for Africa confirms Coale's (1969: 19) point that the process of fertility decline is 'more complex, subtle and diverse than anticipated'.

The information available on fertility has greatly improved as a consequence of the World Fertility Survey which covers forty-two developing countries of which ten are in sub-Saharan Africa (Lightbourne & Singh 1982). By 1983 initial reports had been published by Benin, Kenya, Lesotho, Nigeria, Senegal and Sudan. Coupled with national survey detailed case study provides an important means by which to identify both the range and complexity of the factors involved. One of the most extensive is the Changing African Family Project begun in 1972 as a micro-level inter-disciplinary study into the causes of family change and the consequences for demographic behaviour, fertility patterns in particular. Analyses were conducted in the following countries: Ghana, Nigeria, Senegal, Burkina Faso in West Africa; Cameroon and Zaire in Central Africa; Kenya, Sudan and Uganda in East Africa. (See, for example, Caldwell *et al.* 1975; Caldwell & Ware 1977.)

Given the importance of detailed case studies, on the basis of these attempts have been made to isolate the dominant influences across the continent. Monsted and Walji (1978: 109), for example, argue that 'regional differences in Africa seem to reflect mainly different biological capacities to reproduce, such as differential morbidity and nutritional status, which have an impact on fecundity'. Many studies confirm this view. Adadevoh (1974), McFalls (1979) and Romaniuk (1968), for example, illustrate how in much of Africa a high proportion of women have had an average of only two children or none at all (Fig. 7.2). Among the reasons cited are chronic undernutrition, deficiency diseases, venereal disease, malaria and gynaecological problems. There are also the side effects of abortion and female circumcision. In spatial terms the evidence suggests that these biological problems tend to be more pronounced in rural than in urban areas owing to inequalities in medical provision. For example, in a study of urban and rural sample areas in Nigeria, Morgan and Ohadike (1975) found that foetal (and also early childhood) mortality was substantially higher in the latter for this reason. Valentine and Revson (1979: 470) summarise as follows the benefits to urban women over their rural counterparts of easier access to medical care.

> Urban women are thus less likely to have stillbirths, miscarriages, and other pregnancy wastages. They probably also lead less strenuous lives, avoiding the long hours in the fields, and the heavy burdens that subsistence farming requires. They are less subject to the ravages of parasitic diseases that go with rural living. By inference, they also have easier access to treatment for venereal diseases which causes considerable infertility throughout the continent.

150

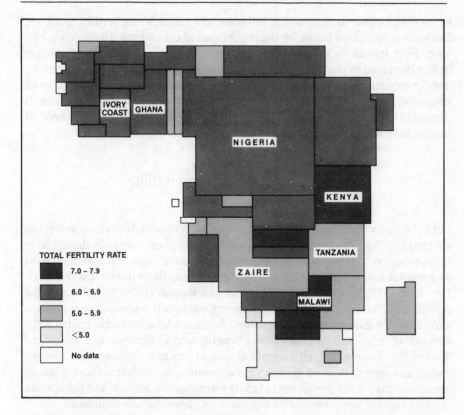

Figure 7.2 Total fertility rates in sub-Saharan Africa. Countries drawn in proportion to the number of births in 1982 (World Bank 1984: 190)

However, given that the most striking differences are between urban and rural areas, even within rural communities disparities arise. Monsted and Walji (1978) suggest that the lower levels of fertility recorded among settled agriculturalists as compared with pastoral people in Africa is accounted for, at least in part, by the easier access of the former to health care facilities.

So, as in the case of mortality, these studies indicate that disease linked to poverty and, with these, spatial inequalities in access to social services, play an important part in explaining fertility differentials. However, this does not tell the whole story as the studies themselves acknowledge. A complex network of biological, socio-economic and institutional factors influence fertility and underlying these is culture. The effects of Africa's political, economic and social transformation on fertility is mediated through fundamental cultural norms and values relating to parenthood, family size and child rearing. It is the way in which these cultural beliefs and practices alter over space and time within the broader

151

politico-economic context which influence the character of fertility patterns. Evidence is presented below for the importance of the cultural dimension in two ways. First, it is shown that total fertility rates in much of sub-Saharan Africa have in fact increased in the recent past, counter to the long-term trend predicted by demographic transition theory.[1] A key factor is the breakdown of traditional social structures and the cultural values which cement them. Second, evidence is presented that family planning programmes which ignore the significance of culture in demographic behaviour achieve only limited success.

Traditional structures and fertility

Let us begin by considering the traditional social system in Africa insofar as it has affected fertility. This system is linked with what has been variously described as the pre-capitalist, non-capitalist, communal or familial mode of production based on rural subsistence and within an environment hostile to human existence (cf. Davidson 1970; Southall 1970). Valentine and Revson (1979: 457) describe the typical social structure as follows: 'The society was tightly organised, communal in nature, with kinship systems in extended families whose members made up the network of relationships that carried benefits and obligations to each other.' Within this loosely defined communal system marked variations in customs, rituals and beliefs evolved between tribal groups. Nevertheless there is broad agreement that 'those pertaining to family formation, childbirth, and the spacing of children have been remarkably similar throughout the sub-continent'.

Many anthropological and sociological studies explore these customs and beliefs in depth through detailed investigation of particular tribal groups (Mitchell 1961; Southall 1961; Molnos 1968; 1972/73). Among hunting and gathering societies particularly valuable demographic information has been collected from members of the Kung Bushmen in the Kalahari Desert of Southern Africa including the cultural practices by which levels of fertility have been maintained (Lee & DeVore 1976; Howell 1979).

The practices which evolved were designed to achieve a comprehensive integrated economic, social and, importantly for the discussion here, demographic system (Meillassoux 1972). As Caldwell (1976a; 1978) emphasises generally and also with illustration from the Yoruba in Nigeria (Caldwell 1976b; 1977) there was a fundamental rationality associated with fertility behaviour. Within the family – the unit of production and reproduction – the inter-generational wealth flow was from children to parents. It was therefore economically rational for fertility to be

---

[1]Short-term rises in the birth rate have been detected in many western countries during different periods and growth cycles (Wrigley & Schofield 1981). Increases in fertility have also been identified in a range of developing countries during the early stages of their transformation (Anker 1978). These have been explained by a rise in life expectancy at birth and a decline in the rates of female participation in the labour force.

high. In making this assessment Caldwell strongly criticises the implications of the demographic transition model that the concept of rationality is a feature only of modern Western society and gives rise to fertility decline. Moreover, he stresses that in traditional African society although high fertility was economically rational the limits were set by non-economic factors. In other words within this familial mode social and cultural practices were critical in defining the demographic regime. Two in particular are discussed here. First, the practice of polygamy which ensured large numbers for the extended family, could therefore reduce the work burden between members and, in the long term, maintained a continuity between generations. The second relates to sexual abstinence during lactation, a custom by which child spacing was effectively controlled. Indeed, Caldwell and Caldwell (1977) report that among the Yoruba in Nigeria it is still not uncommon for post-natal sexual abstinence to extend over a period of three years. (For a detailed analysis of child spacing with case studies from West and Central Africa see Page & Lesthaeghe 1981.)

The impact of an alien mode of production

Given the existence of this apparently stable system what evidence is there of a change in fertility and why? Signs are appearing of declining fertility within selected areas and socio-economic groups. Even in Kenya, with the highest recorded total fertility in Africa, it is apparent that efforts to raise the status of women through improved access to education and employment have influenced attitudes to marriage and the family. Among the small minority who complete secondary and higher education, for example, and who tend to be concentrated in towns, fertility appears to be somewhat lower than among the majority with limited primary schooling or none at all. Total fertility rates are in general lower in the two major metropolitan areas of Nairobi and Mombasa than elsewhere in Kenya (Faruqee 1980; Mott & Mott 1980).

Such trends relating both to specific groups and to broad geographical areas are of course important. However, it cannot automatically be assumed that such trends are common elsewhere or that they will spread to all social groups over time. In rural Kenya, for example, there is little evidence of either economic or emotional nucleation taking place in family structures sufficient to encourage the acceptance of new fertility values or behaviour (Dow & Werner 1983). The urban educated élite maintain a standard of living and opportunity of access to social facilities which are unlikely to be matched by the majority in the foreseeable future. Moreover, even within this élite minority a decline in total fertility is not universal. Findings in Nigeria, for example, contradict those in Kenya. Adegbola et al. (1977) record for metropolitan Lagos as a whole a higher total fertility rate than in the more traditional towns and rural areas. Coupled with this, total fertility appears to increase with a rise in female education. These findings are confirmed for Zaire where Tabutin (1979) reports higher fertility rates among those with greater socio-economic status such as government employees than among those outside the formal sector.

It is apparent that urban growth and access to Western education, both of which are associated with the wage labour mode of production, are not in themselves sufficient to bring about a decline in fertility. Caldwell (1978) indicates that it is the social and cultural processes enshrined in this mode relating to family structure and size which matter. With the adoption of the nuclear family norm typical of industrialised society, so the decision-making unit regarding fertility behaviour becomes synonymous with the co-residential family in contrast to the spatially separate extended family of immediate relatives under the familial mode. The inter-generational wealth flow is directed to children from the parents and with this a positive material advantage to be gained from low rather than high fertility. (For a detailed discussion of wealth flow theory see Caldwell 1982: Ch. 11.)

However, we observe in both rural and urban Africa today several modes of production operating side by side, with members of the same household engaged in more than one system (Ch. 8). Moreover, cultural and social changes rarely coincide with economic change. The evidence above suggests that even among the well-educated in towns, who are perhaps more fully integrated than any others into the capitalist mode, there are many deviations from the 'expected' fertility behaviour. Moreover, for the majority the nuclear family is not the norm: the extended family remains an important unit of distribution. Traditional obligations between family members continue as do certain of the beliefs and customs attached to marriage, fertility and child rearing. From small signs of change in family structure and a decline in fertility rates (as outlined above) it cannot be assumed that the process of change in Africa's socio-economic and demographic structures is either simple and unilinear as implied by the modernisation school or that it will take place according to the consensus model of society with minimal disruption (Peil 1977).

It is widely recognised that the economic system which has evolved in the developing countries is different from Western capitalism and indeed from all other alien modes. It is therefore unlikely that the social system and the accompanying demographic regime will be the same in the foreseeable future if at all. As case studies have shown in Nigeria (Caldwell & Caldwell 1978) and rural Kenya (Dow & Werner 1983) the economic and social advantages of a nuclear family structure are not available to the majority. The values which it enshrines are alien. The basis on which traditional values remain and the strains which are developing within the traditional system are important considerations. Any apparent continuity with the past occurs today under the influence of a different set of forces and within a totally different politico-economic environment. The individual is caught between opposing systems. He/she must of necessity be part of the market economy but is not fully integrated with it. Confrontation with its associated values is indeed producing a unique response. On the one hand certain traditional family loyalties are being conserved though in a different form and for a different purpose than in the past. On the other hand there are signs of a breakdown in many of the cultural values which have maintained social stability and security over time. This has resulted in considerable social disruption. It is this disruption which accounts in part for the increase in fertility observed in much of the continent in the recent past.

Social change and rising fertility

Fertility rates are believed to have been stable in sub-Saharan Africa before 1914, to have risen slightly over the next thirty years and, in many rural and urban areas, to have increased markedly since 1945 (Adegbola 1977; Condé 1973b). Valentine and Revson (1979: 456) describe as follows the context within which change has taken place: 'A forerunner and accompaniment of this increase in fertility rates has been a considerable disorganisation of society.' This 'social disorganisation' is attributed to the penetration of the money economy which began with European contact in the pre-colonial and colonial periods (Ch. 4). Four interlinked characteristics of it are emphasised in particular. First, the physical separation of the household for long periods due to labour migration which has weakened the kinship bond and the control of the extended family over fertility behaviour (Caldwell 1978). Second, the spread of materialist values as reflected in the personal desire for money and possessions and with it a relaxation of the principles of reciprocity and redistribution on which traditional society was based. Third, inequalities in opportunity of access to wage employment and housing in towns and, as a result, the growth of spontaneous settlements, their inhabitants lacking essential basic needs (Sandbrook 1982). Finally, changes in the social role and status of women (Epstein 1975). Each of these processes is central to our understanding of the pressures on African society in general and changes in fertility behaviour in particular. Not least of these are the constraints on women as child bearers and rearers.

Among the social problems which have affected fertility behaviour are marital instability, a rise in divorce rates and prostitution particularly in towns. Marital breakdown has not, however, been the sole outcome of capitalist penetration. In many cases the erosion of the old polygamous union which provided social stability and social security for members of the extended family has been replaced by monogamy. This trend alone is not necessarily harmful. However, in many cases it has been accompanied by a decline in the length of lactation and in post-partum abstinence, the system by which fertility was in the past most effectively controlled. It is the decline in these processes in particular which has been attributed to rising fertility. Many researchers in both rural and urban areas of Africa have identified a close correlation between monogamy, a decline in the length of lactation and postpartum abstinence and increased fertility but, as with marital stability, the breakdown of these customs is particularly significant in the towns (cf. Caldwell & Caldwell [1977] in Nigeria; Pool & Coulibaly [1975] in Ghana; and Romaniuk [1980] in Zaire). A study by Adegbola *et al.* (1977) in metropolitan Lagos found that a reduction in the length of lactation and in postpartum abstinence among women explained at least in part the higher recorded fertility in the city than elsewhere.[2]

This case study is particularly useful in focusing on what is the largest city in Africa and the most cosmopolitan in Nigeria. Table 7.2 summarises the authors' reasons for expecting breast feeding and abstinence to decline with increasing urbanisation and 'Westernisation'. On the basis of these reasons they postulated that variations would be greatest between rural and urban areas and between different education groups within towns. Their results confirmed this hypothesis. However, while traditional fertility control methods were declining among all the education groups sampled and among primary and post-primary educated women in particular, the use of alternative contraceptive techniques was most common among those with at least secondary education. In view of the major thrust of education policy in Nigeria towards compulsory primary education the authors concluded that 'We should not expect education and other modernisation–westernisation related variables to lead to a reduction in fertility rates in the near future' (Adegbola *et al.* 1977: 35).

Within the context of social change the findings imply that while the traditional practices which control fertility and child spacing are weakened in towns, the motivation for a reduction in family size, as reflected at least in the use

Table 7.2 Reasons for a decline in breast feeding and abstinence with increasing urbanisation and westernisation (Source: Adegbola *et al.* 1977: 17–18)

Breast feeding is less attractive because:
  (i)   more job opportunities are available which are incompatible with full breast feeding;
  (ii) baby foods and tinned milk are more widely available and are
        actively marketed (in addition, they become safer to use where
        piped water is also available);
  (iii) public breast feeding is increasingly associated with low social status.

The link between breast feeding and abstinence is weaker because:
  (i)   beliefs linking intercourse (as opposed to pregnancy) with the
        spoiling of the mother's milk weaken as education increases;
  (ii) the availability of contraceptives provides an alternative means
        of postponing the next pregnancy.

Prolonged abstinence is less attractive because:
  (i)   wives may feel more apprehensive of their husbands seeking sexual gratification with
        other women as Western life styles and family nucleation progress;
  (ii) a preference for a family building pattern based on a more rapid succession of births
        followed by a definite stopping after the desired family size is reached, may be seen by
        younger women as more compatible with their employment aspirations.

[2]It should be emphasised that while high urban fertility in many African countries in relation to the figures recorded for rural areas (Condé 1973b) reflects a greater tendency towards monogamy and a reduction in the length of lactation in the former (Harrington 1979), additional social factors come into play in towns. These include a younger age structure due to selective migration and easier access to medical care.

of contraceptives, is confined to a small élite minority. While the employment characteristics of the respondents or their families were not discussed in the Lagos study it can be assumed that a large proportion of the women with limited education had failed to gain access to secure wage jobs. If we accept Caldwell's (1978) view that fertility decline ultimately depends upon the adoption of the small nuclear family which is associated with the wage labour mode of production, then any large-scale decline cannot be anticipated in the foreseeable future.

Social change is one result of the changing politico-economic environment in Africa influenced by external forces. Orthodox theory suggests that modernisation leads to a reduction in fertility and that the focuses of these new social forces are the towns. Environmental, political and economic pressures for change are indeed great in towns. But no simple cultural and demographic transition is taking place manifest in a simple rural–urban duality. For example, in both rural and urban areas differential fertility has been identified among different ethnic groups. Such evidence confirms that there are indeed important alternative ways of dividing African society other than by education, income, class or location (Allen & Williams 1982). Nevertheless, as many studies indicate, access to education for women in particular is among the most important factors influencing attitudes to family formation and child rearing. That progress within the education system orientates a woman to urban wage employment cannot be denied. However such women are a fortunate few. Inequalities in opportunity to progress within the education system and to gain access to secure urban employment act particularly strongly against women. Moreover, the concept of the nuclear family is not within their perception or experience. Indeed, for the majority towns are not centres of freedom and hope. For these women, particularly sigificant of all the trends identified above is the decline in a practice – breast feeding – which is now regarded as vital to the short-term improvement in child health. Under these circumstances the role of the State becomes central in diffusing knowledge of and increasing opportunity of access, both spatial and social, to alternative methods of birth spacing.

Population policy and family planning

All African governments have policies which indirectly affect family size, population structure and growth. Their national development plans include measures to improve the social and economic conditions – education, environmental health, employment – which influence fertility and mortality. Such policies and plans have received considerable impetus since the mid-1970s through their association with the so-called 'basic needs' approach to development which has been strongly advocated by international agencies (Ch. 2).

Among the projects and programmes which arise from this approach reference has already been made to schemes for improved water supply and sanitation. But what of an explicit population policy based on measures to affect population growth rates directly? Since independence the adoption of anti-natalism in Africa through family planning has been a slow process both at government and community levels. Indeed, many states have expressed pro-natalist intentions. The United Nations Economic Commission for Africa (1974) recorded that by the end of 1974 only three countries in the sub-Saharan region – Botswana, Ghana, Kenya – had official policies to reduce population growth. Family planning services are now provided by approximately half the governments for health and human rights reasons but without any explicit demographic purpose (Table 7.3).

Table 7.3 Family planning policy in selected African countries (Source: World Bank 1984: 200)

	SUPPORT FOR DEMOGRAPHIC AND OTHER REASONS	SUPPORT FOR HUMAN RIGHTS REASONS ONLY	NO SUPPORT
Chad			X
Ethiopia		X	
Mali		X	
Zaire		X	
Malawi			X
Burkina Faso (formerly Upper Volta)			X
Uganda	X		
Tanzania		X	
Guinea			X
Niger			X
Madagascar			X
Togo		X	
Ghana	X		
Kenya	X		
Sierra Leone		X	
Mauritania			X
Liberia		X	
Senegal	X		
Zambia		X	
Zimbabwe		X	
Nigeria		X	
Cameroon			X
Ivory Coast			X
Angola			X

Controlling population numbers – established views

State policies which directly affect fertility cannot be discussed without some reference to the theoretical context within which they are formulated, namely, to the debate over the relationship between population and development. (See World Bank 1984). As with all theoretical formulations there are of course opposing views. These are reflected in, for example, the historical analyses of European population by Malthus and Marx (Woods 1982: 36–45). Reference is made to these in particular since despite the spatial and temporal specificity of their works they have proved to be highly influential in shaping contemporary thinking on the developing countries (Bondestam 1980a: 1–38; Monsted & Walji 1978: 24–33). The work of Samir Amin (1972b) on underpopulated Africa reflects the more radical Marxian position. By contrast, Africa's rapid population growth in recent years has given cause for concern among some academics, aid agencies and policy-makers reflecting more closely the Malthusian view (cf. Thomas 1976; Udo 1979a: 138–70).

Lewis (1980: 36), for example, in the Annual Report of the Development Assistance Committee (DAC) of the Organisation for Economic Co-operation and Development (OECD), lists what he regards as seven symptoms of the development problem in low-income Africa of which two are related to population: the first to high fertility, the second to the quality of the human resources. His comments, quoted below, provide a useful summary of this influential view on Africa's development problems. High fertility, he claims,

> is one of the pervasive retardants to low-income Africa's development performance. It causes given amounts of investment to be spread over more people, and thereby, on average, diminishes the per-capita gains in output. In particular, it thins out the per-capita rates of investment being made directly in 'human capital' ... [and slows down] progress toward agricultural self-reliance.

The World Bank (1984: 105) reaffirms this view.

> The evidence ... points overwhelmingly to the conclusion that population growth at the rapid rates common in most of the developing world slows development. At the family level ... high fertility can reduce the amount of time and money devoted to each child's development. It makes it harder to tackle poverty, because poor people tend to have large families, and because they benefit less from government spending on the programmes they use most – health and education, for example – when public services cannot keep pace with population growth. At the societal level ... it weakens macro-economic performance by making it more difficult to finance the investments in education and infrastructure that ensure economic growth.

Interpretations such as these of population and development have formed the basis on which family planning programmes have been formulated. But that reductions in fertility depend upon more than just family planning is also acknowledged. A range of improvements – basic needs – are required in which social policy has a central role to play. Lewis (1980: 36) points to the poverty in

159

which the mass of the African rural people live. 'Their malnutrition, the missing or weak primary health services and protected water supplies, the resulting infant mortality, the massive illiteracy, especially among women: these things are not just intrinsically bad. They impede reductions in fertility, erode productivity and diminish the energy available for self-reliant local development.' Thus population growth is as much a symptom as a cause of Africa's development problems.

A balanced view such as this of the relationship between population and development is strongly advocated by Monsted and Walji (1978: 11). They urge the need for caution in adopting a narrow demographic approach to Africa's development problems – common in macro-economic planning – in view of its neo-Malthusian implications. 'Thus population, which is the *target* of development efforts, may in many cases appear to be the major *constraint* in development, whereas other *structural* phenomena are not given as much explanatory value as they deserve, since they are much more complex and cannot be limited to simplistic quantitative indices or equations, such as the rough population data.' In other words the availability of statistics determines the analysis and the interpretations made.

While this extreme neo-Malthusian view has occasionally been expressed outside the continent (e.g. Pearson *et al.* 1969) hitherto within it pro-natalism has tended to prevail. This is due at least in part to the interplay of population, politics and culture at national and intra-national levels. A dominant factor in the lack of support for a population policy and for family planning in twelve sub-Saharan countries is political adherence to the legacy of colonial culture. 'Most are in Francophone Africa – Chad, Gabon, Guinea, Ivory Coast, Madagascar, Mauritania, Niger and Upper Volta [Burkina Faso] – where anti-contraception laws from the colonial period are still in effect' (World Bank 1984: 163). Indeed, Zaire is one of the few Francophone sub-Saharan countries where official government policy supports family planning for birth spacing although this is not yet reflected in a strong family planning programme (Bertrand *et al.* 1983). Cutting across the boundaries of colonial cultures Udo (1979b: 172–81) discusses the dominance of Nigeria over its neighbours in West Africa arising not only from its great wealth but also from its total population – the largest in Africa. Within individual countries difficulties have been observed where politics are associated with traditional cultural groupings. Power struggles between the major political parties are frequently linked to ethnic rivalries with the result that the pattern of voting on ethnic lines makes population size an emotive political issue. Unsuccessful attempts at census enumeration in Nigeria in 1963, 1973 and again in 1978 illustrate the difficulties involved.

Even in the face of this close association between political power, population numbers and culture it can nevertheless be argued that on two grounds in particular family planning programmes are justified as part of a broad social policy. First, as indicated in the previous section traditional methods of birth spacing are breaking down. Second, a change in family structure towards the nuclear norm, which brings with it a reassessment of the ideal family size, is not within either the perception or the experience of the majority of African people.

Given that one product of these changes is a rise in fertility, for maternal and child health reasons there is a need for policies which permit the introduction of knowledge about and access to modern contraceptive techniques (Valentine & Revson 1979; World Bank 1984: 127–81). The importance of this idea, at least in principle, is now widely accepted within the continent.

The interplay of politics, the bureaucracy and culture

There are many studies which discuss family planning programmes in particular countries. Henin (1979), for example, concentrates on Ghana and Tanzania while Kenya is discussed by Mott and Mott (1980). However, in considering these strategies a framework is needed within which to proceed (Table 7.4). To consider government involvement in changing fertility patterns through family planning raises many of the theoretical and practical issues which were introduced above in connection with programmes for environmental health. It is now appropriate that these issues should be expanded in more detail in view of their importance in geographical study. Both types of programme introduce what is a major theme for the geographer concerned with explaining the processes of demographic change across the continent, namely, the role and function of the State in social service provision as a matter of national and regional policy. In reaffirming that our central concern is with the African people themselves, we must recall that among the many forces which influence standards of health and welfare the political context is vitally important. A central feature of the money economy is that many

Table 7.4 Issues in social service provision (After Warwick 1982: 5–6)

Background:
   What distinctive theories, agencies and events have shaped the values underlying the
   country's population policies?
   (Sources: public documents and other published materials including interviews reported
   with political figures, bureaucrats, agency representatives.)

Policy formulation and presentation:
   What is the process of policy formulation including the key actors involved, the values and
   interests represented, the data base, the degree of attention given to ethnic and religious
   differences and cultural practices?

Policy implementation:
   Have the programmes been introduced as planned? Who have been the key actors in the
   implementation process at national, regional and local levels (senior officials, field workers,
   local social activists)? Who and what have been the leading forces in achieving success or in
   creating obstacles and conflict?

Social response:
   What have been the outcomes for the African people? Who gain access to the facilities? Are
   there social and/or spatial inequalities in opportunity of access? Are the programmes
   socially acceptable? If not, why not?

of the welfare functions formerly performed by the extended family (including birth control and child spacing) gradually break down and that they increasingly become the responsibility of the State. Exploration of state policy and practice is therefore essential.

A striking feature of much development activity is the substantial difference between stated policies on the one hand and the projects and programmes implemented on the other. The former reflect what may be rather lofty intentions by governments, for social and economic development, under the influence of various interest groups. However, only by following these policies through to the implementation stage and by analysing the effects, both social and spatial, can their impact on the welfare of the African people be assessed. For example, while the stated aims behind population policy may be to promote maternal and child health in both rural and urban areas and to encourage freedom of reproductive choice, in practice, for locational (distance from services) and socio-cultural reasons (unfamiliarity with modern medicine), opportunity of access may be limited. In effect both physical and social distance may act as constraints, so much so that the unintended consequences of state policies are to intensify social and spatial inequalities. Identifying the reasons for this gulf between policy and practice must therefore form an essential part of any study. Its importance from a geographical viewpoint is emphasised by Warwick (1982: 7). He points out that it

> forces analysis to move beyond the capital city. Many earlier studies seemed to assume that the most critical actions on the population front took place in the office of the president, the Ministry of Health, or the central headquarters of the Commission on Population. Those offices are indeed important, but as programmes move from concept to operational reality the action shifts to the countryside, for it is there that the majority of the people live.

A central challenge is therefore to investigate the nature of the links between 'concept' and 'operational reality'. In order to do so and bearing in mind Table 7.4, detailed study of decision-making at capital city level is thus required since official attitudes to family planning must be seen within the context of national ideologies (Ch. 6). Equally important is the need to investigate the implementers and their clients with due regard to the local circumstances which influence reactions to decisions made centrally.

In order to illustrate the use of this framework reference is made below to the findings of a study in Kenya carried out during the 1970s as part of a major cross-national project on Cultural Values and Population Policies (Warwick 1982). Mounted by the Hastings Center, New York, with financial support from the United Nations Fund for Population Activities (UNFPA), it is particularly appropriate to the present discussion for two main reasons. First, in following the general framework for study outlined above it reiterates what is a central theme of these chapters, namely, that international pressures are mediated by national goals and development priorities and that these are in turn influenced by the beliefs and behaviour patterns of the African people. Warwick (1982: 189) stresses that 'Most important of all for the implementation of most social service programs are the clients.' Second, in demonstrating the links between population theory, policy and practice the study emphasises the limitations of the assumptions on which much population planning has been based, in particular a failure to recognise the interactions between the political and bureaucratic dimensions and the underlying cultural context.

By way of introduction to the links between population theory, policy and practice Warwick (1982: 31) points out that 'Every social policy rests on some theory of how individuals, societies, governments and organisations operate. A good theory is practical because it points to areas of intervention likely to produce the desired results, correctly indicates how those results can be brought about, and warns of undesired consequences.' He does, however, acknowledge the problems of linking policy and practice. 'Policies built on sound theories may fail because of barriers to implementation, but they stand some chance of success at the beginning'. On the other hand 'there is nothing so impractical as a bad theory'. Regrettably it is this interpretation which he claims is most appropriate to explaining the problems of family planning programmes in the majority of the developing countries.

Kenya's experience

Development in Kenya reflects this view. It is one of the few countries in sub-Saharan Africa with long experience in family planning. Indeed, in 1966 it was the first country in the continent to adopt an official family planning programme as the active ingredient of its population policy. However, in common with many other developing countries, its impact in practice has been limited. Kenya records the highest rate of natural increase (4 per cent) in the world and the highest total fertility rate of eight births per woman (Kenya Central Bureau of Statistics 1979). Two major reasons for the programme's limited success should be noted. It is apparent that the basic concept of population control was out of tune with national values and aspirations at a time when Kenya had so recently gained independence from colonial rule. As regards the design of the programme itself, evidence suggests that at local level it lacked adequate sensitivity to the cultural context of family decisions and, more particularly, to regional variations in cultural traditions.

At national level Warwick (1982) demonstrated that the interaction of history, politics and culture militated against any widespread support for family planning. Initiated by foreign aid donors with the co-operation of expatriate personnel in the Kenyan bureaucracy, notably the Ministry of Economic Planning and Development, it was based on totally unacceptable assumptions regarding the relationship between population growth and economic development. Although these assumptions were initially given tacit political support in the influential

Government Sessional Paper No. 10 (Republic of Kenya 1965: 37) discussed in detail in Chapter 6: 'A high rate of population growth means a large dependent population, reduces the money available for development, lowers the rate of economic growth and makes exceedingly difficult the task of increasing social services.' Nevertheless, it quickly became apparent that such foreign-inspired views were out of tune with the prevailing national feelings (Bondestam 1980b). Depicting population policy as an instrument of control not only raised fears of an external threat – genocide and neo-colonialism – but also renewed internal fears of tribal scheming and with it political power struggles. Moreover, the concept of population control was regarded by many influential leaders as fundamentally alien to established values on fertility. Freedom for the individual and control for the State of population numbers were incompatible. Thus the intermeshing of history, politics and culture at national level rendered inherently controversial the substance of family planning. In doing so it not only raised problems with the formulation and declaration of official government policy (the publicly declared aim of the project was ultimately changed from birth control to the promotion of maternal and child health), but it also weakened the motivation for implementation.

In suggesting that the client is central to the success of family planning Warwick's (1982: 31) view that a bad theory is also impractical – in this case regarding the context and motivation for family formation and fertility change – is particularly apposite. Among the most fundamental mistakes were the assumptions that women of reproductive age were already motivated to practise birth control; that this motivation could be accurately measured through survey techniques (notably the widely used Knowledge–Attitude–Practice survey); that given the means to do so (voluntary family planning services) any social obstacles to adoption would be overcome. These assumptions implied that the delivery of such services was primarily a technical matter and that cultural traditions could be subordinated to an apparently universally applicable programme. The following quotation from the report of the advisory mission to Kenya from the Population Council in New York (1965) illustrates their dismissive attitude towards existing cultural norms (quoted in Warwick 1982: 78).

> Traditional attitudes and values – although likely to change rapidly in the relatively near future – will probably be a hindrance to family planning for some time. Particularly relevant are value systems that assign the subservient status to women, that favour high fertility, that rely on land and family relations for social security, and that are oriented more toward maintaining the past than improving the future ... The extended family system tends to weaken the motivation for family planning by decreasing individual responsibility for children and spreading it over a large number of adults.

The dominant culture was therefore seen as a barrier to implementation. Instead of taking seriously the cultural setting of decisions regarding marriage and reproduction, notably that such decisions are not an individual matter and that

164

they cannot be easily measured or changed, rather traditional authority structures tended to be ignored.

It is reported that by 1978 there were 505 integrated maternal and child health/family planning clinics across the country (Mott & Mott 1980). However, problems of both spatial and social access to these were acute. In Nairobi province, for example, forty-eight clinics each served an estimated target population of 2418 married women aged 15–49 while by contrast in the North-Eastern province four clinics each served more than 10,000 women scattered over an area of some 32,475 square kilometres. Coupled with the distance constraint, failure to adopt the programme to local circumstances was reflected in the client response.

Warwick (1982) points out that in rural areas in particular although clinics would be used for prenatal and postpartum care the family planning sections were often underused. Moral fears and suspicions regarding the basic principle of birth control and the specific techniques used were an understandable response by women with their lack of experience of modern medicine and government services. Thus while the IUD was believed to be applicable to the overwhelming majority of women Bondestam (1980b) reports that although in 1970 it was used by 33 per cent of all acceptors by 1972 this figure had dropped to 11 per cent. Initial doubts on the part of the clients were further compounded in many instances by the attitude of the implementers. The demeanour of officialdom coupled with the imparting of inadequate or inappropriate information to clients unaccustomed to dealing with the bureaucracy produced an unfortunate cultural gulf between agency and client. This further inhibited the implementation process.

Evidence of the overall lack of success of the programme is reflected in the findings of the Kenya Fertility Survey. By 1978 only 5.8 per cent of currently married, non-pregnant and fecund women were using modern contraceptive methods while only 6.3 per cent of women had visited a source of family planning supplies in the preceding twelve months (Mott & Mott 1980). It is apparent that these were primarily better educated women with at least some secondary education employed in non-traditional occupations in the metropolitan centres. The programme did not meet the needs of the poor and those who delivered many children but was rather 'a voluntary choice of the urban middle class' (Bondestam 1980b: 174).

Kenya's experience with family planning is not unusual either in Africa or in the developing countries as a whole. (See, for example, the findings of the Changing African Family Project in Nigeria including Caldwell 1967; 1973; Caldwell & Ware 1977; Ware 1976.) The case study demonstrates how state participation in the process of population change involves the interplay of politics, the bureaucracy and culture. While the stated aims behind family planning must be in sympathy with national political and cultural ideas, successful implementation will depend upon its adaptation to local cultural traditions.

In the case of Kenya despite the acquisition of many of the physical and institutional trappings of the modern nation state, the internal response to the principle of birth control did not conform to the pattern to be 'expected' under these conditions. It offended not only certain national political ideals but also national and local cultural values. In these circumstances both policy formulation and declaration were controversial which added to the difficulties of implementation. Since the late 1970s certain national leaders have become increasingly vocal over the need to curb Kenya's population growth rate and indeed the opening section of the country's national Development Plan for 1979-83 clearly states that 'The higher rate of population growth in turn has magnified the problem of creating income-earning opportunities for the larger numbers seeking work, and postpones the date at which all Kenyans can have primary education, decent housing and adequate medical care. High population growth rates mean lower average levels of living' (Republic of Kenya 1979: 3). Nevertheless, as Mott and Mott (1980: 34) point out, a somewhat ambivalent attitude prevails. No leaders 'have ventured to make explicit statements about the need for substantial numbers of Kenyan couples to reduce their family size significantly below their current desires'. While emphasising this lack of commitment at the highest level they also reaffirm Warwick's findings at local level, namely, family planning is unlikely to be successful within an environment where a 'high value [is] placed on children by Kenya's vast majority of rural households, and especially its women' (Mott & Mott 1980: 7).

Conclusion

The voluntary introduction of family planning programmes in any country implies that certain behaviour is desired by and indeed expected of the national population. This behaviour has become associated with Western values on ideal family size. Thus if we focus on individuals it is clear that providing the service is not enough. It must be accompanied by a latent demand or motivation for family limitation. It may be observed that within the modern nation state in Africa which is alien both in concept and in its physical expression to the traditions of its citizens, the introduction of formal family planning by government is also alien. This fact alone, however, does not render it unacceptable. Increased motivation for family limitation involves a combination of short-term and long-term issues. In the short term, within the existing socio-economic environment, more effective use of family planning services depends both on physical and social access to these services. Assuming that opportunity of physical access is improved, Mott and Mott (1980: 39) point out with respect to Kenya that 'its cultural diversity makes it an almost perfect country for considering a variety of family planning approaches consistent with the varied traditional values of its population'.

In the long term more fundamental economic, social and cultural changes are involved. Evidence in Africa and elsewhere suggests that the opportunity to progress within the education system, particularly for women, together with the spread of urban wage labour employment brings with it the adoption of a nuclear family structure, a change in the value attached to children and with these a greater desire for family limitation. A link is therefore implied between demographic behaviour and the change in life-style occasioned by access to new social and economic opportunities. In spatial terms it suggests that the catalyst can be found in the towns. But this should not be interpreted as a simple or clear-cut economic, social and cultural duality between rural and urban communities. The association between means of earning a living, social organisation and culture is far more complex and has an important influence on the way in which people use and overcome the constraints imposed by space in their efforts to obtain a livelihood. Questions relating to work, employment and incomes are examined in the next chapter.

Further reading

Detailed discussion of demographic processes can be found in Caldwell (1982) and in Woods (1982: Chs 1 & 5 in particular). It also forms the core of the recent World Development Report (World Bank 1984). As regards changes in mortality, the importance of traditional beliefs relating to health and medicine are outlined by Okediji (1975). White (1981) discusses the role of water and sanitation in improving environmental health with particular reference to community participation. The extensive work of Caldwell *et al.* on fertility change in West Africa provides an excellent source of further reading on theory and methodology. In East Africa, case studies are provided by Dow & Werner (1983) and Mott and Mott (1980). Population policy including family planning are presented by Bondestam (1980a; b) and Warwick (1982).

———— Chapter 8 ————

MIGRATION AND RURAL–URBAN INTERACTIONS

Introduction

> The process of urbanisation ... involves the redistribution of popula-
> tion as people move from rural to urban areas ... [It] refers to
> participation in social relations in town and the changes in behavioural
> patterns which such participation involves ... The third aspect of
> urbanisation is a 'feedback' process; it is concerned with the influence
> of town on country and the implications of urban growth for social
> change. (Epstein 1967: 282.)

Although the African continent is the least urbanised, present rates of urban
growth are among the highest in the world (World Bank 1984). This recent urban
development is perhaps the most visible symbol of the processes of political,
economic and social change. But as Epstein (1967) points out urbanisation is
closely related to changes in the countryside. A fundamental question in
development theory concerns the extent and nature of the interactions between
rural and urban areas. Is there a dichotomy between them which reflects two
separate and distinct modes of production? Or, by contrast, is there a continuum
in terms of economic activity and social relations? If so, what is the nature of the
rural–urban relationship – is it, for example, progressive or exploitative? It is the
purpose of this chapter to demonstrate the importance of both structural and
cultural issues in explaining the nature of the interaction process.

Work lies at the base of this discussion. How do men and women earn a
living? What are the economic activities which sustain them? An important
distinction exists between these two questions in relation to African economic and
social life. It is apparent that the politico-economic system introduced from
outside and based on the principle of work–produce–consume, has had a profound
effect on the livelihood of different groups including their access to and use of
scarce resources. Thus the economic activities of individuals and their means of
earning an income cannot be separated from the broader regional, national and
international context within which they take place. The response of individuals to
the opportunities presented and to the constraints imposed involves interaction
with space in a variety of different ways: through the land resources it offers for
food production; through the perceived employment opportunities it provides
elsewhere; through the distance constraint it imposes on satisfying perceived
goals.

However, within the economic and social environment of the nation state the
behaviour 'expected' of individuals is not always evident. It has been shown with

respect to fertility and mortality (Ch. 7) that the underlying influence of cultural values, beliefs and practices is critical. There seems to be a rural–urban dichotomy in life-style, economic activities and social service provision which in combination profoundly affect life expectancy and attitudes to fertility. Does this, however, imply the existence of different systems of production and social relations between the two areas? It is certainly more reasonable to distinguish rural from urban society in the developing countries than in the West. However, such a simple dichotomy implied by proponents of the traditional dual economy model (Lewis 1954; Seidman 1972) is clearly inadequate. The division between the urban privileged and the urban poor is equally striking. Moreover, if we view people as active agents in the processes of change and explore their responses to changing economic opportunities then our concept of social, economic and spatial duality within the African countries must be modified.

Rural–urban migration represents one important demographic response to the new economic and spatial order in Africa. Moreover, it is one symptom of the wider processes by which rural and urban areas interact (O'Connor 1983). In the past, case studies of particular tribal groups have interpreted this interaction as an instrument of social transformation in the countryside (Wilson 1941–42). Others have identified rather a rural–urban continuum in which town–country relations 'are in a state of relatively stable equilibrium' through the network of rural ties which is maintained in towns and which prevents the disintegration of the rural social system (Epstein 1967: 283). In West Africa, for example, a cultural continuity between the old-established towns and cities and the surrounding rural areas has long been acknowledged (Gugler & Flanagan 1978). By contrast some writers have drawn attention to the exploitative role of urban centres in Africa through their association with the expansion of colonial capitalism and the extraction of a rural surplus (Bardinet 1977; Doherty 1977) – an interpretation which has also been challenged (Adepoju 1977).

It is from the perspective of different groups in African society that these issues are discussed here. It is emphasised that migration and the rural–urban social and economic ties with which it is associated cannot be adequately explained either in terms of the economic rationality of the individual decision-maker or merely as the behaviour 'expected' of passive victims manipulated by global forces (Swindell 1979). Rather it is stressed that these processes must also be placed in the socio-cultural context within which individuals live. It is suggested here that in explaining their use of space in response to changes in the politico-economic environment reference should be made to the most basic social and cultural unit to which individuals owe allegiance, the family.

Work, mobility and the family

It is apparent that in their daily lives men and women may be involved in more than one economic activity within or between modes of production within or between rural and urban areas. Moreover, evidence suggests the presence of important gender differences in economic roles. However, in order to make sense of these in terms of the distribution of income and welfare among the African people and so inform our discussion of rural–urban interrelationships, we need to explore how individuals come together within the family unit. Economic activities in African society cannot be separated from the social context within which they take place. The family cuts across class categories. It is the most basic unit within which tensions have developed as a result of external influence. Conflicts of loyalty have arisen between family members and role relationships questioned under the influence of national and international change. It is therefore an important focus which brings together the various forces affecting the behaviour of individuals. In adopting this focus of particular significance is the pattern of continuity and change in the contemporary African family and in its internal social relations. It is the elements of continuity and change in family formation, structure and pattern of loyalties which play an active role in the use made of space by men and women in their economic activities and the social constraints upon them which limit their opportunities for action. It is thus at the level of the family group and below this, the households of which it is made up, that questions relating to who are the disadvantaged and why must be ultimately resolved.

The African family comprises a number of households which represent the everyday units of social viability. While each may have access to very different resources, through the network of ties and obligations between family members they are linked together. New forms of spatial mobility arising from Africa's changing political economy influence directly the demographic composition of the household at any point in time and profoundly affect the social and economic interactions between family members. In terms of development theory, by studying the causes and consequences of migration from the perspective of the family and household the limitations inherent in models based on the concept of a dual economy are clearly displayed (Ch. 2). It is from the household that a range of social networks emanate which influence the ability of individuals to perceive and take advantage of economic opportunities. It is in turn through the household that the benefits derived from the economic activities in which individuals engage are brought together and redistributed. The significance of these household functions to different groups in the organisation and maintenance of their economic activities, both inside and outside the formal sector within and between rural and urban areas, needs to be established. In this way the social and cultural processes which underlie the economic organisation of space are firmly displayed and a more complete explanation of the problems of poverty and inequality within the African countries obtained (Bienefeld & Godfrey 1975).

As important as the theoretical perspective, however, is the need for an awareness of the regional significance of the forces involved. Case study provides an essential means by which to highlight this regional experience. In this chapter the Southern African periphery is selected for detailed study where harsh environmental conditions in combination with a geo-political position adjacent to South Africa renders it a particularly interesting and distinctive region. The

170

traditional system of social and spatial organisation adapted to the vagaries of the environment is outlined followed by a discussion of capitalist penetration and the importance of the cultural context in influencing the response of different groups. Three major themes are considered, each one concerned with different forms of rural–urban interaction: international migration to South Africa and the associated changes in family structure and survival strategies; the problems of women 'left behind' and as migrants; rural investment by an urban élite and its particular impact on a distinctive cultural group, the remote area dwellers. To set this case study in context we explore patterns of economic activity more widely.

Wage employment and the division of labour

For the African people wage employment as a means of earning an income and as a basis on which to engage in certain economic activities is both a symptom and a cause of the politico-economic transformation of Africa. It is the outcome of a change in ownership and control of factors of production which took place with the penetration of capitalism into Africa during the colonial period (Ch. 4). While formal employment continues to absorb only a small minority of the labour force, typically under 20 per cent, the effects of this type and location of economic opportunity on rural communities have been profound. It has led to a change in the division of labour within the family and has altered the basis on which status is ascribed and wealth accumulated. Within traditional communalism in Africa the private accumulation of much capital for investment was generally absent. Land, rights to which were usually acquired through the authority of the chief, and labour power were therefore vital means of production (Mabogunje 1980a). While some specialisation in production for exchange based on barter was not uncommon, most rural households were engaged primarily in production for their own subsistence needs. As a result any division of labour was limited, based chiefly on hereditary position, age and sex (Epstein 1975). In many societies the tradition continues today of men having control over cattle, of wives with responsibility for food farming, while children from five years onwards, as in the past, engage in tasks commensurate with their ability and size. Caldwell (1976b: 228) reports that among the Yoruba 'young children copy the activities of their parents in play and it is hard to distinguish a borderline between such play and subsequent useful work'.

This division of labour was traditionally important to the functioning of the household and family group as production units and was supported by co-operation with, rather than competition between, kin. This element of mutual support is discussed in detail by Watts (1983) in a study of Hausaland in what is now Northern Nigeria. He outlines how the complex socio-economic system which evolved in the pre-colonial era could cope with the harsh ecological conditions. With the household as its base 'peasant reproduction in the face of a hazardous climatic environment was secured through a network of horizontal and vertical relationships and reciprocities' (Watts 1983: 27) embracing the domestic sphere of the family group, and beyond this village community and regional/state levels.

By contrast the penetration of the capitalist mode of production, based on a much higher degree of product specialisation and a more sophisticated division of labour than the African non-capitalist mode, has required wage workers in fixed locations. A change in the scale and nature of population mobility has been one inevitable result (Gould & Prothero 1975). Indeed, it can be argued that among the many external stimuli to social and economic change in African rural communities the selective movement of household members from these communities to centres of cash income has been among the most potent. In analysing its consequences for different groups in African society it is with the relationship between structure and culture that we should be concerned.

Southern Africa

In the Southern African periphery which includes the three former British Protectorates of Botswana (Bechuanaland), Lesotho (Basutoland) and Swaziland, the development of a male dominated migrant labour system must be seen within the context of changes in that region in the politico-economic and social organisation of space. As a region it forms part of what Amin (1972a) refers to as Africa of the 'labour reserves', namely, those parts of southern and East Africa where, during the colonial period, mining and settler agriculture required large supplies of cheap labour. From the end of the nineteenth century the exploitation of the industrial and agricultural resources of the southern African territories by expatriate Europeans extending from Zambia (Northern Rhodesia) to South Africa, led to much male labour movement both within and between territories. Lionel Cliffe (1977: 326) describes the effects of this distinctive form of capitalist penetration as follows:

> The terms on which most of the African people of most of the areas of Southern and Central Africa have been integrated into the capitalist world economy have been through labour migration rather than the direct production of commodities. In all the countries immediately to the north of the Zambezi, as well as the well-known examples to the south, not only have large numbers of African men come as gästarbeiter in mines, farms and industries installed by whites and run as capitalist production units; but the communities from which these migrants come have become geared to the production and reproduction of this special form of exported labour power.

Classic accounts of the rural communities from which labour migrants came together with the circular pattern of movement which evolved and its effects upon the rural economy are provided by Gulliver (1955; 1957; 1971), Richards (1939),

Watson (1958) and Van Velsen (1960). The form of urban settlement to which this labour migration gave rise is analysed for the Zambian Copperbelt in particular by Wilson (1941–42) and Mitchell (1954; 1964). Labour migration in this major region of the continent is therefore old-established and well researched.

The particular significance of the Southern African periphery, notably Botswana and Lesotho, in this labour migration process lies in its environmental conditions and geo-political position adjacent to South Africa. Botswana is semi-arid and dominated by the Kalahari Desert with the result that some 80 per cent of its total population of close to one million live on 20 per cent of the land area – the line of rail from South Africa to Zimbabwe in the east of the country. Periodic droughts have in the recent past brought acute suffering to many rural households. The kingdom of Lesotho is barren and mountainous with some 70 per cent of its 1.25 million population concentrated on the narrow lowland strip (less than 20 per cent of the total land area) lying to the west of the mountain ranges. In this small country pressure on limited land resources is particularly acute with densities ranging from 80 to 219 persons per square kilometre in the lowlands. Harsh environmental conditions coupled with the location of these countries adjacent to, and in the case of Lesotho surrounded by, South Africa have forced them to function as labour reserve economies for their powerful neighbour, a function promoted by official policy in the Republic. Following the passage of an Immigration Act in South Africa in 1913 which prohibited Rand mines from employing labour north of latitude 22 degrees south, Basutoland, Swaziland and the southern half of Bechuanaland became key sources of labour.

It should not be assumed that South Africa has traditionally drawn workers solely from these adjacent territories. Indeed, following the repeal of the Immigration Act in 1936 migrant workers to the South African mines in particular were recruited from as far north as Malawi and Zambia. Despite political and economic pressures within South Africa since the 1970s to 'internalise' mine labour recruitment this pattern of long-distance migration continues albeit much reduced in scale (Taylor 1982). However, it is within the countries of the periphery that economic dependence on South Africa in general and as a labour market for foreign workers in particular is most significant. Colclough (1980) points out that in the late 1970s one-third and one-fifth of the labour force of Lesotho and Botswana respectively were working abroad at any one time, mainly in the Republic. The vulnerability of these countries – and the households of which they are made up – to policy changes within South Africa is now acknowledged both by governments in Southern Africa and international agencies (Böhning & Stahl 1979).

Labour reserve economies

It is against this background of scarce physical resources – notably land and water – and the powerful influence of South Africa that we can begin to explore the elements of continuity and change which characterise the social relations of production among the predominantly Sotho speaking peoples of the periphery (Doke 1967). While recognising that any classification both in space and time is of necessity a gross simplification, Fig. 8.1 summarises the alternate spatial scales at which the forces influencing the household and family group have operated since the pre-colonial period. Two interrelated aspects of Sotho traditional culture found among the Basotho in Lesotho and the Tswana in Botswana are particularly

Figure 8.1 Changing social and spatial relations in Southern Africa

PRE-COLONIAL TRIBAL AUTONOMY (FOR FURTHER DETAILS
SEE FIGURE 8.2)

REGIONAL	TRIBAL STATE	COMMUNITY AND HOUSEHOLD
Trade and warfare	Social hierarchy based on ascribed status	Oscillating migration between village/lands/cattlepost

COLONIAL CAPITALISM

SUPRA-NATIONAL	NATIONAL	COMMUNITY AND HOUSEHOLD
Southern African political economy	Colonial state	Social and spatial differentiation between households in access to income earning opportunities.
Demands for migrant labour	Introduction of: taxation social services commercialisation of livestock	Tswana social hierarchy strengthened while new patterns of social differentiation emerge. International male labour migration from poor households. Changes in the division of labour within the household – conjugal relationship strained (emergence of female-headed households).

POST-COLONIAL CONTINUITY AND CHANGE

SUPRA-NATIONAL	NATIONAL	COMMUNITY AND HOUSEHOLD
Recruitment of male migrant labour continues but under threat.	Independent nation state. Capital investment in livestock supplemented by economic and social investment in towns. Rural–urban migration for men and women.	Differentiation between and within households intensified. Social hierarchy – ascribed status extended through achieved status. Problems for women in education and the labour market. Rural–urban interactions among urban-based élite. Investment in cattle through purchase of land and boreholes – financial ability to withstand drought. Rural–urban interdependence of poor households – natal tie strengthened – vulnerable to drought.

174

relevant to this discussion: a relatively concentrated settlement pattern compatible with the physical environment and Sotho political tradition (Kuper 1975) requiring that household members be geographically split for periods of the year in order to sustain a combined agricultural and pastoral economy; and a form of social organisation operating at interlocking social and spatial scales to provide for the mutual support and economic interdependence of household members.

Tswana social and spatial relations

The Tswana have traditionally had three dwellings, one at the village, one at the lands area and one at the cattlepost. Schapera (1953) indicates how within the eight major Tswana tribes maintenance of authority by the chiefs could be most effectively achieved through a concentrated settlement pattern. Thus the permanent home of Tswana families was located in the tribal capital or an adjacent large compact village. An area around was designated for cultivation and apportioned to each married man by the chief. Beyond the arable zones was pastoral land where people could establish their cattlepost. Schapera (1953: 21) points out that in the early days 'Natural waters and grazing [were] used in common, but any man sinking a well or building a dam [had] exclusive rights over the water it contains.' Thus within the context of communal tenure some priority access to scarce resources was possible.

With the first rains, usually in November, family members would move to their fields for the beginning of the cultivating season returning again in July/August. A sexual division of labour operated so that men would plough the land and broadcast the seed, chiefly sorghum; women and girls would then do the weeding, bird scaring and frequently also the harvesting. Cattle were the preserve of men and boys, and would be herded for much of the year often far from the permanent home. They were, and still are, an important source of wealth and status; they represented the standard medium of exchange and were given as bogadi (bridewealth). A sample survey of six tribal areas in 1943 indicated that although at that time the size of herd varied widely among cattle-owners – chiefs in particular having the largest number – nevertheless only 7.4 per cent of families had no cattle at all (Schapera 1947).

Thus temporary migration was an established feature of the Tswana economy. But the unity of the society was not weakened owing to a system of reciprocity, redistribution and economic interdependence which operated at a series of interlocking scales (Fig. 8.2). Comaroff (1976: 71) points out that it was in the permanent settlement that 'the enduring groupings of Tswana society' were formed and took on 'their politico-administrative and structural identity'. These included the household and the family group at the domestic level. The household continues to be the smallest well-defined social unit, having its own compound or lolwapa. In the past it comprised a man, his wife or wives, their unmarried children and often, in addition, married sons, brothers or daughters with their

175

Figure 8.2 Traditional system of collective security adapted to the environment (adapted from Schapera 1953)

DOMESTIC LEVEL	COMMUNITY LEVEL	TRIBAL STATE
Integrated crop production and pastoralism.	Siting of villages accessible to water.	Payment of tribute to chief (cattle, corn, animal skins, ivory).
Cycle of activity – timing of planting, weeding, harvesting in relation to onset of rains – crop mixtures.	Kin support through gift giving and social exchange (food, agricultural implements).	Serfdom (Basarwa). Reciprocal gift giving to retainers and councillors.
Division of labour.	Work Parties.	State relief – mafisa cattle – corn from Chief's granaries during famine.
Exploitation of local environment (hunting and gathering).	Elite support for poor (eg. loaning of cattle – mafisa).	
Food storage.		
Domestic self help and support.		

respective families (Schapera 1953: 39). The household would produce most of its own food, clothing and domestic utensils. The family group comprised related households living adjacent to each other in the permanent settlement. Schapera (1953: 40) described its functions as follows: 'its members associate together constantly, co-operate in such major tasks as building and thatching huts, clearing new fields, weeding and reaping, and help one another with gifts or loans of food, livestock and other commodities'. It was at this domestic level that the strongest bonds of support were sustained.

Operating at community level were the ward and the kinship system. Several adjacent family groups within a village would form the ward. This represented the basic unit of administration under the leadership and authority of a headman. The Tswana kinship system extended from near relatives living in close proximity (the family group) to distant relatives dispersed throughout the community and tribe. Finally, extending over the entire area of the tribal state, was what may be described as the 'moral economy' (Scott 1976) involving the payment of tribute by tribespeople to the chief and, in turn, some redistribution of wealth by the chief to his subjects. Thus it can be suggested that the unique pattern of settlement characteristic of the Tswana people which involved the temporary migration of individuals kept together by a web of interdependence, was a product of the functional relationship between the Tswana political order centred on the chief and the system of social organisation centred on the household.

It would be incorrect to assume that the Tswana was an egalitarian society. Indeed, Schapera (1953) and, more recently, Parsons (1977) clearly describe its internal class structure based on the Tswana nobility and commoners together with two groups of recently assimilated peoples: aliens or settlers and serfs, of whom the latter were attached to the nobility and included the original inhabitants of the area, namely, the nomadic hunters and gatherers known as the San, the Basarwa or more popularly as the Bushmen (Silberbauer & Kuper 1966).

However, alongside this differentiation the three-tier social organisation of space described above provided an effective form of collective security against the vagaries of the environment. It formed the basis on which social life was organised and economic activities sustained. Moreover, the redistributive mechanisms provided an essential means by which households could compensate for poverty or seasonal under-production. It could be argued that any breakdown in part of this support system might lead to a more general dissolution of the structure as a whole and with it acute suffering for the most vulnerable groups and poverty in the most marginal areas.

Significant changes were indeed to come about with the creation in 1885 of the Bechuanaland Protectorate south of latitude 22 degrees to the Molopo river and of a British colony south of the Molopo to Cape Colony under the name of British Bechuanaland (Fig. 8.3). In economic terms it promoted the capitalist mode of production which upset the social relations on which the Tswana settlement pattern and system of collective security had been based.

The migrant labour system with particular reference to Botswana

Among the most significant of all changes to come about in traditional social and economic life as a result of capitalist penetration are those associated with male labour migration which was initially encouraged by the search for a means of earning money to pay taxes imposed by the protectorate administration. Since the end of the nineteenth century international migration has taken place to the mines, farms and towns of South Africa supplemented since independence in the case of Botswana in particular by internal migration to the country's own rapidly growing towns. The changes wrought by this migrant labour system have been accelerated since the 1930s, and intensified since the 1950s in particular, by the progressive attacks on traditional land tenure and on the village, lands, cattlepost settlement pattern.

Thus two further destinations – both urban rather than rural based – have been added to the traditional migratory behaviour of Tswana household members. It is not only in this pattern of migration but also, and more particularly, in its association with the capitalist mode of production that its significance lies. Migration to mines and towns by individual household members has provided income earning opportunities outside the traditional sector. Rural areas have therefore become an important source of labour. Capital has in turn entered the rural areas through the remittance system and, in the case of Botswana, through the investments made in cattle by urban dwellers. And what of the impact of this interaction between sectors and areas? It has exaggerated social differentiation between households and unequal access to economic opportunities within households – certain groups of women have suffered in particular. The function of the household as a unit of production, reproduction and social welfare has been modified as the economic activities and income earning opportunities of

177

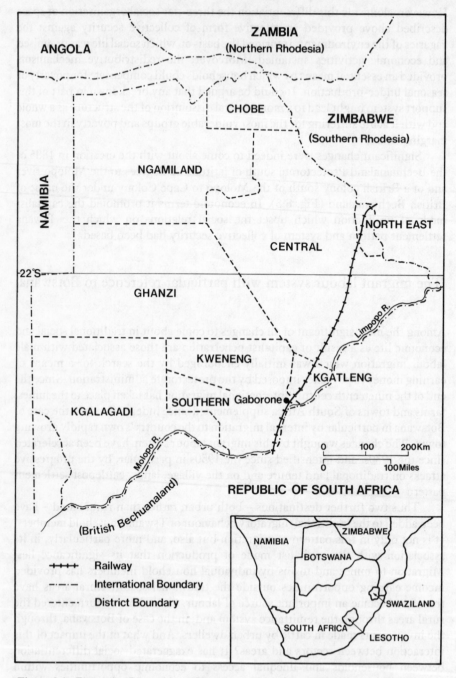

Figure 8.3 Republic of Botswana in Southern Africa (after Colclough and McCarthy 1980)

individual members have changed. These modifications within the household have in turn influenced the economic and spatial strategies adopted by different groups to maintain a living. Finally, coupled with and providing a further stimulus to differentiation within and between households has been the growing problem of environmental degradation.

Interactions between sectors and regions

It is with the process of male migration to the South African mines that rural social change in the periphery began. The history of this migration is well documented (Parsons 1977; Taylor 1982; Wilson 1972). The composition of the migration stream indicates that in the late nineteenth century male members of age regiments were sent to obtain cash for the purchase of firearms to be used for hunting and defence. By the 1930s, when a massive expansion in mine labour recruitment took place from Bechuanaland, Schapera (1947) reports that the young and unschooled males began their adult working lives as mine workers. Moreover, their social background indicates what has become a hallmark of the history of the periphery, namely, the close association between migration and environmental and economic stress. Coming principally from poorer families with few cattle from which to derive an income, mine migrants tapped a critical alternative source of cash and an important buffer against the devastating 1930s drought from which their families with few assets to sink wells or boreholes suffered most severely. In seeking to understand the significance of this labour migration we must study not only the migrants' demographic characteristics but also the social system which migration helped to mould and of which migration formed an essential part – in particular the relationship between the migrant and his/her home community.

Since the colonial period legal constraints on entry to South Africa for the purpose of seeking work have necessitated that international migrants are recruited through a labour contract (of approximately one year's duration) made in their home country to which they must return on its completion, usually to take up a further contract some months later. Thus in the words of Murray (1981: 41) any study of the labour histories of mine migrants reveals 'variations on a single theme: the repetitive movement between a rural home in Lesotho [or Botswana] and an industrial centre in South Africa'. While it is not intended to draw any direct comparisons between the conditions in Lesotho and Botswana (Peters 1983), it is nevertheless apparent that, given the statutory obligation upon miners to return home, mining employment as a major form of wage work in this part of the continent has become one of the essential 'pillars of subsistence' of thousands of Botswana and Basotho domestic economies. The familial relationships necessarily maintained by miners with their home communities have created an integrated system comprising three distinct economic activities – wage labour, subsistence agriculture and small-scale pastoralism – within the same social setting, the context for which Parson (1980) identifies a 'peasantariat' class. Under the influence of these social forces conventional divisions between wage and non-wage, urban and rural have little significance. Any assessment of the impact of this labour migration (both international and, since independence, internal as well) on the distribution of income and welfare requires that in our analysis of the household allowance be made not only for temporary absentees engaged in agriculture at the lands or at the cattlepost but also, and more particularly, for workers employed in the formal sector. Household membership is in a constant state of flux. Thus *de jure* household membership may be taken to include more or less temporary absentees while *de facto* membership refers only to individuals present in the village homestead at any one time and identified, for example, at the time of a survey.

Differentiation between households

On the basis of this operational definition Murray (1981: 51) calculates that during the 1970s almost two-thirds of rural households in Lesotho had at least one absentee wage labourer with a continuing responsibility to contribute towards the maintenance of the household to which he/she belonged. The overwhelming majority were employed in South Africa. Most of the remaining households he regarded as economically disadvantaged in this respect, contending that 'the actual distribution of wage labourers between households is the most important single variable which determines particular households' income and also their capacity to invest in agriculture and other economic activities'. A similar differentiation between households has been identified by Cooper (1981) and Field (1981) in Botswana. On the basis of data from the National Migration Study (Kerven 1982) conducted in that country during 1978-79 Cooper calculated that remittances from mine labour formed one of several sources of income for two-thirds of rural households. At that time it was estimated that some 30 per cent of citizen employment was in South Africa, of which 66 per cent was in the mines (Republic of Botswana 1980). Only a minority - the poorest rural dwellers - were viewed as solely farming units or without assets at all.

On disaggregating the national statistics Cooper (1981) also revealed important regional variations in the character and distribution of 'worker-farmer' households (Fig. 8.3). With the exception of Ngamiland in the remote north-west of the country, in all regions some 70 per cent of permanent rural dwellings - essentially village dwellings - had one or more absent wage earner at the time of the study. However spatial variations occurred in the direction of the migration stream. In the North-Eastern and Central regions, for example, the vast majority of absent wage earners were working in Botswana towns while the Southern region, closest to South Africa's industrial heartland, in addition to supplying internal migrants also provided the main source of labour to the South African mines (Field 1981). Some 56 per cent of all absent miners came from this region which lies within the traditional recruitment zone south of latitude 22 degrees. By contrast migrant wage earners from Ngamiland and Kgalagadi in the west away from the main centres of population tended to be absorbed into Tswana villages.

Within regions, further spatial and related socio-economic variations in the source of wage earners were apparent. In the Centre and the South, the larger villages of the eastern hardveld rather than the more remote western sandveld and non-village areas provided the major source of wage earners chiefly to the Botswana towns. Given that the former areas have traditionally been wealthier than the latter and have also become the focuses of recent rural investment, it is apparent that the development of urban wage employment has tended to reinforce socio-economic and spatial inequalities between households. Only in the case of mine migration, associated chiefly with the Southern region, was the pattern somewhat different. Households in the smallest (and, by implication, the poorest) settlements, together with the poorer households in the large villages were the major sources of mine workers. Thus, in the case of this region of Botswana at least, poor households could benefit from a wage income by taking advantage of the opportunities, albeit tough and unreliable, for employment for the unskilled and poorly educated in South Africa.

Analyses such as these have important theoretical and practical implications. By acknowledging the rural homestead rather than the individual as the key unit of decision-making, distribution and redistribution, the interaction between rural and urban modes of production is clearly displayed. Evidence in support of a strong economic and social link between sectors and regions forged through the medium of the household and familial responsibilities is overwhelming. Large-scale studies undertaken in Botswana during the 1970s including the Rural Income Distribution Study (Central Statistics Office 1976) and the National Migration Study, together with in-depth investigations by individual researchers, have sought to probe these relationships. (See Kerven & Simmons 1981.) The interdependence of rural and urban modes of production has been demonstrated by Kerven with reference to Francistown migrants (1977), by Cooper (1980) in relation to wage earners in Selebi-Phikwe, by Izzard (1982), Bell (1980) and Bryant *et al.* (1978) in Gaborone. On the rural side detailed studies by Field (1980), Gulbrandsen (1980) and Molenaar (1980) among others confirm the importance of urban income to rural households.

Interaction – constructive or destructive?

By analysing the character and location of households with and without migrant wage earners as household members we begin to uncover a picture of the social and cultural basis on which income is generated and redistributed both socially and spatially within countries. But the links between migration and fundamental social and economic processes need to be further explored. The spatial mobility of household members and, in turn, the interaction between sectors and regions, has caused different types of household to emerge and is also an important strategy for these different types of household. Its significance for and impact upon these households does, however, vary. Two questions lie at the root of the following discussion. To what extent are absentee wage earners beneficial/necessary to rural households? Who are the disadvantaged groups and why? In effect we are asking which groups gain and lose from the opportunities for migrant labour movement. Important distinctions need to be made between those households for which a wage income is a complementary source of capital to that accumulated through rural production, notably through cattle ownership; those for which participation in wage labour movement is critical to the maintenance of the household and those most vulnerable households which are unable to participate in the wage economy.

A way forward may be found in returning to the concept of continuity and change in household structure and organisation under the influence of capitalist penetration in which differences between households and also between members within households are identified. Both the household as a unit and the individuals which it comprises have been integrated into and affected by the capitalist mode of production in different ways. Migration and the opportunities for wage employment affect and are affected by the household as a cultural and economic unit. The individual and the household in turn influence and are influenced by the broader issues of access to productive assets in rural areas – notably cattle, land and water. By studying the way in which the migration of individuals relates to changes in the household as a cultural and economic unit and to changes in the broader rural economy a better understanding of the processes underlying patterns of inequality and poverty are revealed. These points will be demonstrated by means of three themes: mine migration and family change; the social and economic constraints on women and female-headed households in particular; and patterns of rural investment among the urban élite.

Mine migration and family change – the case of Lesotho

It is from individual labour histories that we can learn about the career pattern of male migrants including the effects of repetitive movement between home country and South Africa on their own lives and those of their families. For this purpose the excellent studies of Colin Murray in Lesotho provide a valuable source of information. Basotho migrants provide a particularly appropriate focus of study in view of the overwhelming importance of mine labour as a source of wage employment for men. The following statistics illustrate this point.

In 1976 there were only 27,500 Basotho employed inside the country ... Perhaps 200,000 migrants from Lesotho are regularly employed in South Africa, out of the country's total (1976) population of 1,217,000. In 1977 nearly 130,000 men were employed in South African mines alone, supplying more than a quarter of the industry's complement of black labour ... About 70 per cent of mean rural household incomes is derived from migrant earnings. (Murray 1981: 19)

182

The majority of miners recruited in the past have been young – in the age range of 20–39 years – with little or no formal education. But with a growing trend towards the 'internalisation' and 'stabilisation' of the workforce within South Africa the insecurity of their future careers as mine workers is becoming increasingly apparent (Lipton 1980). This vulnerability may indeed be extended to their position as employees in the formal sector in general given the limited and highly competitive nature of the alternatives both in their home country and elsewhere.

It is against this uncertain background that we can consider the experience of mining employment. The model of a successful career to which migrants aspire is described by one wife and reported by Murray (1981: 60) as follows: 'On your first trip to the place of the whites you support those who brought you up. On your second trip, you take out money that counts as cattle for marrying a wife. On your third trip, you look after everything in your own homestead.' The events behind the formation and search for domestic autonomy of this homestead, including the important cultural dimension underlying the need to migrate, are thus:

> Malefetsane was born in 1914. Coming from a poor family which had lost all its livestock he took his first mine contract in 1934 and retired from an active migrant career in 1963. He had accumulated a number of animals and his eldest son (D) had just embarked on his migrant career. By the early 1970s, however, bridewealth payments on behalf of his two sons had deprived the household of all its livestock, and Malefetsane took up a further gold-mine contract in January 1973, from which he returned home in August 1974. His wife is permanently resident in the household. She received irregular remittances from Malefetsane during 1973–74 and also occasional help from her two sons, both married migrants. The eldest (D), employed in a Natal coal mine, had not yet built his own homestead. D's wife (E) was resident in the household in May 1973 together with her three children, of whom the two eldest were D's but the third, as her mother-in-law put it, 'she had simply made in the veld' during his absence. She disappeared with all three children in June 1973, after eight years of marriage. However, more than sufficient bridewealth transfers had taken place to secure D's paternity of all her children, and in 1974, following negotiations with E's parents, the two eldest boys were returned to their paternal grandparents.
>
> Not long after, between mine contracts, D found himself another young wife, who bore him a daughter in 1976. He finished building his own homestead next to his parents' yard, and installed his new wife there, so that by 1978 there were two separate households. His young wife told me in September 1978 that he had already transferred nine head of bridewealth 'cattle' in cash to her parents. (Murray 1981: 59–60).

This example serves to illustrate two points: the economic dependence of particular households on the income derived from mine migration, and the variability in the composition of particular households over time under the influence of labour migration. Such evidence emphasises the importance of exploring the impact of labour loss in greater depth. In particular we need to distinguish between the economic and social processes with which it is associated and the interrelations between the two.

Migration studies offer alternative perspectives on this issue (Swindell 1979, van Binsbergen & Meilink 1978). The utility maximisation approach assumes that the potential migrant and/or the family unit are in a position to allocate labour resources in such a way that the returns to labour will be maximised (Harris & Todaro 1970; Harris 1981). On this basis, therefore, the decision to participate in mine work reflects the outcome of a range of perceived choices. Alternative more radical explanations of labour migration place greater emphasis on the economic necessity for movement from the household and on the surpluses which accrue to the employer and receiving political economy rather than to the sending community (Amin 1974b; Massey 1980). Critical to the validity of both approaches are the effects of labour migration on the family unit. To assess the significance of these alternatives, detailed study is required for different types of household. This should include not only the economic effects in terms of the monetary benefit received as compared to the loss of labour but also the social processes associated with migrant labour movement and the influence of these processes on the economic returns.

Social organisation and agriculture

In so far as productive activities on the land no longer provide an adequate livelihood for the majority of Basotho and Botswana families, the search for alternative sources of income through, in many cases, the physical separation of family members may be regarded as an economic necessity. However, in determining the impact of labour loss through migration upon the rural household, fundamental issues of social organisation are involved. The significance of these issues can be illustrated by reference to agriculture.

There is only a minority of Basotho and Botswana households who are not still engaged in arable and/or livestock activities, however small in scale. Despite increasing land shortages, climatic uncertainties and declining agricultural productivity a continuing adherence to the apparent stability of the rural social system in the face of the insecurity of urban life remains strong. In view of this one way in which to measure the economic impact of labour loss is through its effects upon household strategies of participation in domestic production. It has become a much researched and debated topic in the developing countries as a whole (Boserup 1970; Findley 1977; Lipton 1980b) and in Southern Africa in particular (cf. Kerven 1979a; 1980; Lucas 1983; Schapera 1940; 1947).

Among the most important inputs to subsistence agriculture are draught power, labour and cash. Migrant labour may play a dual role in securing these

184

inputs. It may be both beneficial and detrimental. In determining this the social context is vital and decisive. For example, an absolute scarcity of any one resource, particularly during the ploughing season, may be compensated for by co-operation and pooling of resources between households. The following strategy adopted by a Lesotho family, to which reference has already been made earlier in this chapter, illustrates that as in the past effective crop production depends upon efficient social organisation and mutual support at community level. It also emphasises, however, the complexity and fragility of this organisation and with it the vulnerability of households in terms of the contributions they are able to make under the influence of the cash economy and the migrant labour system.

Three neighbouring households pooled their resources in the seasons 1972–73 and 1973–74. T (household 1) and Malefetsane (household 2) each held two fields; and Malefetsane's elder brother's widow F (household 3) held three. In October 1972 T possessed three beasts fit for yoking to F's plough. Together with three beasts belonging to Malefetsane these made up a full ploughing team of six animals. With this team, and the labour of Malefetsane and of his elder son D, they cultivated one of T's fields, both of Malefetsane's and two of F's. They also used the team to plough for Malefetsane's younger son, an absent migrant, who had his own household elsewhere; and for a distant kinsman of T with whom T had made a share-cropping contract.

In October 1973 Malefetsane no longer owned any cattle, having transferred his three animals in an instalment of bridewealth for his son D's marriage; and both he and his son were absent migrants during the ploughing season. However, T's sister's son (R), was home from a mine contract and the labour for ploughing was provided by R and by T's adolescent son. The widow (F) had two beasts which the previous year had been herded out elsewhere but which she brought back in 1973. T was able to borrow a beast from someone else 'through friendship' and once again they were able to make up a ploughing team.

In October 1974 it became apparent that the network was going to break down. F no longer kept her animals in the village because her younger sister's son who had been herding them had returned to his own home. In November 1974, at the end of the ploughing season, T had slaughtered an ox to make a marriage feast for his daughter's husband's people, and the households were thus quite unable to constitute a ploughing team. R was absent on another mine contract, Malefetsane and his son were both absent, and T himself was in no physical condition for holding the plough. It seemed likely that they would have to abandon the co-operative effort and each household would have to make its own contractual arrangements for 1974–75. (Murray 1981: 81–82)

The dual elements of continuity and change in traditional social relations in the modern world – in this case at community level – are clearly displayed. The economic necessity of maintaining such relationships is counterbalanced by the threat to these relationships arising from a social system which must contend with two modes of production.

One way in which this vulnerability may be reduced and with it a measure of security and economic independence for rural households is through access to cash for the purchase or hire of essential inputs like draught power and labour to compensate for any losses through migration. Exchanges based on kin may be replaced therefore by monetary exchange. This cash may in turn be derived from the migrant's earnings. However, the realisation of monetary rewards by rural households is conditioned once again by the social dimension. It depends upon the interactions maintained by spatially divided families and through these the remittances of which they form an essential part together with the uses to which these remittances are put. Evidence suggests that returning migrants together with their remittances can encourage the adoption and assist in the purchase of new agricultural technology (Low 1981) and in turn improve agricultural productivity. However, this tends to occur only after basic subsistence needs of the receiving household have been met and indeed circumstantial evidence points also to the irregular and unpredictable way in which remittances are received (Cooper 1979; Gay 1980a; Van der Wiel 1977). Once again the theme of continuity and change is relevant here – in this case at the domestic level. While it is essential for the migrant but more particularly for his family that these financial obligations are maintained, the element of economic independence secured by the migrant while he is fit to work and has employment – in contrast to the economic interdependence maintained by temporary migrants under the traditional system – places a strain on the fulfilment of these obligations.

Household structures

Accepting that the reliability of remittances from miners varies, as indeed does the earning capacity with the type of mine work in which they are engaged, it can be suggested that the ultimate significance of any remittance received by rural households depends also on two basic household characteristics: what Murray (1981) refers to as the demography of household composition and the nature of residential associations over time. The first he defines as the ratio of *de facto* household members (rural consumers) to paid employees who are *de jure* household members. The second refers to the domestic cycle – namely, the fluidity of residential associations during the lifetime of households from their creation to ultimate dissolution. Both features arise from the particular characteristics of oscillating migration in the labour reserves of Southern Africa. Exploring their causes and consequences throws further light on the impact of migration on the participants and their families and with it the relationship between migration and changing social relations. In particular it is by reference to these features that we are able to identify the disadvantaged groups and to explain why they are so.

Differences in income and wealth between households as reflected in inequalities in the distribution of productive assets must take into account variations in the internal structure of households, notably size and composition at any one time, and also changes in these characteristics over time with the developmental cycle of the household. A wide range of household types are characteristic of the labour reserves of Southern Africa. It is a region where

> thousands of husbands and wives are forced to live apart; where frequency distributions of household sizes commonly exhibit several distinct modes; where the boundaries of the *de jure* household coincide with those of the nuclear family in only a small minority of households ... ; where a significant number of women bear children but remain unmarried; where many households are headed by widows; and where many children are reared by grandparents in multi-generation households because their parents are absent migrants. (Murray 1981: 102)

Evidence of this kind calls into question yet again the simplistic notion that the transition from subsistence to capitalist mode of production is accompanied by the movement from extended to nuclear family norm (Ch. 7). It is also from within this diversity of household types, and by reference to the phase reached in the development cycle of particular households within each type, that we can identify the most vulnerable groups.

In a survey by Van der Wiel (1977) of 1286 households in Lesotho in the mid-1970s he confirmed that migrant earning capacity was critical to household income and that this was in turn dependent on the age and sex composition of household members, in particular the association of an able-bodied male with the household. Multi-generation households of 'widows living with little children, thereby lacking a potential wage earner' he regarded as most vulnerable (Van der Wiel 1977: 88). Similar findings were obtained by Murray (1981) on the basis of field evidence in 1978. He identified a continuum of relative advantage-disadvantage with small female-headed households the most disadvantaged in this respect (Table 8.1). Their income from crops and livestock was also lower than

Table 8.1 Household structures derived from field study in Lesotho (Source: Murray 1981: 56

DE JURE HOUSEHOLD SIZE	DEPENDENCY RATIO* SEX OF HEAD		
	MALE	FEMALE	ALL
Small (1 to 4)	3.18	6.33	4.29
Large (>4)	4.79	5.40	4.98
All households	4.39	5.67	4.80

*De facto *household members*
paid employees

that of other groups. Comprising perhaps one quarter of all households in Lesotho, Murray emphasised the importance of these household types as a legitimate focus for programmes designed to relieve absolute poverty.

Women in social change

Findings such as these require that we explore the position of women in Southern Africa's migrant labour system. In so doing the focus of study shifts from comparison between households to individuals within the household, in particular to differences in the economic and social roles of men and women.

Over the last decade the analysis of gender roles and, with it, women studies have become much discussed topics in geographical enquiry forming part of the wider feminist movement (IBG 1984). Anthropologists and sociologists have for long been engaged in such studies overseas. (See, for example, Goddard 1973; Hill 1972; Little 1973.) However, a recent flourishing of interest by a wide range of social scientists, including geographers, in the developing countries and Africa in particular, reflects a concern with the changing roles and status of women within the broad context of politico-economic transformation (Schuster 1982). Research and published work adopt both a liberal and more radical perspective. (See, for example, Cutrufelli 1983; *IDS Bulletin* [Brighton] 1981 vol. 12, no. 3; 1984 vol 15, no. 1; *Review of African Political Economy* 1984 nos. 27 & 28.)

In Southern Africa this interest in and concern over the problems and position of women is well represented in recent literature. (See, for example, Gay 1980b; Izzard 1982; 1985; *Journal of Southern African Studies* 1983 vol. 10, no. 1; Kerven 1984.) It is now widely acknowledged that studies of the migrant labour system have paid undue attention to the men who oscillate between urban and rural areas. The following statistics illustrate the demographic, social and economic importance of women in sustaining male migration and as active participants in the migration process. Botswana's National Development Plan for 1979–85 (Republic of Botswana 1980: 9) records that in all age groups over fifteen years there are more women than men in both the *de jure* and *de facto* population. Women 'left behind' in rural areas comprise the majority of the rural population. Izzard (1982) reports that in 1979 the male to female sex ratio in the rural areas for the *de facto* population was 82. In consequence, women play a crucial role in agriculture 'being responsible for a large part of arable operations' and in addition are at the head of some '30 per cent of all rural households' (Republic of Botswana 1980: 165). Furthermore, and perhaps most often forgotten, women are themselves active participants in the migration process frequently seeking a cash income on their own account. The Lesotho 1976 national population census recorded that 9.4 per cent of the population in wage employment in South Africa were women. We should add to this figure those who also migrate both internally and internationally in search of employment and/or to stay with relatives. As a

188

major demographic group both participating in and with a key role to play in sustaining the labour force women are worthy of study. Our particular interest in them here is in their position as the head of a household and the tendency for this role to be associated with economic disadvantage. In proceeding, it should be stressed that it is not the fact of their being headed by women which makes these households disadvantaged, rather it is the structural and cultural circumstances surrounding their formation and governing their survival. This is the context within which the impact of male migration on women and the contemporary significance of female migration needs to be considered.

In traditional society spatial mobility was desirable and necessary for most women during their lifetime. It was through marriage, and associated with it their adoption of the multiple roles of wife, mother and food producer, that women gained status and acquired access to the means of production (Schapera 1940; 1943). Thus at the most simple level migration from the natal to the marital home would take place coupled with short-term movement to the lands area during the active agricultural seasons. Their pattern of mobility has become more complex, however, with the penetration of the capitalist mode of production. A change in the sexual division of labour within the household and in the status of marriage have altered the significance of the roles which women traditionally perform, notably as wives and mothers, and have introduced the additional role of income earner. Under these circumstances mobility for many women has become more diverse involving movement both within and between rural and urban areas related to the search for income earning opportunities, and the maintenance of links with and possibly a return to the natal home. It will be demonstrated below that the politico-economic circumstances of the Southern African periphery mediated by prevailing cultural values and practices lie at the base of the contemporary problems faced by many women as a disadvantaged group and, in turn, the migration strategies which they adopt.

Emergence of female-headed households

The model of a successful male migrant's career has already been described earlier in this chapter. While related here to mine workers it could be applied equally well to the vast majority of male migrants who seek a money income. Fulfilling this ideal career pattern depends among other things on maintaining two types of link with the home community; an association with kin through which access to land is secured, and a conjugal link. It is this latter association which the migrant labour system has rendered most unstable. The dual role of migration as economically advantageous but destructive in its impact on certain social ties is once again confirmed. It is within this context of conjugal instability that the most critical problems faced by women lie since it is they who are most vulnerable to the effects of changes in the ratio of consumers to wage workers within the household.

Among the major outcomes of male labour migration in this part of the

189

continent has been a change in family structures, notably the emergence of the female-headed household, accompanied by a change in the social and economic roles of women. With reference to what is now Botswana, Izzard (1981) points out that male labour migration led initially to wives 'acting' as household heads (on a so-called *de facto* basis), a practice which was essentially alien to Tswana custom. The prolonged separation of spouses, however, had yet more significant long-term social consequences. It was observed some forty years ago that while rural areas traded labour for cash the exchange was frequently unequal as remittances became irregular, wives were often abandoned and the distributional role of the household came under threat (Wilson 1941–42; Schapera 1947). The significance of a woman's role as mother – as reproducer of the labour force – increased and was accompanied by, among other things, a rise in the incidence of illegitimacy as the importance of the role of wife declined (Comaroff & Roberts 1977). It is these circumstances which have contributed to a restructuring of the household as a social and economic unit and, in sharp contrast to the past, to the emergence of women as household heads in their own right (*de jure*).

Women may form their own household or become the head of an existing household either in their own right or in the absence of the real head (husband, father, son, brother) at varying points in their lives and for many different reasons. The diversity of household types to which this social and temporal process gives rise has been the subject of much discussion (Kerven 1979b; Izzard 1982). Various classifications have been drawn up based on, for example, marital status of the female head and household composition. Applying this second criterion to data from the Botswana National Migration Study, Izzard (1981) drew up a typology of female-headed households distinguished by whether adult males were associated with the dwelling unit and if so whether they were present or absent (Table 8.2). In

Table 8.2 Household types by composition and sex of head (Izzard 1981: 37)

	(%)
Female-headed household without adult males (FH–NM)	8
Female-headed household with adult males (FH–M)	18
De facto female-headed household (DFFH)	10
Male-headed household (MH)	64

stressing that any classification is necessarily a simplification of reality, Izzard also emphasised the need to interpret these 'types' within the context of the development cycle of the household. Given that the majority of women heading households without adult males (FH–NM) had never married, Izzard (1981: 42–43) discussed a hypothetical case as follows:

It is clear that not all single women will remain so, since some will, at a later stage in their lives, become married and assume the role of wife. At a later stage she may be left as a de facto household-head whilst her husband migrates in search of employment. Subsequently the husband may die, and the woman assumes permanent headship. Her sons may initially remain as members of the household, and she therefore could be described as an FH–M. In later years these sons may leave and the, by then, elderly woman will be the head of a household lacking adult males (FH–NM).

Bearing these features in mind, in determining the extent to which households within each 'type' were economically disadvantaged it was apparent that the categories had to be further refined. Geographical location of households needed to be considered, notably whether they were in rural or urban areas (Table 8.3). The broad framework of opportunities available to and the constraints upon women in these settings is very different. Within this framework it was also apparent that the internal demographic characteristics of households were important. Reference is made below to two features: the association of an adult male with the dwelling unit and the stage in the life cycle of the household. It is these features which influence the nature of the resources by which households can be sustained and, by implication, their income and welfare.

Table 8.3 Location of different household types (Izzard 1981: 45)

HOUSEHOLD TYPE	RURAL		URBAN	
	ROW %	COLUMN %	ROW %	COLUMN %
FH–NM	66	6	34	17
FH–M	88	19	12	14
DFFH	94	11	6	4
MH	84	64	16	65
Total	84	100	16	100

The rural environment – women 'left behind'

In rural and urban areas economic conditions mediated by cultural practices influence the opportunities available to women and the roles which they perform. Both areas play a dual role in providing positive benefits and also limitations. For most Botswana and Basotho women and men the countryside is still perceived to offer the social and economic security necessary for the rearing of the next generation and for old age. As wives, women have responsibility for managing the rural household in the absence of their husbands. In the domestic sphere they reproduce and socialise the future labour force. In agriculture they make many key decisions (Bond 1974). But it is also in rural areas, under the influence of

191

capitalism, that cultural attitudes towards the rights and status of women and the sexual division of labour have adapted only slowly to the absence of males (Cliffe 1977). Within the context of the migrant labour system two social constraints on women render them particularly vulnerable. First, the persistence of traditional attitudes towards control over resources within the household. Second, the penetration of capitalist values regarding unpaid work.

As regards the rights and status of women, under customary law rural wives had limited control over the resources – land, cattle, cash – needed to run the household effectively in the absence of the husband in whom authority was vested. In the case of unmarried women, customarily they were not eligible to hold land in their own right (Schapera 1943) and although in Botswana they can now legally apply to the Land Boards the practice does not seem to be common. Turning to the social and economic roles of women, a combination of cultural and physical problems arise in coping with traditionally specialist male tasks (associated with, for example, livestock and ploughing), in the prolonged absence of men. Furthermore, in view of the low status attached to work which cannot easily be assigned a monetary value – often described as women's work – improvements in technology which might compensate for the loss of male labour frequently receive low priority by governments (Carr 1982; Lipton 1980b). In cases where technological improvements have been encouraged, women farmers are not surprisingly often reluctant and/or unable to adopt innovations requiring a level of training and skill to which they have not received access (Boserup 1970; Kerven 1977). Nevertheless, representing as they do the majority of the rural population, they are frequently required to participate in self-help rural development projects and as such constitute a vital labour force (Carr 1982). Under these circumstances the workload of women has greatly increased and in the absence of regular remittances the presence of or access to an adult male is critical to household welfare. This is particularly the case for older women who constitute a significant proportion of the rural population. Indeed, as a result of the out-migration of young adults Izzard (1982) reports that in rural Botswana in 1979 almost two-thirds of the population were in the age groups below fifteen or above fifty-four years.

With data from the Botswana National Migration Study, Kerven (1981) emphasised the importance of adult males to rural households. She demonstrated that female-headed households with no males present were less likely to plough their own lands. 'No one here to help' or 'couldn't afford labour' were more important reasons given than the environmental constraint of 'lack of rain'. These households were also less likely to own cattle which continue to occupy the male sphere. Most disadvantaged of all in these respects was the group of female heads with no adult males associated with the household, either present or absent (FH–NM). In rural areas these comprised, in the main, the elderly and the very young. Thus, as Kerven (1981: 6) points out, it is clear that 'The beneficial or detrimental effects of migration upon agriculture are mediated by a range of natural, social and economic variables, and are not uniformly distributed amongst all farming families.' In a country like Botswana where much of the land is agriculturally marginal 'climatic factors are a *necessary but not a sufficient condition* for the success of arable production' (Kerven 1981: 39). Other inputs, notably access to labour, are critical. It is female-headed households without access to these additional inputs or to wage labour remittances which are most vulnerable to the constraints of the physical environment and least able to cope with the uncertainties they cause.

The urban setting – women migrants

Rural–urban migration, and with it the very different social and economic environment of the towns, presents possibilities, therefore, for many kinds of women at different stages in their life cycle. In Gay's (1980a: 22) study of Lesotho women migrants to South Africa she found that while a small number went with their husbands, the majority were women on their own: young girls 'seeking experiences and earning opportunities which they could not find in Lesotho'; older widows 'who went to seek work only after their husbands had died, leaving them with children but with inadequate assets in Lesotho to manage without a cash income'; and women whose marital relations had been unstable and for whom 'employment in the Republic offered both an alternative to the frustrations of rural life and the means to support their children and make a fresh start in a new community'. Thus urban migration, in these illustrations at international level, was important in providing an alternative to the social constraints and economic insecurity of rural life. Access to male labour within the household was not vital to their economic well-being. In these circumstances, returning to the Botswana National Migration study, female-headed households without adult males (FH-NM), who comprised almost 50 per cent of all urban female-headed households (Table 8.3) and who tended to be in the age range 15–34 years, were not at this stage in their lives, in contrast to their older rural counterparts, unduly disadvantaged.

But towns, like the countryside, perform a dual function. They provide opportunities and also present many problems. Women in towns are faced with a highly unstable and competitive labour market. The unequal opportunities to progress within the education system associated with established values regarding the role of women (Kann 1981) ensure that much female labour commands a low wage and that only a limited range of formal sector job opportunities tend to be available. In Botswana the National Migration Study found that female participation in the formal sector was considerably lower than that of males and confined largely to domestic service and clerical work (Bell 1981b). In these circumstances, as Bienefeld (1981) has pointed out more generally, the informal sector plays a vital role in the welfare of independent women with little education. Data from the National Migration Study confirmed this point. Informal activities were the preserve of women, notably the making and selling of food (chiefly beer), clothing and the sale of firewood (Bell 1981b).

But maintaining economic security in towns also depends upon cultural practices. Although urban women are released from many of the social obligations associated with rural life their economic well-being depends upon fundamental social and cultural ties. The following quotation from Gay (1980a: 23) indicates why. She reports with reference to Basotho women in South Africa that lacking the opportunity for skilled employment or further education

> it was almost exclusively in their domestic roles that black women could obtain employment. However the domestic lives of these women were split. Cleaning, washing, child-minding and cooking could be sold on the legitimate labour market in the service of white family life. Brewing, sewing, sex and hospitality could provide supplementary income in the 'informal sector' serving the needs of black workers separated from their own families. But the care of their children had to be delegated to others if they were to earn the money to support them.

Two points arise from this description. First, the need for many urban women to engage in more than one economic activity in order to make a living. This may, as the quotation suggests, involve interacting between the formal and informal sectors in town. It may also involve retaining some participation in agriculture which depends, significantly, on continued social contact with and support from rural kin (Cooper 1979; Izzard 1985; Kerven 1977; 1979b). Second, for many urban women the primacy of their economic role necessitates that the role of mother is postponed. Evidence suggests that on these social grounds also, retaining rural links is critical. Results from the Botswana National Migration Study and related in-depth studies indicate a high degree of absenteeism among children from urban female-headed households (Izzard 1982). Continued childbearing for urban women depends upon maintaining a rural base for the rearing and education of their children.

For the purposes of this discussion it is the cultural form of this rural link which is particularly significant. While traditional social relations in the form of conjugal and affinal ties have been weakened by labour migration, it is apparent that links with natal kin have been strengthened. It is the mothers of female migrants (or a close natal kinswoman) to whom responsibility for raising their children is given. Moreover, this reliance on natal kin is not confined to urban women. The relationship between generations of women who are spatially divided and the cycle of mutual dependence on which it is based, are illustrated as follows: 'Many migrant women spend all their earnings to support and educate their children and return to care for their daughter's children so that the daughter in turn may seek wage employment' (Gay 1980a: 26). For many older rural-based female-headed households without adult males (FH–NM), those identified by the Botswana National Migration Study as lacking essential agricultural resources (referred to on page 192), it is their younger female counterparts, those who are also their natal kin, on whom they depend.

This pattern of return/retirement migration by urban women to the countryside reinforces the essentially circular character of labour mobility which is typical also of men in Southern Africa. It confirms in addition the interdependence of family members between rural and urban areas. However, while the pattern of mobility may be similar, for women the distinctive feature of rural–urban interdependence is its association with the development of family forms in which the role of father is marginal both in social and economic terms (Izzard 1982).

Rural investment and the urban élite

Finally, rural–urban interdependence of modes of production forged through the social unit of the household and discussed above should be distinguished from the interrelated rural and urban investments of a small élite minority: those who by virtue of ascribed or achieved status have secured preferential access to the means of production in rural areas and also to lucrative income-earning opportunities in towns – typically under 20 per cent of households. For the majority of Botswana and Basotho families for whom an additional income outside agriculture is critical but for whom the rural economy and society continue to offer essential security, explaining this paradox requires that we return to the regional scale once again and to the broader set of forces influencing changes in the countryside, notably the encroachment of capitalist relations from the towns. In doing so we shall concentrate on conditions in Botswana.

The ability of Tswana households to cope with the vagaries of a physical environment which is agriculturally marginal and prone to successive droughts, cannot be separated from their socio-economic circumstances. It is the poor who are most vulnerable. Income distribution is in turn a product of the interaction between culture and structure. Traditional stratification patterns within Tswana society have been strengthened by the penetration of capitalism while the support system which protected poor households from an unpredictable environment has come under threat.

Capitalist relations have penetrated the countryside not only through the exchange of labour for cash but also through the conversion, at least in part, of essential environmental resources – land and water – into commodities for livestock production. A traditionally integrated economy of agriculture and cattle has thus become split between on the one hand crop production which remains largely at subsistence level and on the other the commercialisation of livestock. This division within the rural economy has been initiated and sustained by a form of rural–urban interaction somewhat different from the kind discussed above – the involvement of an urban-based élite in cattle rearing and exchange as a highly profitable form of capital investment. It is this interaction in a drought-prone environment which has increased the reliance of poor households on a social support system between kin and community which has itself been subject to

195

change. In these circumstances the vulnerability of these households to environmental hazards such as drought has intensified and their rural–urban dependence increased.

Commercialisation of livestock production

The distinction being made between rural–urban interactions and interdependence and at the same time the structural links between the two, can best be appreciated by an historical review. An important continuity between the wealth of Tswana households in the past and the present lies in ownership of cattle and the association between this and access to land and water resources in rural areas. In traditionally stratified Tswana society cattle were under the control of the nobility who in turn lent them to their tribespeople. Cliffe and Moorsom (1979: 36) record that some very large herders, often chiefs, owned 'hundreds and even thousands' of cattle symbolising their wealth and status. Those with herds were in turn allocated the use of cattleposts and had exclusive rights over the water from any well dug or dam built. Thus preferential access to the means of production existed under the supervision and control of the chief. However, through a complex set of social relationships and institutions, safeguards were provided for those with limited resources against the hazards of drought and famine. Among these safeguards, reference should be made to the mafisa system whereby wealthy men including the chief would loan out cattle to relatives and kinsmen with few beasts of their own and, in return for rendering services to the owner, the latter could 'use the oxen for ploughing and transport [of water and firewood] take the milk of cows, and usually receive a heifer for themselves' (Schapera 1953: 28).

Against this background, since the turn of the century, commercial cattle production has been encouraged as the mainstay of the Botswana economy. In the light of the political and socio-economic changes which have taken place since then, however, it remains so for only a minority and indeed a declining number of Tswana households. Public investment in technology (drilling rigs) and research (vaccination, improved pasture) during the colonial period contributed to the development of the livestock sector. Borehole drilling for communal grazing funded by the tribal treasuries was supplemented by the sinking of private boreholes for those who could afford them, notably existing large cattleowners who, by virtue of a steady increase in the monetary value of livestock during the colonial period, had the ability to pay. Thus as Roe (1980: 27) points out 'The skewed distribution of livestock holdings and borehole ownership grew mutually reinforcing through time'. In geographical terms a distinction emerged between the land occupied by large herds with access to permanent water supplies, chiefly in the sand veld, and smaller herds confined to communal sources in the east susceptible to drought and overgrazing.

In this commercialisation process inequalities were intensified by environmental constraints. For example, a devastating drought during the 1930s and again in the 1960s increased the skewed distribution of livestock holdings (Campbell 1979). It was 'those livestock holders with larger herds [who] were better able to endure the hardship of drought since they often had the assets with which to sink wells or boreholes in *new* grazing areas during these times' (Roe 1980: 33). By contrast, for small herders the opportunities were more limited and, within the context of an increasingly monetarised economy, the sale of livestock which survived in order to buy food became an important strategy (Vierich & Sheppard 1980). Thus while in a survey of six tribal areas in 1943 it was found that only 7 per cent of households had no cattle and 10.5 per cent less than ten head each (Schapera 1953: 23), by 1974/75 45 per cent of rural households were recorded without cattle while 66 per cent owned ten or less (Central Statistics Office 1976).

The development of commercial livestock production in a drought-prone environment has modified the relations of production in rural areas such that access to additional land and water resources and, by implication, the ability to survive as a livestock owner, has become increasingly dependent on ability to pay. However the impact of these trends on the income and welfare of Botswana households cannot be explained merely in economic terms. Nor indeed can the response of different groups. It is with the relationship between culture and structure that we should be concerned. By way of illustration reference will be made below to the effects of commercial production on social exchange among the Tswana people; to the character of the new élite; and finally to the impact of changing land ownership and use on remote area dwellers.

Social exchange, the environment and the 'successful' career pattern

For a growing number of Tswana households with few or no cattle the socio-economic significance of the increasing inequalities in the distribution of cattle, land and water lies in the effects of commercial livestock production on the traditionally integrated lands/cattlepost system. Both public and private investment in livestock has taken place alongside a relatively neglected and subordinate agricultural sector which, under the environmental conditions of Botswana, is not suited to intensive arable production. Technological improvements have been limited to the replacement of the hoe by the plough while the traditional geographical split between lands and cattlepost has meant that in the provision of permanent water supplies it is at the lands areas that comparative shortages have occurred (Fortmann & Roe 1980; Silitshena 1981). In these circumstances two interlinked effects of the growing division between crop and livestock production should be mentioned. First, for small herders a financial dependence on cattle sales in drought years has impaired the self sufficiency of these households since 'profitable crop production relies heavily upon the ability to plough independently of other households' (Vierich & Sheppard 1980: 1).

197

Second, lacking adequate draught power an important contradiction has emerged between on the one hand the growing reliance of poor households on the web of social exchange in order to plough and on the other the threat to this form of exchange from an increasingly monetarised rural economy. Reference to the mafisa system illustrates this point.

Evidence suggests that the use of cattle for ploughing reduces their monetary value and that in the case of market-orientated cattleowners with access to alternative means like tractors fewer oxen are being trained for this purpose. As Solway (1979) observes with reference to the western Kweneng this commercial-isation in turn threatens the mafisa system. Furthermore, in view of the persistence of traditionally negative attitudes towards women as cattle managers they are effectively prevented from receiving mafisa cattle at all. Female-headed households are therefore particularly disadvantaged if there is no resident male. It is within the context of changes in the countryside such as these that the rural-urban interdependence of Tswana households takes on its significance.

Rural-urban interdependence is in turn structurally linked to the rural-urban interactions of a small minority. In exploring these beneficiaries from both modes of production it is apparent that the development of commercial livestock has been shaped by the traditional hierarchical structure of Tswana society and that this hierarchical structure has in turn been both consolidated and modified in the process. Those with ascribed status, representatives and close associates of the tribal chieftaincy with large cattle herds, were best placed to benefit initially from the commercial opportunities available. Moreover, as Schapera (1970) points out in his book *Tribal Innovators*, through their legislative and judicial power this Tswana élite could in turn control the speed and character of commercial development among tribal members.

More recently it is through the status acquired by means of formal education that the traditional hierarchical structure has been modified. The close association between education and income in the formal sector has enabled those with adequate qualifications to accumulate sufficient financial capital to invest in large cattle holdings (Cooper 1980; Parsons 1977). For this new urban élite (those with upper and post secondary schooling), however, the socio-economic significance of their rural-urban links stands in sharp contrast to that of the majority. While family and kinship networks provide an important initial means of acquiring rural housing and cattle – also occasionally, but much less important for this group, land for relatively unprofitable crop production – in the long term the maintenance of these interests relies less upon kinship links and obligations than upon the financial security derived from an urban income (Bell 1980; 1981c). It is this security which provides the essential buffer against the potentially destructive effects of drought (Devitt 1979). Thus the assets available in rural and urban economic systems can be exploited as complementary and integrated rather than as an interdependent whole. If we return to the model of the successful migrant career pattern outlined earlier in this chapter, it is worth noting that it is members of this group more than any other who, in the course of their working lives, are able to secure the substantial and reliable urban income needed to achieve an economic independence from kin which marks the achievement of what is perceived to be a successful career.

Finally, in discussing the links between capitalist relations, culture and the environment reference should be made to the Basarwa (Bushmen), a distinctive hunter–gatherer society and the focus of much anthropological research (Hitchcock 1978a; Lee 1968). As the original occupants of the veld they retreated into the Kgalagadi desert following the penetration of Tswana immigrants into the area. Since then their economy and society have been progressively threatened by external influence. Some became serfs for their Tswana conquerors acting as cattle herders and trackers, and with few legal rights they were among the most oppressed groups. But perhaps the greatest threat to their survival has come from commercial ranching and with it competing interests for the use of their most valuable resource – land.

Helga Vierich (1980: 151) suggests that among the most important reasons for the steady disappearance of hunting and gathering from Southern Africa and the rest of the world 'are the cumulative effects of environmental degradation due to over-stocking of domestic animals, and competition over veld foods, game and ultimately over the rights to the land itself between hunter–gatherers and peoples with different and in some senses more "efficient" extractive technologies'. An increase in livestock numbers and in population density in the Kalahari since the beginning of the borehole drilling programme has upset the fine balance achieved by the Basarwa between social organisation and the environment and has necessitated some adaptation to these external forces (Hitchcock 1977; 1978b; Wilmsen 1981). Among the strategies adopted, seasonal employment in agricultural areas and at cattleposts has provided a means of meeting basic subsistence needs but it has also increased their dependence on an alien economic system. In times of drought when the productivity of veld food is at its lowest it is this dependency which renders the Basarwa particularly vulnerable since the opportunities for hired labour are seriously reduced. Thus, under harsh climatic conditions and in the absence of adequate opportunities for remote area dwellers to adjust, these clashes between the hunter–gatherer economy and that of more complex societies speeds the eventual destruction of the security of the hunting and gathering way of life.

Conclusion

If we return to the two features discussed earlier in this chapter that are characteristic of traditional society in this part of the continent, namely, spatial mobility and mutual support, it is apparent that both persist. However, within the context of Southern Africa's politico-economic transformation the character and significance of their various forms display elements of both continuity and radical change. Labour migration has become the most economically significant form of mobility for the household, supplementing traditional movement to the lands and cattlepost. Moreover, contrary to the ideology of the migrant labour system women too are migrants and income earners. They too interact between economic sectors and oscillate between rural and urban areas.

However, whether we focus on male or female mobility, of fundamental importance in theoretical and practical terms is the household as the key unit of decision-making, distribution and redistribution and with this the concept of the spatially divided household characteristic of both traditional and contemporary African society. By focusing on the household the strength of the rural–urban economic and social links forged by men and women are clearly displayed. But merely to confirm in this way a continuity between rural and urban areas in terms of modes of production and social relations and firmly to reject the concept of the rural–urban dichotomy is clearly not enough. In analysing the distribution of income and welfare within the African countries what matters is the significance of these links for different groups. In broad terms we can distinguish between the economic and social interdependence of rural and urban areas for the majority of households which is sustained through a pattern of labour circulation and the interrelated rural–urban investments of a small élite minority. To explain how these links are forged and maintained reference needs to be made to the continuity and change in household structure and organisation under the distinctive conditions of the Southern African political economy. The regional context is vitally important.

It has been shown that the household as a unit and the individuals which it comprises have been integrated within and modified by the capitalist mode of production in different ways. Reference to mine migration, to the activities of women and to the urban élite illustrates this point. However, within the framework of opportunities and constraints defined by the politico-economic system these case studies also emphasise the vital and decisive role played by cultural values and practices in shaping the spatial interactions which take place and in determining in turn the survival strategies adopted by different groups.

With reference to mine migrants and female-headed households, while for both groups the interdependence of kin between rural and urban areas is critical, important differences also arise in the interplay between structure and culture. In the case of female-headed households variations occur in their demographic characteristics by location which may be regarded as the outcome of alternative migration strategies open to women at different stages in their life cycle: to 'remain behind' or to return to the rural environment; to become participants in urban migration either internal or international. The combination of opportunities and constraints varies in each setting and also with the internal characteristics of the household. But shared in common by the majority is the importance of natal ties. Within the context of a powerful and persistent mutual support system it is the natal link which has been strengthened as the conjugal relationship has weakened. These dual elements of continuity and change in social relations reflect the particular politico-economic circumstances of the Southern African periphery mediated by prevailing cultural values and practices affecting the roles and status of women. In these circumstances, while there are similarities in the pattern of male and female migration, for female-headed households the conditions which promote and sustain interaction between kin together with the family context and the networks on which this interaction is based are different from those of their male counterparts.

Finally, it has been emphasised that the interdependence of spatially divided family members must be seen within the context of important changes in the countryside, notably the encroachment of capitalist relations from the towns. The rural–urban interactions of an urban-oriented élite based on the conversion of land and water to commodities for commercial livestock production have profoundly affected the value attached to essential environmental resources. Under these conditions it is the interplay between structure and culture which influences opportunity of access to these resources and the survival strategies adopted by different groups. The character of the new élite reflects a combination of ascribed and achieved status. Problems faced by the most vulnerable groups engaged in agriculture relate not only to economic forces but more particularly to the ways in which they are affected by changes in the web of social exchange. As regards hunter–gatherer societies the threat posed by external forces to their way of life derives not merely from competing land uses associated with changing patterns of tenure but from the way in which these changes have upset the fine balance achieved by these communities between social organisation and the environment. Thus the opportunities for gradual cultural change have been destroyed.

Further reading

Analyses of migration in Africa are provided by Van Binsbergen and Meilink (1978) and Swindell (1979) while urbanisation and rural–urban interactions are the subject of O'Connor's recent text (1983). The extensive work of Isaac Schapera in Southern Africa, including a short ethnographic survey of the Tswana (1953), provides an excellent basis for contemporary study. Kerven and Simmons (1981) have compiled a bibliography of research on the society, culture and political economy of post-independence Botswana. Murray (1981) presents the results of detailed investigation into migration and family change in Lesotho while, in the case of Botswana, the findings of a national migration study based on the household are edited by Kerven (1982).

———— Chapter 9————

CONCLUSIONS

Changes in African economies have been accompanied by both social and demographic change. The penetration of alien modes of production have brought about new ways of dividing society, notably by class and gender, beyond those of ethnicity and tribe and new ways of dividing territories – the nation state, administrative regions, perhaps most significantly, the rural–urban divide. External forces have altered the terms on which African people gain access to scarce resources while control over these resources has become increasingly concentrated both socially and spatially. While the majority of Africa's population continues to be concentrated in rural areas the centre of power and decision-making lies in the towns. But Africa is not characterised by a social and spatial dualism. Nor can we identify a linear progression within countries between modes of production. While international politico-economic forces have a powerful influence on the development of national economies their impact is shaped in particular instances by the cultural context. It has been the purpose of this book to illustrate the nature and impact of these interrelationships between structure and culture. The previous chapter, which is in large measure a regional case study, is therefore appropriate for it represents the culmination of the argument on which this book is based. Africa is marked by both politico-economic and cultural variety. Only through detailed case study are these similarities and differences and their impact on the organisation of space identified and explained.

Historically, the penetration of colonial capitalism gave rise to a diversity of political, economic and social structures across the continent as a result of the interaction which took place between local and external institutions. It is the form of this interaction which has shaped the national values, beliefs and ideals of Africa's independent leadership and the nature of their external relations. In considering conditions within the African countries the central theme throughout has been the power of the African people in influencing the processes of change. While the administrative and economic organisation of space laid down during colonial rule has since independence been strongly influenced by political decision-making and bureaucratic planning at the centre, it has been demonstrated that both in the formulation and implementation of spatial planning local cultural values and practices play a crucial role.

Africans are not passive agents in the processes of change. Their responses to the opportunities presented and to the constraints imposed by the politico-

202

economic context are mediated by culture and it is through this cultural filter that their behaviour in turn reproduces the system. The relationship between culture and the behaviour of the African people has formed the central focus of Chapters 7 and 8. In seeking to understand changes in the social organisation of space – how people use space in the economic activities which maintain them and in the social ties which sustain them – it has been emphasised that the household as the primary social and cultural unit, the traditional focus of production, reproduction, sentiment and social welfare, provides an essential starting point. By adopting this focus two notions well-established in the development literature are firmly challenged and rejected: that there is a steady progression from the extended to nuclear family norm with the penetration of capitalism; and that rural and urban areas represent separate social spheres.

With reference to demographic processes, it is apparent that changes in mortality and fertility are influenced by fundamental social and cultural beliefs associated with, for example, sickness, disease, child spacing and childrearing and that in both rural and urban areas geographical access to the social services and facilities which are designed to modify these demographic processes is in turn mediated by the cultural environment of the household and close kin. Similarly, with reference to work and employment it is clear that in order to understand the use made of space by individuals in their economic activities reference should be made to the links between economic and social processes and cultural values. While income-earning opportunities vary between the countryside and the towns strong links exist between sectors and areas which are forged through the medium of the household and kin. In these circumstances the labour force should not be interpreted merely as a set of individuals but as households whose members may be geographically split and engaged in more than one mode of production.

But the household is not a static unit of production and reproduction and among the critical forces stimulating change is labour mobility. Both international and internal migration reflect the outcome of capitalist penetration and have provided an essential means by which to increase household income. At the same time this mobility has had a profound effect on household structure. Analysing the links between migration and the household raises a number of important points. The focus adopted directs the analysis to the micro-scale. But at the same time it provides an essential link with alternative spatial scales since our explanations of migration must recognise the structures of opportunity and constraint within which household decisions are made. The diversity of household types associated with labour migration challenges once again any evidence in support of a movement towards the nuclear family norm. Furthermore, in seeking to identify inequalities in income and domestic productive capacity between households their internal demographic characteristics and location are of critical importance. Cultural prejudices against the education and employment of women coupled with the tradition of male-dominated labour migration renders them a particularly vulnerable group. However, contrary to the ideology of the Southern African migrant labour system, they too are participants in the labour migration process. Like the majority of male migrants, for independent women involvement in more than one economic sector together with movement between rural and urban areas represents a form of economic interdependence which is critical to the maintenance of the household. But the family context and the social networks on which they depend are significantly different.

Finally, reference should be made to the relationship between the development process and the environment. The problems of environmental degradation, drought and famine in much of Africa are now major research topics in which the interaction between natural conditions and politico-economic forces is fundamental. The penetration of capitalist relations into the countryside has altered the terms on which the African people gain access to essential environmental resources and has intensified pressure on these increasingly scarce resources. But in explaining the effects of this pressure on the incidence and distribution of poverty it is with the cultural context that we should also be concerned. The adaptive strategies by which the African people have traditionally coped with the uncertainties of the environment are under threat. It is the breakdown of the system of social and spatial organisation and of the mechanisms of social support which, in the absence of adequate opportunities for adjustment, renders most vulnerable the untrained, the unskilled and poorly educated, and which also plays such a key and damaging role in Africa's current environmental crisis.

BIBLIOGRAPHY

Adadevoh, K. (ed) 1974   *Subfertility and Infertility in Africa.* Caxton Press, Ibadan.

Adedeji, A. (ed) 1981   *Indigenisation of African Economies.* Hutchinson.

Adegbola, O. 1977   'New estimates of fertility and child mortality in Africa south of the Sahara', *Population Studies* vol. 31, no. 3, 467–86.

Adegbola, O., Page, H. J. & Lesthaeghe, R. 1977   'Breast feeding and post-partum abstinence in metropolitan Lagos'. Annual meeting of the Population Association of America, St Louis, April.

Adepoju, O. 1977   'Migration and development in tropical Africa: some research priorities', *African Affairs* vol. 76, 210–25.

Agarwal, A., Kimondo, J., Moreno, G. & Tinker, J. 1981   *Water Sanitation, Health–for all?* Earthscan.

Ageni, B. 1981   'Lagos' in Pacione, M. (ed)   *Problems and Planning in Third World Cities.* Croom Helm, pp. 127–55.

Agnew, S. & Stubbs, M. (eds) 1972   *Malawi in Maps.* Hodder & Stoughton.

Ajayi, J. F. A. & Crowder, M. (eds) 1976   *History of West Africa*   vol. 1, *Pre-History–1800.* Longman.

Ajayi, J. F. A. & Crowder, M. (eds) 1974   *History of West Africa* vol. 2, *19th and 20th centuries.* Longman.

Ake, C. 1981a   *A Political Economy of Africa.* Longman.

Ake, C. 1981b   'Kenya' in Adedeji, A. (ed)   *Indigenisation of African Economies.* Hutchinson, pp. 186–203.

Akintoye, S. A. 1980   *Emergent African States.* Longman.

Akpovi, S. U., Johnson, D. C. & Brieger, W. R. 1981   'Guinea worm control: testing the efficacy of health education in primary health care', *International Journal of Health Education* vol. 24 (4), 229–37.

Allan, W. 1965   *The African Husbandman.* Greenwood Press, Westport, Connecticut.

Allen, C. & Williams, G. (eds) 1982   *Sub-Saharan Africa.* Macmillan.

Amin, S. 1971   'The class struggle in Africa', *Revolution* vol. 1, no. 9, 23–47.

Amin, S. 1972a   'Underdevelopment and dependence in black Africa – origins and contemporary forms', *Journal of Modern African Studies* vol. 10, no. 4, 503–24.

Amin, S. 1972b   'L'Afrique sous-peuplée', *Developpement et Civilisation* no. 47/48, 59–67.

Amin, S. 1973   *Neo-colonialism in West Africa.* Penguin.

Amin, S. 1974a   *Accumulation on a World Scale.* Monthly Review Press.

Amin, S. 1974b   *Modern Migrations in Western Africa.* OUP.

Anker, R. 1978   'An analysis of fertility differentials in developing countries', *Review of Economics and Statistics* vol. 60, 58–69.

Anker, R. & Knowles, J. C. 1977   'An empirical analysis of mortality differential in Kenya at the macro and micro levels', *ILO Working Paper No. 60,* Geneva.

Anker, R. & Knowles, J. C. 1983 *Population Growth, Employment and Economic-Demographic Interactions in Kenya: Bachue-Kenya.* Gower, St Martin's Press, New York.

Anthony, K. R. M., Johnson, B. F., Jones, W. O. & Uchendu, V. C. 1979 *Agricultural Change in Tropical Africa.* Cornell University Press, Ithaca.

Arnold, G. 1979 *Aid in Africa.* Kogan Page.

Arnold, G. 1981 *Modern Kenya.* Longman.

Arrighi, G. 1970 'Labour supplies in historical perspective: a study of the proletarianisation of the African peasantry in Rhodesia', *Journal of Development Studies* vol. 6, no. 3, 197–234.

Arrighi, G. & Saul, I. 1968 'Socialism and economic development in tropical Africa', *Journal of Modern African Studies* vol. 6, no. 2, 141–69.

Arrighi, G. & Saul, I. (eds) 1973 *Essays on the Political Economy of Africa.* Monthly Review Press.

Bakpetu Thompson, V. 1969 *Africa and Unity: The Evolution of Pan-Africanism.* Longman.

Baran, P. A. 1957 *The Political Economy of Growth.* Monthly Review Press.

Barber, W. J. 1961 *The Economy of British Central Africa: A Case of Development in a Dual Economy.* OUP.

Barbour, M. *et al.* 1982 *Nigeria in Maps.* Hodder & Stoughton.

Bardinet, C. 1977 'City responsibilities in the structural dependence of sub-industrialised economies in Africa', *Antipode* vol. 9, no. 3, 43–48.

Bates, R. H. 1983 *Essays on the Political Economy of Rural Africa.* CUP.

Belay, H. 1980 *European Economic Community aid in Africa.* Institute of Social Studies, The Hague.

Bell, M. 1980 'Rural-urban migration among Botswana's skilled manpower: Some observations on the two sector model', *Africa* vol. 50, no. 4, 404–21.

Bell, M. 1981a 'Transition to urban life – the role of indigenous enterprise in Naledi, Botswana', *Geography* vol. 66, no. 290, 63–65.

Bell, M. 1981b 'The influence of education on migration'. Paper presented at the National Migration Study Conference, 7–11 December, Gaborone, Botswana.

Bell, M. 1981c 'Modern sector employment and urban social change: A case study from Gaborone, Botswana', *Canadian Journal of African Studies* vol. 15, no. 2, 259–76.

Bell, M. 1982 'Botswana's way with self-help housing', *Development Forum* vol. 10, no. 8, 5.

Belshaw, D. G. R. 1979 'Decentralised regional planning in Tanzania' in Kim, K. S., Mabele, R. B. & Schultheis, M. J. (eds) *Papers on the Political Economy of Tanzania.* Heinemann, Nairobi, pp. 47–64.

Berman, B. 1984 'Structure and process in the bureaucratic states of colonial Africa', *Development and Change* vol. 15, 161–202.

Bernstein, H. 1978 'Notes on capital and peasantry', *Review of African Political Economy* no. 10, 60–73.

Berry, B. J. L. 1960 'An inductive approach to the regionalisation of economic development' in Ginsburg, N. (ed) *Essays on Geography and Economic Development.* University of Chicago Press, pp. 78–107.

Berry, L. 1971 *Tanzania in Maps.* Hodder & Stoughton.

Bertrand, J. T., Bertrand, W. E. & Malonga, M. 1983 'The use of traditional and modern methods of fertility control in Kinshasa, Zaire', *Population Studies* vol. 37, 129–36.

Bettelheim, C. 1972 'Theoretical comments' in Emmanuel, A. (ed) *Unequal Exchange: A Study of the Imperialism of World Trade.* New Left Books.

Bewayo, E. D. 1979 'Local government in different images: Kenya and Zambia'. Paper presented at the 22nd Annual Meeting of the African Studies Association, 31 Oct.–3 Nov., Los Angeles, California.

Bienefeld, M. 1981 'The informal sector and women's oppression', *IDS Bulletin* (Brighton) vol. 12, no. 3, 8–13.

Bienefeld, M. & Godfrey, M. 1975 'Measuring unemployment and the informal sector: Conceptual and statistical problems', *IDS Bulletin* (Brighton) vol. 7, no. 3, 4–10.

Binns, J. A. & Funnell, D. C. 1983 'Geography and integrated rural development', *Geografiska Annaler* vol. 65 B, no. 1, 57–63.

Birmingham, D. & Martin, P. M. (eds) 1983 *History of Central Africa* vols. 1 and 2. Longman.

Bohannan, P. 1964 *African Outline: A General Introduction.* Penguin.

Böhning, W. R. & Stahl, C. W. 1979 *Reducing Migration Dependence in Southern Africa.* International Labour Organisation, Geneva.

Bond, C. 1974 *Women's Involvement in Agriculture.* Ministry of Agriculture, Gaborone, Botswana.

Bondestam, L. 1980a 'The political ideology of population control' in Bondestam, L. & Bergstrom, S. (eds) *Poverty and Population Control.* Academic Press, pp. 1–38.

Bondestam, L. 1980b 'The foreign control of Kenyan population' in Bondestam, L. & Bergstrom, S. (eds) *Poverty and Population Control,* Academic Press, pp. 157–78.

Boserup, E. 1970 *Women's Role in Economic Development.* Allen & Unwin.

Bradley, D. J. 1977a 'The health implications of irrigation schemes and manmade lakes in tropical environments' in Feachem, R., McGarry, M. & Mara, D. (eds) *Water, Wastes and Health in Hot Climates.* Wiley, pp. 18–29.

Bradley, D. J. 1977b 'Health aspects of water supplies in tropical countries' in Feachem, R., McGarry, M. & Mara, D. (eds) *Water, Wastes and Health in Hot Climates.* Wiley, pp. 3–17.

Brain, R. 1981 *Art and Society in Africa.* Longman.

Bray, J. M. 1969 'The economics of traditional cloth production in Iseyin, Ghana', *Economic Development and Cultural Change* vol. 17, 540–51.

Brett, E. A. 1973 *Colonialism and Underdevelopment in East Africa: The Politics of Economic Change 1919–39.* Heinemann.

Brookfield, H. 1978 'Third World development', *Progress in Human Geography* vol. 2, 121–32.

Browne, A. W. 1981 'Appropriate technology and the dynamics of village industry: a case study of pottery in Ghana', *Transactions of the Institute of British Geographers* vol. 6, no. 3, 313–23.

Bryant, C., Stevens, B. & McLiver, S. 1978 'Rural to urban migration: some data from Botswana', *African Studies Review* vol. 21, no. 2, 85–99.

Bwibo, N. W. 1981 'Utilisation of health services by children in Kenya and some aspects of deterrent factors'. Symposium on Development and the Reduction of Inequalities in Different Socio-Cultural Contexts regarding Children and Family Life-Styles, 9–12 May, Doha, Qatar.

Cabral, A. 1973 *Return to the Source.* Africa Information Service, New York.

Caldwell, J. C. 1967 'Fertility attitudes in three economically contrasting rural regions of Ghana', *Economic Development and Cultural Change* vol. 15, 217–38.

Caldwell, J. C. 1973 'Family planning in continental sub-Saharan Africa' in Smith, T. E. (ed) *The Politics of Family Planning in the Third World.* Allen & Unwin, pp. 50–66.

Caldwell, J. C. 1975 'The Sahelian drought and its demographic implications'. American Council of Education, *Overseas Liaison Committee Paper no. 8,* Washington.

Caldwell, J. C. 1976a 'Toward a restatement of demographic transition theory', *Population and Development Review* vol. 2, 321–66.

Caldwell, J. C. 1976b 'Fertility and the household economy in Nigeria', *Journal of Comparative Family Studies* vol. 7, no. 2, 193–253.

Caldwell, J. C. 1977 'The economic rationality of high fertility: an investigation illustrated with Nigerian survey data', *Population Studies* vol. 31, 5–27.

Caldwell, J. C. 1978 'A theory of fertility: from high plateau to destabilisation', *Population and Development Review* vol. 4, 553–77.

Caldwell, J. C. 1979 'Education as a factor in mortality decline: an examination of Nigerian data', *Population Studies* vol. 3, no. 3, 395–413.

Caldwell, J. C. 1982 *Theory of Fertility Decline.* Academic Press.

Caldwell, J. C. et al. (eds) 1975 *Population Growth and Socio-Economic Change in West Africa.* Columbia University Press, New York.

Caldwell, J. C. & Caldwell, P. 1977 'The role of marital sexual abstinence in determining fertility: a study of the Yoruba in Nigeria', *Population Studies* vol. 31, 193–217.

Caldwell, J. C. & Caldwell, P. 1978 'The achieved small family: early fertility transition in an African city', *Studies in Family Planning* vol. 9, no. 1, 2–18.

Caldwell, J. C. & Okonjo, C. (eds) 1968 *The Population of Tropical Africa.* Longman.

Caldwell, J. C. & Ware, H. 1977 'The evolution of family planning in an African city: Ibadan, Nigeria', *Population Studies* vol. 31, 487–507.

Campbell, A. C. 1979 'The 1960s drought in Botswana' in Hinchey, M. T. (ed) *Symposium on Drought in Botswana, 5–8 June 1978.* Botswana Society in collaboration with Clark University Press, Hanover, New Hampshire, pp. 98–109.

Carr, M. 1982 'Appropriate technology for rural African women', *Development Digest* vol. 20, no. 1, 87–98.

Cassen, R. H. 1976 'Population and development: a survey', *World Development* vol. 4, 785–830.

Cassen, R. H. 1978 'Current trends in population change and their causes', *Population and Development Review* vol. 4, 331–53.

Central Statistics Office 1972 *Report on the Population Census 1971.* Government Printer, Gaborone, Botswana.

Central Statistics Office 1976 *The Rural Income Distribution Survey in Botswana 1974–75.* Gaborone, Botswana.

Chamberlain, M. E. 1974 *The scramble for Africa.* Longman.

Chenery, H., Ahluwalia, M. S., Bell, C. L. G., Duloy, J. H. & Jolly, R. 1974 *Redistribution with Growth: Policies to Improve Income Distribution in Developing Countries in the Context of Economic Growth.* OUP.

Clarke, J. I. 1970 *Sierra Leone in Maps.* Hodder & Stoughton.

Clarke, J. I. & Kosinski, L. A. (eds) 1983 *Redistribution of Population in Africa.* Heinemann.

Cliffe, L. 1975 'Underdevelopment or socialism? A comparative analysis of Kenya and Tanzania' in Harris, R. (ed) 1975 *The Political Economy of Africa.* Wiley, pp. 139–85.

Cliffe, L. 1976 'Rural political economy of Africa' in Gutkind, P. C. W. & Wallerstein, I. (eds) *Political Economy of Contemporary Africa.* Sage, pp. 112–30.

Cliffe, L. 1977 'Labour migration and peasant differentiation: Zambian experiences', *Journal of Peasant Studies* vol. 5, 326–46.

Cliffe, L. & Moorsom, R. 1979 'Rural class formation and ecological collapse in Botswana', *Review of African Political Economy* no. 15/16, 35–52.

Coale, A. J. 1969 'The decline in fertility in Europe from the French Revolution to World War II' in Behrman, S. et al. (eds) *Fertility and Family Planning: A World View.* University of Michigan Press, Ann Arbor, pp. 3–24.

Cohen, D. L. 1981 'Class and the analysis of African politics: problems and prospects' in Cohen, D. L. & Daniel, J. (eds) *Political Economy of Africa: Selected Readings.* Longman, pp. 85–111.

Cohen, D. L. & Daniel, J. 1981 *Political Economy of Africa: Selected Readings.* Longman.

208

Cohen, R. 1972 'Class in Africa: analytical problems and perspectives' in Miliband, R. & Saville, J. (eds) *The Socialist Register*. Merlin Press, pp. 231–55.

Cohen, R. 1975 'From peasants to workers in Africa' in Gutkind, P. C. W. & Wallerstein, I. (eds) *The Political Economy of Contemporary Africa*. Sage, pp. 155–68.

Colclough, C. 1980 'Some aspects of labour use in Southern Africa – problems and policies', *IDS Bulletin* (Brighton) vol. 11, no. 4, 29–39.

Colclough, C. & McCarthy, S. 1980 *The Political Economy of Botswana. A Study of Growth and Distribution*. OUP.

Comaroff, J. L. 1976 'Tswana transformations 1953–1975', supplementary chapter in Schapera, I. *The Tswana*. International African Institute, pp. 67–76.

Comaroff, J. L. & Roberts, S. 1977 'Marriage and extra-marital sexuality: the dialectics of legal change among the Kgatla', *Journal of African Law* vol. 21, no. 1, 97–123.

Commission of the European Communities 1977 *The European Community and the Third World*. Office for Official Publications of the EC, Luxemburg.

Conde, J. 1971 *The Demographic Transition as Applied to Tropical Africa*. OECD, Paris.

Conde, J. 1973a *Some Demographic Aspects of Human Resources in Africa*. OECD, Paris.

Conde, J. 1973b 'The effects of changes in fertility and mortality on the socio-economic structures of African population'. Proceedings of an expert group meeting. OECD, Paris.

Conyers, D. 1982 *An Introduction to Social Planning in the Third World*. Wiley.

Cooney, S. 1980 'Overseas companies as transnational actors during the European conquest of Africa', *British Journal of International Studies* vol. 6, 154–79.

Cooper, D. M. 1979 'Economy and society in Botswana: some basic national socio-economic coordinates relevant to an interpretation of national migration study statistics'. Working Paper no. 2, National Migration Study, Central Statistics Office, Gaborone.

Cooper, D. M. 1980 'How urban workers in Botswana manage their cattle and lands: Selebi-Phikwe case studies'. *Working Paper no. 4* National Migration Study, Central Statistics Office, Gaborone.

Cooper, D. M. 1981 'A Socio-economic-geographical perspective on the causes of migration'. Paper presented at the National Migration Study Conference, 7–11 December, Gaborone, Botswana.

Cooperstock, H. 1979 'Some methodological and substantive issues in the study of social stratification in tropical Africa' in Shaw, T. M. & Heard, K. A. (eds) *The Politics of Africa: Dependence and Development*. Longman, pp. 5–38.

Coquery-Vidrovitch, C. 1976 'The political economy of the African peasantry and modes of production' in Gutkind, P. C. W. & Wallerstein, I. (eds) *The Political Economy of Contemporary Africa*. Sage, pp. 90–111.

Coulson, A. 1977 'Agricultural policies in mainland Tanzania, 1946–1976', *Review of African Political Economy*, no. 10, 74–100.

Coulson, A. (ed) 1979 *African Socialism in Practice: The Tanzania Experiment*. Spokesman, Nottingham.

Coulson, A. 1981 *Tanzania 1800–1980. A Political Economy*. OUP.

Creech Jones, A. 1951 'British colonial policy, with particular reference to Africa', *International Affairs* vol. 27, no. 2, 176–83.

Crowder, M. 1962 *Senegal: A Study in French Assimilation Policy*. OUP.

Crowder, M. 1964 'Indirect rule – French and British style', *Africa* vol. 34, 197–205.

Cruise O'Brien, R. 1980 'Evaluation of technical assistance awarded by the Commission to the ACP states'. Research report for the EEC Development Directorate, Institute of Development Studies, University of Sussex.

Crummey, D. & Stewart, C.C. 1981 *Modes of Production in Africa: The Pre-Colonial Era*. Sage.

Crush, J. S. & Riddell, J. B. 1980 'Third World misunderstandings?' *AREA* vol. 12, no. 3, 204–6.

Crush, J. & Rogerson, C. 1983 'New wave African historiography and African historical geography', *Progress in Human Geography* vol. 7, no. 2, 203–31.

Curtin, P. D., Feierman, S., Thompson, L. & Vansina, J. 1979 *African History*. Longman.

Cutrufelli, M.R. 1983 *Women of Africa: Roots of Oppression*. Zed Press.

Daaku, K. Y. 1968 'The slave trade and African society' in Ranger, T. O. (ed) *Emerging Themes of African History*. East African Publishing House Nairobi, Kenya, pp. 134–40.

Daniel, J. 1981 'The culture of dependency: introduction and selected bibliography' in Cohen, D. L. & Daniel, J. (eds) *Political Economy of Africa*. Longman, pp. 164–70.

Dasgupta, B. & Seers, D. 1975 *Statistical Policy in Less Developed Countries*. IDS (Brighton) Communications Series no. 114.

Davidson, B. 1955 *The African Awakening*. Jonathan Cape.

Davidson, B. 1961 'The African personality' in Legum, C. (ed) *Africa: A Handbook*. Anthony Blond, pp. 408–12.

Davidson, B. 1967 *Which Way Africa? The Search for a New Society*. Penguin.

Davidson, B. 1970 *The African Genius: An Introduction to African Cultural and Social History*. Atlantic Monthly Press, Boston.

Davidson, B. 1975 *Can Africa Survive? Arguments against Growth without Development*. Heinemann.

Davies, D. H. 1971 *Zambia in Maps*. Hodder & Stoughton.

Davies, P. N. 1976 *Trading in West Africa 1840–1920*. Croom Helm.

De Kadt, E. 1976 'Wrong priorities in health', *New Society* no. 3, 525–26.

Devitt, P. 1979 'Drought and poverty, in Hinchey, M. T. (ed) *Symposium on Drought in Botswana, 5–6 June 1978*. Botswana Society in collaboration with Clark University Press, Hanover, New Hampshire, pp. 121–27.

De Vries 1978 'Agricultural extension and development – Ujamaa villages and the problems of institutional change', *Community Development Journal* vol. 13, no. 1, 11–19.

Doherty, J. 1977 'Urban places and Third World development: the case of Tanzania', *Antipode* vol. 9, no. 3, 32–42.

Doke, C. M. 1967 *The Southern Bantu Languages*. International African Institute.

Dore, R. 1978 *The Diploma Disease: Education, Qualification and Development*. Allen & Unwin.

Dore, R. & Mars, Z. 1981 *Community Development*. Croom Helm.

Dossier 1984 'Food strategy: new hope for the hungry?' *The Courier* no. 84, 46–69.

Dow, T. E. & Werner, L. H. 1983 'Prospects for fertility decline in rural Kenya', *Population and Development Review* vol. 9, no. 1, 77–97.

Dumont, R. 1966 *False Start in Africa*. Deutsch.

Dumont, R. & Mottin, Marie-France 1983 *Stranglehold on Africa*. Deutsch.

Dupriez, H. 1978 'Integrated rural development projects carried out in Black Africa with EDF aid. Evaluation and outlook for the future'. Commission of the European Communities, *Development Series no. 1*.

East Africa Royal Commission 1955 'Report 1953–55'. Cmd. 9475 HMSO.

Ebong, M. O. 1982 'Spatial dynamics of population in Nigeria: implications for rational migration policies' in Findlay, A. (ed) *Recent National Population Change (Conference Proceedings)*. Department of Geography, University of Durham, pp. 126–41.

Elkan, W. 1960 *Migrants and Proletarians: Urban Labour in the Economic Development of Uganda*. OUP.

Epstein, A. L. 1967 'Urbanisation and social change in Africa', *Current Anthropology* vol. 8, no. 4 275–95.

Epstein, T. S. 1975 'The role of women in the development of Third World countries', *Internationale Entwicklung* vol. 3, 7–12.

Europe Information 10/1978 *Industrial Co-operation and the Lomé Convention*. Office for Official Publications of the EC, Luxemburg.

European Economic Community (EEC) 1958 *The Treaty of Rome and Related Documents*. Brussels.

European Economic Community (EEC) 1975 *The Lomé Convention and Related Documents*. Brussels.

European Economic Community (EEC) 1980a *The Second ACP–EEC Convention and Related Documents*. Com(79) 315 Final. Brussels.

European Economic Community (EEC) 1980b *Report of the Commission on the Implementation of Microprojects under the Lomé Convention*. Brussels.

Evans, P. 1979 *Dependent Development: The Alliance of Multinational, State and Local Capital in Brazil*. Princeton University Press, Princeton.

Ezeife, E. 1981 'Nigeria' in Adedeji, A. (ed) *Indigenisation of African Economies*. Hutchinson, pp. 164–85.

Ezenwe, U. 1982 'Trade and growth in West Africa in the 1980s', *Journal of Modern African Studies* vol. 20, no. 2, 305–22.

Fage, J. & Verity, M. 1978 (2nd edn) *An Atlas of African History*. Arnold.

Fagana. O. 1979 'Trade and growth: the Nigerian experience', *World Development* vol. 7, no. 1, 73–79.

Fallers, L. A. 1973 *Inequality: Social Stratification Reconsidered*. Chicago University Press.

Fanon, F. 1967 *The Wretched of the Earth*. Penguin.

Faruqee, K. C. 1980 *Kenya: Population and Development*. World Bank.

Faulkingham, R. & Thorbahn, P. 1975 'Population dynamics and drought: a village in Niger', *Population Studies* vol. 29, 463–77.

Feachem, R. *et al.* 1978 *Water, Health and Development: An Interdisciplinary Evaluation*. Tre-Mid.

Field, R. F. 1980 *Patterns of Settlement at the Lands: Family Strategy in a Variegated Economy*. Ministry of Agriculture, Gaborone, Botswana.

Field, R. F. 1981 'Botswana Labour in South Africa'. Paper presented at the National Migration Study Conference, 7–11 December, Gaborone, Botswana.

Findley, S. 1977 *Planning for Internal Migration: A Review of Issues and Policies in Developing Countries*. US Bureau of the Census, Washington DC.

Flew, A. (ed) 1970 *Thomas Robert Malthus: An Essay on the Principle of Population and a Summary View of the Principle of Population*. Penguin.

Foley, D. E. 1977 'Anthropological studies of schooling in developing countries: some recent findings and trends', *Comparative Education Review* vol. 21, 311–28.

Forbes, D. K. 1984 *The Geography of Underdevelopment: a critical survey*. Croom Helm.

Fordham, P. 1965 *The Geography of African Affairs*. Pelican.

Forrest, T. 1977 'Notes on the political economy of state intervention in Nigeria'. *IDS Bulletin* (Brighton) vol. 9, no. 1, 42–47.

Fortes, M. 1975 'Isaac Schapera: an appreciation' in Fortes, M. & Patterson, S. (eds) *Studies in Social Anthropology*. Academic Press, pp. 1–16.

Fortmann, L. & Roe, E. 1980 'Settlement on tap: the role of water in permanent settlement at the lands'. Paper presented at the Symposium on Settlement, 4–8 August, Gaborone, Botswana.

Foster, P. 1977 'Education and social differentiation in less developed countries', *Comparative Education Review* vol. 21, 211–28.

Frank, A.G. 1967 *Capitalism and Underdevelopment in Latin America: Historical Studies of Chile and Brazil.* Monthly Review Press, New York.

Frank, A. G. 1974 *Latin America: Underdevelopment or Revolution.* Monthly Review Press, New York.

Von Freyhold, M. 1977 'The post-colonial state and its Tanzanian version', *Review of African Political Economy* no. 8, 75–89.

Von Freyhold, M. 1979 *Ujamaa Villages in Tanzania: Analysis of a Social Experiment.* Heinemann, Nairobi.

Funnell, D. 1976 'The role of small service centres in regional and rural development with special reference to Eastern Africa' in Gilbert, A. G. (ed) *Development Planning and Spatial Structure.* Wiley, pp. 77–112.

Fyfe, C. 1974 'Reform in West Africa: the abolition of the slave trade' in Ajayi, J.F. & Crowder, M. (eds) *History of West Africa* vol. 2. Longman, pp. 30–56.

Galbraith, G. K. 1967 *The New Industrial State.* Hamilton.

Galtung, J. 1976 'The Lomé Convention and neo-capitalism', *The African Review* vol. 5, no. 1, 33–42.

Gay, J. S. 1980a 'Basotho women migrants: a case study', *IDS Bulletin* (Brighton) vol. 11, no. 4, 19–28.

Gay, J. S. 1980b 'Basotho women's options: a study of marital careers in rural Lesotho'. Unpublished Ph.D. dissertation, University of Cambridge.

Ghai, D., Godfrey, M. & Lisk, F. 1979 *Planning for Basic Needs in Kenya: Performance, Policies and Prospects.* ILO, Geneva.

Gilbert, A. 1982 'Urban and regional systems: a suitable case for treatment' In Gilbert, A. & Gugler, J. (eds) *Cities, Poverty and Development: Urbanisation in the Third World.* OUP, pp. 134–61.

Glennie, C. 1983 *Village Water Supply in the Decade: Lessons from Field Experience.* Wiley.

Goddard, A. D. 1973 'Changing family structures among rural Hausa', *Africa* vol. 43, no. 3, 207–18.

Golladay, F. 1980 'Health problems and policies in the developing countries'. *World Bank Staff Working Paper, no. 412.*

Goody, J. 1971 *Technology, Tradition and the State in Africa.* Hutchinson.

Gould, P. R. 1970 'Tanzania 1920–63: the spatial impress of the modernisation process', *World Politics* vol. 22, 149–70.

Gould, W. T. S. & Prothero, R. M. 1975 'Space and time in African population mobility' in Kosinski, L.A. & Prothero, R. M. (eds) *People on the Move.* Methuen, pp 39–50.

Great Britain Advisory Committee on Native Education in British Tropical African Dependencies 1925 *Education policy in British Tropical Africa.* HMSO, London (Cmd. 2374).

Green, R. H. 1965 'Four African development plans: Ghana, Kenya, Nigeria and Tanzania', *Journal of Modern African Studies* vol. 3, no. 2, 249–79.

Green, R. H. 1975 'Redistribution with growth – and/or transition to socialist development – some jottings on Tanzania 1961–74', *IDS Bulletin* (Brighton) vol. 7, no. 2, 22–28.

Green, R. H. 1976 'The Lomé Convention: updated dependence or departure towards collective self-reliance', *The African Review* vol. 6, no. 1, 43–54.

Green, R. H. & Seidman, A. 1968 *Unity or Poverty: The Economics of Pan-Africanism.* Penguin.

Grigg, D. 1981 'The historiography of hunger: changing views on the world food problem 1945–80', *Transactions of the Institute of British Geographers* vol. 6, no. 3, 279–92.

Grindle, M. S. 1980 'The implementor: political constraints on rural development in

Mexico' in Grindle, M. S. (ed) *Politics and Policy Implementation in the Third World*. Princeton University Press, pp. 197–223.

Gruhn, I. V. 1979 *Regionalism Reconsidered: the Economic Commission for Africa*. Westview Press, Boulder, Colorado.

Gugler, J. 1982 'The urban-rural interface and migration' in Gilbert, A. & Gugler, J. *Cities, Poverty and Development: Urbanisation in the Third World*. OUP, pp. 49–64.

Gugler, J. & Flanagan, W. G. 1978 *Urbanisation and Social Change in West Africa*. CUP.

Gulbrandsen, O. 1980 *Agro-pastoral Production and Communal Land Use: A Socio-economic Study of the Bangwaketse*. Rural Sociology Unit, Ministry of Agriculture, Gaborone, Botswana.

Gulliver, P. H. 1955 'Labour migration in a rural economy'. *East African Studies 6*, East African Institute of Social Research, Kampala.

Gulliver, P. H. 1957 'Nyakusa labour migration', *Human Problems of British Central Africa* no. 21, 32–63.

Gulliver, P. H. 1971 *Neighbours and Networks*. University of California Press, Berkeley.

Gutkind, P. C. W. 1970 *The Passing of Tribal Man in Africa*. Brill, Leiden.

Gutkind, P. C. W. & Wallerstein, I. 1976 'Editor's introduction' in *The Political Economy of Contemporary Africa*. Sage, pp. 7–29.

Gutkind, P. C. W. & Waterman, P. (eds) 1977 *African Social Studies: A Radical Reader*. Heinemann.

Hamilton, F. E. I. & Linge, G. J. R. (eds) 1981 *Spatial Analysis, Industry and the Industrial Environment: Progress in Research and Applications* vol. 2, *International Industrial Systems*. Wiley.

Hance, W. A. 1972 'The crudeness of crude densities' in Ominde, S. H. & Ejiogu, C. N. (eds) *Population Growth and Economic Development in Africa*. Heinemann, pp. 36–40.

Harlow, V. & Chilver, E. M. 1965 *History of East Africa* vol. 2. OUP.

Harrington, J. A. 1979 'Mortality in infancy and childhood in a developing economy: the example of West Africa', in Udo, R. K. (ed) *Population Education Source Book for Sub-Saharan Africa*. Heinemann, pp. 125–36.

Harris, J. 1981 'A conceptual framework for the study of migration in Botswana', *Working Paper no. 42*, African Studies Centre, Boston University.

Harris, J. & Todaro, M. 1970 'Migration, unemployment and development: a two sector model', *American Economic Review* vol. 60, 126–42.

Harris, R. (ed) 1975 *The Political Economy of Africa*. Wiley.

Harriss, J. & Harriss, B. 1979 'Development studies', *Progress in Human Geography* vol. 3, no. 4, 576–84.

Harriss, B. & Harriss, J. 1981 'Development studies' *Progress in Human Geography* vol. 5, 572–81.

Hazelwood, A. 1975 *Economic Integration: An East African Experience*. Heinemann.

Helleiner, G. K. 1975 'The role of multinational corporation in the less developed countries' Trade in Technology' *World Development* vol. 3, no. 4, 161–190.

Henin, R. S. 1979 'Government approaches to the population issue' in Udo, R. K. (ed) *Population Education Source Book for Sub-Saharan Africa*. Heinemann, pp. 184–99.

Hetherington, P. 1978 *British Paternalism and Africa 1920–40*. Cass.

Hewitt, A. 1979 'The European Development Fund as a development agent: some results of EDF aid to the Cameroon', *ODI Review* vol. 7, no. 2, 41–56.

Hewitt, A. 1982a 'The EEC policies towards the least developed: an analysis' in Stevens, C. (ed) *EEC and the Third World: A Survey* (part 2). ODI/IDS, pp. 125–36.

213

Hewitt, A. 1982b 'The EDF and its function in the EEC's development and policy'. *ODI Working Paper no. 11.*

Hill, C. R. 1983 'Regional co-operation in Southern Africa', *African Affairs* vol. 82, no. 327, 215–40.

Hill, P. 1972 *Rural Hausa: A Village and a Setting.* CUP.

Hill, P. 1977 *Population Prosperity and Poverty: Rural Kano 1900–1970.* CUP.

Hinderink, J. & Sterkenburg, J. J. 1978 'Spatial inequality: an attempt to define the concept', *Tijdschrift voor Economische en Sociale Geografie* vol. 69, nos. 1/2, 5–16.

Hitchcock, R. K. 1977 'Hunter-gatherers, boreholes and lands: a reconnaissance survey of the northern Kweneng'. *Consultancy report no. 3,* Ministry of Local Government and Lands, Gaborone, Botswana.

Hitchcock, R. K. 1978a 'A history of research among the Baswara in Botswana'. *Working Paper no. 19,* National Institute for Research in Development and African Studies, University College of Botswana, Gaborone.

Hitchcock, R. K. 1978b *Kalahari Cattleposts. A Regional Study of Hunter Gatherers, Pastoralists and Agriculturalists in the Western Sandveld Region, Central District, Botswana.* Ministry of Local Government and Lands, Gaborone, Botswana.

Hoogvelt, A. 1982 *The Third World in Global Development.* Macmillan.

Hopkins, A. G. 1973 *An Economic History of West Africa.* Longman.

Hopkins, A. G. 1976 'Imperial business in Africa. Part I: Sources; Part II: Interpretations', *Journal of African History* vol. 17, no. 1, 29–48; vol. 18, no. 2, 267–90.

Howard, R. 1978 *Colonialism and Underdevelopment in Ghana.* Croom Helm.

Howell, N. 1979 *Demography of the Dobe !Kung.* Academic Press.

Huddleston, B., Merry, F., Raikes, P. & Stevens, C. 1982 'The EEC and Third World food and agriculture' in Stevens, C. (ed) *EEC and the Third World: A Survey 2. Hunger in the World.* Hodder & Stoughton, pp. 15–46.

Hunton, W. A. 1959 *Decision in Africa.* Calder.

Hyden, G. 1980 *Beyond Ujamaa in Tanzania: Underdevelopment and an Uncaptured Peasantry.* Heinemann.

Hynes, W. 1979 *The Economics of Empire: Britain, Africa and the New Imperialism 1870–95.* Longman.

IBG: Women and Geography Study Group 1984 *Geography and Gender.* Hutchinson.

ICIDI (Independent Commission on International Development Issues) 1980 *North–South: A Programme for Survival.* Pan.

Ikime, O. 1977 *The Fall of Nigeria: The British Conquest.* Heinemann.

Iliffe, J. 1983 *The Emergence of African Capitalism.* Macmillan.

International Labour Organisation (ILO) 1972 *Employment Incomes and Inequality. A Strategy for Increasing Productive employment in Kenya.* International Labour Office, Geneva.

Isaksen, J. 1981 'Macro-economic management and bureaucracy: the case of Botswana'. *Research Report no. 59,* Scandinavian Institute of African Studies, Uppsala.

Isichei, E. 1983 *A History of Nigeria.* Longman.

Izzard, W. J. 1981 'The impact of migration on the roles of women'. Paper presented at the National Migration Study Conference, 7–11 December, Gaborone, Botswana.

Izzard, W. J. 1982 'Rural-urban migration in a developing country: the case of women migrants in Botswana'. Unpublished D.Phil. thesis, Oxford University.

Izzard, W. J. 1985 'Migrants and mothers: case studies from Botswana'. *Journal of Southern African Studies* vol. 11, no. 2, 258–80.

Jackson, R. H. 1973 'Political stratification in tropical Africa', *Canadian Journal of African Studies* vol. 7, no. 3, 381–400.

Jahn, Samia al Azharia 1981 *Traditional Water Purification in Tropical Developing*

Countries - Existing Methods and Potential Application. German Agency for Technical Co-operation, Eschborn.

Janes, M. D. 1974 'Physical growth of Nigerian Yoruba children', *Tropical and Geographical Medicine* vol. 26, 389–98.

Johnston, R. J. (ed) 1985 *The Dictionary of Human Geography.* Blackwell (2nd Edition).

Jones, D. 1973 *Europe's Chosen Few: Policy and Practice of the EEC Aid Programme.* Overseas Development Institute.

Jones H. R. 1981 *Population Geography.* Harper & Row.

Kabagambe, D. & Moughtin, C. 1983 'Housing the poor: a case study in Nairobi', *Third World Planning Review* vol. 5, no. 3, 227–48.

Kabuage, S. I. 1983 'Community participation in rural water supplies in Kenya', Proceedings of the 9th WEDC Conference on Sanitation and Water for Development in Africa, 12–15 April, Harare, Zimbabwe, pp. 67–69.

Kandeke, T. K. 1977 *Fundamentals of Zambian Humanism.* National Education Company of Zambia, Lusaka.

Kanesa-Thasan, S. 1981 The Fund and adjustment policies in Africa. *Finance and Development* vol. 18, no. 3, pp. 20–24.

Kann, U. 1981 'Career development in a changing society: the case of Botswana'. *Studies in Comparative Education no. 4.* Institute of International Education, University of Stockholm, Sweden.

Kaplinsky, R. (ed) 1978 *Readings on the Multinational Corporations in Kenya.* OUP.

Kaunda, K. D. 1967; 1974 *Humanism in Zambia and a Guide to its Implementation Part I and Part 2.* Zambia Information Service, Lusaka.

Kay, G. 1975 *Development and Underdevelopment: A Marxist Analysis.* Macmillan.

Kennedy, P. 1977 'Indigenous capitalism in Ghana', *Review of African Political Economy* no. 8, 21–38.

Kenya Central Bureau of Statistics 1979 *Kenya Fertility Survey: Major Highlights.* Government Printer, Nairobi.

Kerven, C. 1977 'Underdevelopment, migration and class formation: North East District, Botswana'. Unpublished Ph.D. dissertation, University of Toronto, Canada.

Kerven, C. 1979a 'Rural–urban migration and agricultural productivity in Botswana'. National Migration Study, Central Statistics Office and Rural Sociology Unit, Ministry of Agriculture, Gaborone, Botswana.

Kerven, C. 1979b 'Urban and rural female-headed households dependence on agriculture'. National Migration Study, Central Statistics Office and Rural Sociology Unit, Ministry of Agriculture, Gaborone, Botswana.

Kerven, C. 1980 'Rural–urban interdependence and agricultural development'. Paper presented at Symposium on Settlement in Botswana, 4–8 August, Gaborone, Botswana.

Kerven, C. 1981 'The effects of absenteeism on agricultural production'. Paper presented at the National Migration Study Conference, 7–11 December, Gaborone, Botswana.

Kerven, C. (ed) 1982 *Migration in Botswana: Patterns, Causes and Consequences.* Central Statistics Office, Gaborone, Botswana.

Kerven, C. 1984 'Academics, practitioners and all kinds of women in development: a reply to Peters', *Journal of Southern African Studies* vol. 10, no. 2, 259–68.

Kerven, C. & Simmons, P. 1981 'Bibliography on the society, culture and political economy of post-independence Botswana'. National Migration Study, Central Statistics Office, Gaborone, Botswana.

Kjekshus, H. 1977 'The Tanzanian villagisation policy: implementation lessons and ecological dimensions', *Canadian Journal of African Studies* vol. 11, no. 2, 269–82.

Killick, T. 1973 'The benefits of foreign direct investment and its alternatives: an empirical exploration', *Journal of Development Studies* vol. 9, no. 2, 301–22.

Killick, T. 1980 'Trends in development economics and their relevance to Africa', *Journal of Modern African Studies* vol. 18, no. 3, 367–86.

Kirk, D. 1971 'A new demographic transition?' in *National Academy of Sciences Rapid Population Growth* vol. 2, Research Papers. Johns Hopkins University Press, Baltimore, pp. 123–47.

Kirk, D. 1979 'World population and birth rates: agreements and disagreements', *Population and Development Review* vol. 5, 387–403.

Kirkpatrick, C. & Nixson, F. 1981 'Transnational corporations and economic develop-ment', *Journal of Modern African Studies* vol. 19, no. 3, 367–99.

Kitching, G. N. 1972 'The concept of class and the study of Africa', *African Review* vol. 2, no. 3, 327–50.

Kpedekpo, G.M.K. 1979 'Sources and uses of population data' in Udo, R. K. (ed) *Popula-tion Education Source Book for Sub-Saharan Africa.* Heinemann, pp. 12–23.

Kpedekpo, G. M. K. 1982 *Essentials of Demographic Analysis for Africa.* Heinemann.

Kpedekpo, G. M. K. & Arya, P.L. 1981 *Social and Economic Statistics for Africa.* Allen & Unwin.

Kuper, A. 1975 'The social structure of the Sotho-speaking peoples of Southern Africa', *Africa* vol. 45, nos. 1–2, 67–81, 139–49.

Laclau, E. 1971 'Feudalism and capitalism in Latin America', *New Left Review* vol. 67 (May/June), 19–38.

Langdon, S. 1977a 'The state and capitalism in Kenya', *Review of African Political Economy* no. 8, 90–98.

Langdon, S. W. 1977b 'Multinational firms and the state in Kenya', *IDS Bulletin* (Brighton) vol. 9, no. 1, 36–41.

Langdon, S. W. 1981 *Multinational Corporations in the Political Economy of Kenya.* Macmillan.

Lanning, G. & Mueller, M. 1979 *Africa Undermined: Mining Companies and the Underdevelopment of Africa.* Pelican, Harmondsworth.

Lee, R. B. 1968 'What hunters do for a living, or how to make out on scarce resources' in Lee, R. B. & De Vore (eds) *Man the Hunter.* Aldine, Chicago, pp. 30–48.

Lee, R. B. & DeVore, I. (eds) 1976 *Kalahari Hunter Gatherers.* Harvard University Press, Cambridge, Mass.

Lenin, V. I. 1916; 1964 'Imperialism: the highest stage of capitalism' in Lenin, V. I. *Collected Works* vol. 22. Progress Publishers, Moscow.

Lewis, J. P. 1980 *Development Co-operation: Efforts and Policies of the Members of the Development Assistance Committee.* OECD, Paris.

Lewis, M. D. 1962 'The assimilation theory in French colonial policy', *Comparative Studies in Society and History* vol. 4, no. 2, 129–53.

Lewis, O. 1970 'The culture of poverty in Lewis, O. *Anthropological Essays.* Random House, New York, pp. 67–80.

Lewis, W. A. 1954 'Economic development with unlimited supplies of labour', *Manchester School of Economics and Social Studies* vol. 22, 139–91.

Lewis, W. A. 1955 *The Theory of Economic Growth.* Allen & Unwin.

Leys, C. 1971 'Politics in Kenya: the development of peasant society', *British Journal of Political Science* vol. 1, no. 3, 307–37.

Leys, C. 1972 'A new conception of planning?' in Faber, M. & Seers, D. (eds) *The Crisis in Planning.* Chatto & Windus, pp. 56–80.

Leys, C. 1975 *Underdevelopment in Kenya: The Political Economy of Neo-Colonialism 1964–71.* Heinemann.

Leys, C. 1978 'Capital accumulation, class formation and dependency – the significance of the Kenyan case', *Socialist Register,* 241–66.

Leys, R. & Tostensen, A. 1982 'Regional co-operation in Southern Africa: The Southern African Development Co-ordination Conference (SADCC)', *Review of African Political Economy* no. 23, 52–71.

Lightbourne, R. Jr., Singh, S. with Green, C. P. 1982 'The World fertility survey: charting global childbearing', *Population Bulletin*, vol. 37, no. 1.

Lipton, M. 1977 *Why Poor People Stay Poor: A Study of Urban Bias in World Development.* Temple Smith, London.

Lipton, M. 1980a 'Migration from rural areas of poor countries: the impact on rural productivity and income distribution', *World Development* vol. 8, no. 1, 1–24.

Lipton, M. 1980b 'Minimum wages, exploitation and Botswana's unemployment crisis', *South African Labour Bulletin* vol. 6, no. 1, 53–72.

Lipton, M. 1984 'Urban bias revisited', *Journal of Development Studies* vol. 20, no. 3, 139–66.

Lipton, Merle. 1980 'Men of two worlds: source countries and regions: problems and prospects', *Optima* vol. 29, 172–83.

Little, K. 1973 *African Women in Towns; an Aspect of Africa's Social Revolution.* CUP.

Livingstone, I. & Ord, H. W. 1980 *An Introduction to Economics for Eastern Africa.* Heinemann.

Lloyd, P. C. 1972 *Africa in Social Change: Changing Traditional Societies in the Modern World.* Penguin.

Lloyd, P. C. 1973 'The Yoruba: an urban people?' in Southall, A. (ed) *Urban Anthropology.* OUP, New York, pp. 107–23.

Lloyd, P. 1976 'Marginality: euphemism or concept?' *IDS Bulletin* (Brighton) vol. 8, part 2, 12–16.

Lloyd, P. 1979 *Slums of Hope?* Pelican.

Lofchie, M. F. 1978 'Agrarian crisis and economic liberalisation in Tanzania', *Journal of Modern African Studies* vol. 16, no. 3, 451–75.

Lofchie, M. F. & Commins, S. K. 1982 'Food deficits and agricultural policies in tropical Africa', *Journal of Modern African Studies* vol. 20, no. 1, 1–25.

Low, A. R. C. 1981 'The effects of off-farm employment on farm incomes and production: Taiwan contrasted with Southern Africa', *Economic Development and Cultural Change* vol. 29, no. 4, 749–58.

Low, D. A. 1965 'British East Africa: the establishment of British rule 1895–1912' in Harlow, V. & Chilver, E. M. (eds) *History of East Africa* vol. 2. Clarendon Press, pp. 1–56.

Low, D. A. & Smith, A. 1976 *History of East Africa* vol. 3. Clarendon Press.

Lucas, C. P. 1922 *Partition and Colonisation of Africa.* Clarendon Press.

Lucas, R. E. B. 1983 'Emigration employment and accumulation: the miners of Southern Africa'. Discussion Paper no. 4, Migration and Development Programme, Harvard University, Cambridge, Mass.

Lugard, F. D. 1965 *The Dual Mandate in British Tropical Africa.* Cass.

Luxemburg, R. 1913; 1951 *The Accumulation of Capital.* Routledge & Kegan Paul.

Luxemburg, R. 1921; 1972 *The Accumulation – an Anti-Critique.* Monthly Review Press.

Mabogunje, A. L. 1962 *Yoruba Towns.* Ibadan University Press.

Mabogunje, A. L. 1970 'Migration policy and regional development in Nigeria', *Nigerian Journal of Economic and Social Studies* vol. 12, pp. 243–62.

Mabogunje, A. L. 1972 *Regional mobility and resource development in West Africa.* McGill-Queens University Press, Montreal.

Mabogunje, A. L. 1978 'Growth poles and growth centres in the regional development of Nigeria in Kuklinski, A. (ed) *Regional Policies in Nigeria, India and Brazil.* Mouton, The Hague, pp. 3–93.

Mabogunje, A. L. 1980a *The Development Process.* Hutchinson.

217

Mabogunje, A. L. 1980b 'The dynamics of centre-periphery relations: the need for a geography of resource development', *Transactions of the Institute of British Geographers* vol. 5, no. 3, 277–96.

McFalls, J. 1979 *Psychopathology and subfecundity*. Academic Press, New York.

McMaster, D. N. 1968 'The colonial district town in Uganda' in Beckinsale, R. P. & Houston, J. M. (eds) *Urbanisation and its Problems*. Blackwell, pp. 330–51.

Mafeje, A. 1971 'The ideology of tribalism', *Journal of Modern African Studies* vol. 9, no. 2, 253–63.

Makinwa, P. K. 1976 *Government Policies and Population Growth in Nigeria*. Population Association of America, Washington, D.C.

Mangin, W. 1967 'Latin American squatter settlements: a problem and a solution', *Latin American Research Review* vol. 2, 65–98.

Maquet, J. J. 1961 *The Premise of Inequality in Rwanda*. OUP.

Maro, R. S. & Mlay, W. F. I. 1979 'Decentralisation and organisation of space in Tanzania', *Africa* vol. 49, no. 3, 291–301.

Martin, G. 1982 'Africa and the ideology of Eurafrica: neo-colonialism or Pan-Africanism?' *Journal of Modern African Studies* vol. 20, no. 2, 221–38.

Marx, K. 1867; 1976 'The progressive production of a relative surplus population or industrial reserve army' in Marx, K. *Capital: A Critique of Political Economy* vol. 1. Penguin, pp. 781–94.

Marx, K. 1885; 1967 *Capital* vol. 2. Progress Publishers, Moscow.

Masser, I. & Gould, W. T. S. 1975 *Inter-Regional Migration in Tropical Africa*. Institute of British Geographers Special Publication no. 8.

Massey, D. 1980 'The changing political economy of migrant labour in Botswana', *South African Labour Bulletin* vol. 5, no. 5, 4–26.

Massey, D. 1981 'Labour migration and rural development in Botswana'. Unpublished Ph.D. dissertation, Boston University.

Mauldin, W. P. & Berelson, B. 1978 'Conditions of fertility decline in developing countries 1965–75', *Studies in Family Planning* vol. 9, no. 4, 75–84.

Maxwell, S. J. & Singer, H. W. 1979 'Food aid to developing countries: a survey', *World Development* vol. 7, 225–47.

Mazrui, A. A. 1969 'Pluralism and national integration' in Kuper, L. & Smith, M. G. (eds) *Pluralism in Africa*. University of California Press, Berkeley, pp. 33–330.

Meadows, D. H. *et al.* 1972 *The Limits to Growth: A Report for the Club of Rome's Project on the Predicament of Mankind*. Earth Island.

Meillassoux, C. 1972 'From reproduction to production: a Marxist approach to economic anthropology', *Economy and Society* vol. 1, 93–105.

Metz, S. 1982 'In lieu of orthodoxy: the socialist theories of Nkrumah and Nyerere', *Journal of Modern African Studies* vol. 20, no. 3, 377–92.

Ministry of Health (undated) *1978 Annual Report for the National Family Welfare Centre*. Government Printer, Nairobi.

Mitchell, J. C. 1954 'The distribution of African labour by area of origin in the copper mines of Northern Rhodesia', *Human Problems of British Central Africa* no. 14, 30–36.

Mitchell, J. C. 1959 'Labour migration in Africa south of the Sahara: the causes of labour migration', *Bulletin of the Inter-African Labour Institute* vol. 6, no. 1, 12–46.

Mitchell, J. C. 1961 'Social change and the stability of African marriage in Northern Rhodesia' in Southall, A. W. (ed) *Social Change in Modern Africa*. OUP, pp. 316–29.

Mitchell, J. C. 1964 'Distance and urban involvement in Northern Rhodesia' in *Burg Wartenstein Symposium 26: Cross-Culture Similarities in the Urbanisation Process*. Wenner-Gren Foundation for Anthropological Research, New York City.

Mitchell, J. C. (ed) 1969a *Social Networks in Urban Situations.* Manchester University Press.

Mitchell, J. C. 1969b 'Structural plurality, urbanisation and labour circulation in Southern Rhodesia' in Jackson J. A. (ed) *Migration: Sociological Studies.* CUP, pp. 156–80.

Mohiddin, A. 1981 *African socialism in two countries.* Croom Helm.

Molenaar, M. 1980 *Social Change within a Traditional Pattern: A Case Study of a Tswana Ward.* Leiden, Netherlands.

Molnos, A. 1968 *Attitudes towards Family Planning in East Africa: An Investigation in Schools around Lake Victoria and in Nairobi.* Weltforum Verlag, Munich.

Molnos, A. 1972/73 *Cultural Source Materials for Population Planning in East Africa.* East African Publishing House, Nairobi.

Monsted, M. & Walji, P. 1978 *A Demographic Analysis of East Africa. A Sociological Interpretation.* Scandinavian Institute of African Studies, Uppsala.

Morgan, W. T. W. 1983 *Nigeria.* Longman.

Morgan, R. W. & Ohadike, P. O. 1975 'Fertility levels and fertility change' in Caldwell, J. C. *et al.* (eds) *Population Growth and Socio-Economic Change in West Africa.* Columbia University Press, New York, pp. 187–235.

Morton, K. & Tulloch, P. 1977 *Trade and Developing Countries.* Croom Helm.

Mott, F. L. & Mott, S. H. 1980 'Kenya's record population growth: a dilemma of development', *Population Bulletin* vol. 35, no. 3.

Msukwa, L. A. H. 1983 'Participation in rural water supply – the Malawi experience'. Proceedings of the 9th WEDC Conference on Sanitation and Water for Development in Africa. University of Zimbabwe, Harare, 12–15 April, pp. 81–85.

Muller, M. 1976 'Will the EEC shift the milk mountain?' *New Scientist* vol. 70, 642–43.

Murray, C. 1981 *Families Divided: The Impact of Migrant Labour in Lesotho.* Ravan, Johannesburg.

Mushi, S. S. 1971 'Ujamaa: modernisation by traditionalisation', *Taamuli* vol. 1, no. 2, 13–29.

Mushi, S. S. 1981 'Community development in Tanzania' in Dore, R. & Mars, Z. (eds) *Community Development.* Croom Helm, pp. 139–244.

Myint, H. 1980 (5th edn) *The Economics of the Developing Countries.* Hutchinson.

Nadel, S. F. 1942 *A Black Byzantium.* International African Institute.

Newbury, C. W. 1969 'Trade and authority in West Africa from 1850 to 1880' in Gann, L. H. & Duignan, P. (eds) *Colonialism in Africa 1870–1960* vol. 1, CUP, pp. 66–99.

Newitt, M. 1981 *Portugal in Africa. The Last Hundred Years.* Longman.

Nigerian Ministry of Economic Development 1962 *National Development Plan 1962–68.* Government Printer, Lagos.

Nkrumah, K. 1963 *Africa Must Unite.* Heinemann.

Nkrumah, K. 1965 *Neo-Colonialism: The Last Stage of Imperialism.* Nelson.

Nkrumah, K. 1970a *Africa Must Unite.* International Publishers, New York.

Nkrumah, K. 1970b *Class Struggle in Africa.* International Publishers, New York.

Nyerere, J. K. 1962 *Ujamaa: The Basis of African Socialism.* Government Printer, Dar es Salaam.

Nyerere, J. K. 1967 *Socialism and Rural Development.* Government Printer, Dar es Salaam.

Nyerere, J. K. 1968 *Ujamaa – Essays in Socialism.* Government Printer, Dar es Salaam.

O'Connor, A. M. 1978 (2nd edn) *The Geography of Tropical African Development.* Pergamon.

O'Connor, A. M. 1983 *The African City.* Hutchinson.

Ojo, G. J. A. 1968 'Some cultural factors in the critical density of population in tropical Africa' in Caldwell, J. C. & Okonjo, C. (eds) *The Population of Tropical Africa.* Longman, pp. 312–19.

Okediji, F.O. 1975 'Socio-economic status and attitudes to public health problems in the Western State: a case study of Ibadan' in Caldwell, J. C. *et al.* (eds) *Population Growth and Socio-Economic Change in West Africa.* Columbia University Press, New York, pp. 275–97.

Oliver, R. & Fage, J. D. 1966 *A Short History of Africa.* Penguin.

Ominde, S. H. & Ejiogu, C. N. (eds) 1972 *Population Growth and Economic Development in Africa.* Heinemann.

Organisation of African Unity 1981 *Lagos Plan of Action for the Economic Development of Africa 1980–2000.* Addis Ababa.

Ormsby-Gore, W. G. A. 1924–5 East Africa Commission Report Cmd. 2387.

Ormsby-Gore, W. G. A. 1926 West Africa Commission Report Cmd. 2744.

Orubuloye, I. & Caldwell, J. 1975 'The impact of public health services on mortality differentials in a rural area of Nigeria', *Population Studies* vol. 25, 259–72.

Ottaway, M. 1978 'Soviet Marxism and African socialism', *Journal of Modern African Studies* vol. 16, no. 3, 477–85.

Padmore, G. 1936 *How Britain Rules Africa.* Wishart, London.

Page, H. J. & Lesthaeghe, R. (eds) 1981 *Child Spacing in Tropical Africa: Traditions and Change.* Academic Press.

Palloix, C. 1973 *Les Firmes Multinationales et le Procès d'Internalisation.* Maspero, Paris.

Palmer, R. 1977 'The agricultural history of Rhodesia' in Palmer, R. & Parsons, N. (eds) *The Roots of Rural Poverty in Central and Southern Africa.* Heinemann, pp. 221–54.

Palmer, R. & Parsons, N. 1977 *The Roots of Rural Poverty in Central and Southern Africa.* Heinemann.

Parson, J. 1980 'Botswana in the Southern African periphery: the limits of capitalist transformation in a "labour reserve"', *IDS Bulletin* (Brighton) vol. 11, no. 4, 45–52.

Parsons, N. 1977 'The economic history of Khama's Country in Botswana 1844–1930' in Palmer, R. & Parsons, N. *The Roots of Rural Poverty in Central and Southern Africa.* Heinemann, pp. 113–43.

Pearson, L. B. *et al.* 1969 *Partners in Development (Report of the Commission on International Development).* Pall Mall Press.

Peil, M. 1973 'The influence of formal education on occupational choice', *Canadian Journal of African Studies* vol. 6, 199–214.

Peil, M. 1976 'African squatter settlements: a comparative study', *Urban Studies* vol. 13, 155–66.

Peil, M. 1977 *Consensus and Conflict in African Societies: An Introduction to Sociology.* Longman.

Peters, P. 1983 'Gender, development cycles and historical processes: a critique of recent research on women in Botswana', *Journal of Southern African Studies* vol. 10, no. 1, 100–122.

Phillips. C. S. 1980 'Nigeria's new political institutions 1975–79', *Journal of Modern African Studies* vol. 18, no. 1, 1–22.

Picard, L. A. 1979a 'District councils in Botswana – a remnant of local autonomy', *Journal of Modern African studies* vol. 71, no. 2, 285–308.

Picard, L. A. 1979b 'Rural development in Botswana: administrative structures and public policy', *Journal of Developing Areas* vol. 13, 283–300.

Pinfold, T. & Anderson, D. L. 1981 'Co-ordinating operations and investment expenditures: the need for balance in planning and budgeting' in Norcliffe, G. & Pinfold, T. (eds) *Planning African Development.* Croom Helm, pp. 110–28.

Pisharoti, K. A. 1975 *Health Education in Environmental Health Programmes.* WHO, Geneva.

Pool, D. T. & Coulibaly, S. P. 1975 'Un essai d'explication des variations de la fécondité en Haute-Volta et au Ghana', *Population et Famille* no. 34, 29–54.

Presidential Commission on World Hunger 1980 *Overcoming World Hunger: the Challenge Ahead.* US Government Printing Office, Washington DC.

Preston, S. H. 1976 *Mortality Patterns in National Populations.* Academic Press, New York.

Rajana, C. 1982 'The Lomé Convention: an evaluation of EEC economic assistance to the ACP states', *Journal of Modern African Studies* vol. 20, no. 2, 179–220.

Ranis, G. & Fei, J. C. 1961 'A theory of economic development', *American Economic Review* vol. 51, 533–65.

Redclift, M. 1984 *Development and the Environment Crisis: Red or Green Alternatives?* Methuen.

Republic of Botswana 1980 *National Development Plan 1979–85.* Government Printer, Gaborone.

Republic of Kenya 1965 'African socialism and its application to planning in Kenya', Sessional Paper no. 10. Government Printer, Nairobi.

Republic of Kenya 1966 *Development Plan 1966–70.* Government Printer, Nairobi.

Republic of Kenya 1969 *Development Plan 1970–74.* Government Printer, Nairobi.

Republic of Kenya 1979 *Development Plan 1979–83.* Government Printer, Nairobi.

Republic of Tanzania 1967 *The Arusha Declaration and TANU's Policy on Socialism and Self-Reliance.* Government Printer, Dar es Salaam.

Republic of Tanzania 1969 *Tanzania Second Five-Year Plan for Economic and Social Development, 1st July 1969–30th June 1974.* Government Printer, Dar es Salaam.

Republic of Uganda 1966 *Work for Progress, Uganda's Second Five-Year Plan 1966–71.* Government Printer, Entebbe.

Richards, A. I. 1939 *Land, Labour and Diet in Northern Rhodesia.* OUP.

Richards, A. I. 1960 *East African Chiefs: A Study of Political Development in some Uganda and Tanganyika Tribes.* Faber.

Richards, A. I. 1969 *The Multi-cultural States of East Africa.* McGill-Queens University Press, Montreal.

Richards P. 1979 'Community environmental knowledge and African rural development', *IDS Bulletin* (Brighton) vol. 10, no. 2, 28–36.

Richards, P. 1980 'The environmental factor in African studies', *Progress in Human Geography* vol. 4, 589–600.

Richards, P. 1983 'Farming systems and agrarian change in West Africa', *Progress in Human Geography* vol. 7, 1–39.

Richardson, H. W. 1980 'An urban development strategy for Kenya', *Journal of Developing Areas* vol. 15, 97–118.

Riddell, J. B. 1970 *The Spatial Dynamics Of Modernisation in Sierra Leone.* Northwestern University Press, Evanston.

Rimmer, D. 1984 *The Economics of West Africa.* Weidenfeld & Nicolson.

Robinson, P. 1978 'The political context of regional development in the West African Sahel', *Journal of Modern African Studies* vol. 16, no. 6, 579–95.

Rodney, W. 1972 *How Europe Underdeveloped Africa.* Bogle-L'Ouverture, London.

Roe, E. 1980 'Development of livestock, agriculture and water supplies in Botswana before independence: a short history and policy analysis'. Rural Development Committee, Centre of International Studies, Cornell University, New York.

Romaniuk, A. 1968 'Infertility in tropical Africa' in Caldwell, J. C. & Okonjo, C. (eds) *The Population of Tropical Africa.* Longman, pp. 216–24.

Romaniuk, A. 1980 'Increase in natural fertility during the early stages of modernisation: evidence from an African case study, Zaire', *Population Studies* vol. 34, 293–310.

Rondinelli, D. A. 1983a 'Secondary cities in developing countries. Policies for diffusing urbanisation'. *Sage Library of Social Research, vol. 145.*

Rondinelli, D.A. 1983b 'Decentralisation of development administration in East Africa', in Cheema, G. S. & Rondinelli, D. A. (eds) *Decentralisation and Development. Policy Implementation in Developing Countries.* Sage, pp. 77–126.

Ross, M. H. 1973 *The Political Integration of Urban Squatters.* Northwestern University Press, Evanston.

Rostow, W. W. 1960 *The Stages of Economic Growth: A Non-Communist Manifesto.* CUP.

Rotberg, R. I. 1966 *The Rise of Nationalism in Central Africa: The Making of Malawi and Zambia 1873–1964.* OUP.

Sahlins, M. 1976 *Culture and Practical Reason.* University of Chicago Press.

Samoff, J. 1981 'Crises and socialism in Tanzania', *Journal of Modern African Studies* vol. 19, no. 2, 279–306.

Sandbrook, R. 1982 *The Politics of Basic Needs: Urban Aspects of Assaulting Poverty in Africa.* Heinemann.

Sandbrook, R. & Cohen, R. (eds) 1975 *The Development of an African Working Class: Studies in Class Formation and Class Action.* Longman.

Saul, J. 1979 *The State and Revolution in Eastern Africa.* Heinemann.

Schapera, I. 1940 *Married Life in an African Tribe.* Faber & Faber.

Schapera, I. 1943 *Native Land Tenure in the Bechuanaland Protectorate.* Lovedale Press, Alice, South Africa.

Schapera, I. 1947 *Migrant Labour and Tribal Life: A Study of Conditions in the Bechuanaland Protectorate.* OUP.

Schapera, I. 1953 *The Tswana.* International African Institute.

Schapera, I. 1970 *Tribal Innovators: Tswana Chiefs and Social Change 1795–1940.* Athlone Press, University of London.

Schuster, I. 1982 'Recent research on women in development', *Journal of Development Studies* vol. 18, no. 4, 511–36.

Scott, J. 1976 *The Moral Economy of the Peasant.* Yale University Press, New Haven.

Sebina, D. B. 1980 'Africa and the decade', *World Health,* August–September, pp. 4–7.

Seidman, A. 1972 *Comparative Development Strategies in East Africa.* East African Publishing House, Nairobi.

Seidman, A. 1980 *An Economics Textbook for Africa.* Methuen.

Sène, P. M. 1982 'Africa: the Sahel zone', *World Health* June, 23–27.

Shaw, T. 1982 'Beyond neo-colonialism: varieties of corporatism in Africa', *Journal of Modern African Studies* vol. 20, no. 2, 239–61.

Sheck, M. 1980 *The Lomé Convention and Tanzania's Basic Needs Strategy.* Scandinavian Institute of African Studies, Uppsala.

Shivji, I. G. (ed) 1973 *The Silent Class Struggle.* Tanzania Publishing House, Dar es Salaam.

Shivji, I. G. 1976 *Class Struggles in Tanzania.* Monthly Review Press.

Silberbauer, G. & Kuper A. 1966 'Kgalagadi masters and Bushmen serfs', *African Studies* vol. 25, 171–79.

Silitshena, R. 1981 'Rural settlement patterns'. Paper presented at the National Migration Study Conference, 7–11 December, Gaborone, Botswana.

Singer, H. W. 1976 'Review of C. Leys *Underdevelopment in Kenya: The Political Economy of Neo-Colonialism*', *Economic Development and Cultural Change* vol. 25, 171–76.

Sklar, R. L. 1979 'The nature of class domination in Africa', *Journal of Modern African Studies* vol. 17, no. 4, 531–52.

Smith, A. D. 1983 *State and Nation in the Third World.* Wheatsheaf, Brighton.

Smith, S. 1979 'Colonialism in economic theory: the experience of Nigeria', *Journal of Development Studies* vol. 15, no. 3, 38–59.

Soja, E. W. 1968 *The Geography of Modernisation in Kenya: A Spatial Analysis of Social, Economic and Political Change.* Syracuse University Press.

Solway, J. 1979 *People, Cattle and Drought in the Western Kweneng District.* Rural Sociology Unit, Ministry of Agriculture, Gaborone, Botswana.

Sorrenson, M. P. K. 1967 *Land Reform in Kikuyu Country: A Study in Government Policy.* OUP.

Southall, A. W. 1961 'The position of women and the stability of marriage' in *Social Change in Modern Africa.* OUP, pp. 46-66.

Southall, A. W. 1970 'The illusion of tribe' in Gutkind, P. C. W. (ed) *The Passing of Tribal Man in Africa.* Brill Leiden, pp. 28-50.

Stevens, C. 1979 *Food Aid and the Developing World: Four African Case Studies.* Croom Helm.

Stevens, C. (ed) 1984 *EEC and the Third World: A Survey 4. Renegotiating Lomé.* Hodder & Stoughton.

Stewart, F. 1972 'Choice of technique in developing countries', *Journal of Development Studies* vol. 9, no. 1, 99-121.

Stewart, F. 1979 'International technology transfer: issues and policy options'. *World Bank Staff Working Paper no. 344.*

Stitcher, S. 1982 *Migrant Labour in Kenya: Capitalism and African Response 1895-1975.* Longman.

Streeten, P. 1973 'The multinational enterprise and the theory of development policy', *World Development* vol. 1, no. 10, 1-14.

Stren, R. 1975 'Urban policy and performance in Kenya and Tanzania', *Journal of Modern African Studies* vol. 13, 267-82.

Sunkel, O. 1973 'Transnational capitalism and national disintegration in Latin America', *Social and Economic Studies* vol. 22, no. 1, 132-76.

Sunkel, O. 1974 'External economic relationships and the process of development: suggestions for an alternative analytical framework' in Williamson, R. B. *et al.* (eds) *Latin American-US Economic Interactions.* American Enterprise Institute for Public Policy Research, Washington DC, pp. 27-40.

Sunkel, O. 1977 'The development of development thinking', *IDS Bulletin* (Brighton), vol. 8, no. 3, 6-11.

Sutton, F. X. 1961 'Planning and rationality in the newly independent states in Africa', *Economic Development and Cultural Change* vol. 10, no. 1, 42-50.

Swainson, N. 1977 'The rise of a national bourgeoisie in Kenya', *Review of African Political Economy* no. 8, 39-55.

Swainson, N. 1980 *The Development of Corporate Capitalism in Kenya 1918-77.* Heinemann.

Swindell, K. 1979 'Labour migration in underdeveloped countries: the case of subsaharan Africa', *Progress in Human Geography* vol. 3, no. 2, 239-59.

Swynnerton, R. J. M. 1954 *A Plan to Intensify the Development of African Agriculture in Kenya.* Government Printer, Nairobi.

Szentes, T. 1964 'Migrant-labour system in black Africa', *Indian Journal of Labour Economics* vol. 7, 95-118.

Szentes, T. 1976 'Socio-economic effects of two patterns of foreign capital investments, with special reference to East Africa' in Gutkind, P. C. W. & Wallerstein, I. (eds) *The Political Economy of Contemporary Africa.* Sage, pp. 261-90.

Tabutin, D. 1979 'Tendances et niveau de la fécondité au Zaire'. *Working Paper no. 54,* Département de Demographie Université Catholique de Louvain.

Tarrant, J. R. 1980 'The geography of food aid', *Transactions, Institute of British Geographers,* vol. 5, no. 2, pp. 125-40.

Taylor, D. R. F. 1981 'Conceptualising development space in Africa', *Geografiska Annaler* vol. 63B, 87-93.

Taylor, J. 1982 'Changing patterns of labour supply to the South African gold mines', *Tijdschrift voor Economische en Sociale Geografie* vol. 73, no. 4, 213-20.

Taylor, M. J. & Thrift, N. J. (eds) 1982 *The Geography of Multinationals.* Croom Helm.

223

Tendler, J. 1982 'Rural projects through urban eyes: an interpretation of the World Bank's new-style rural development projects'. *World Bank Staff Working Paper no. 532*, Washington DC.

Thomas, I. D. 1972 'Infant mortality in Tanzania', *East African Geographical Review* vol. 10, 5–26.

Thomas, I. D. 1976 'Planning techniques – physical indicators in Tanzania', *IDS Bulletin* (Norwich) vol. 8, no. 1, 30–35.

Thompson, W. S. 1929 'Population', *American Journal of Sociology* vol. 34, 959–75.

Tipple, M. P. 1976 'Self-help housing policies in a Zambian mining town', *Urban Studies* vol. 13, 167–69.

Turner, J. F. C. 1967 'Barriers and channels for housing development in modernising countries', *Journal of the American Institute of Planners* vol. 33, 167–81.

Turner, J. F. C. 1969 'Uncontrolled urban settlements: problems and policies' in Breese, G. (ed) *The City in Newly Developing Countries: Readings on Urbanism and Urbanisation*. Prentice Hall, pp. 507–31.

Twitchett, C. C. 1978 *Europe and Africa: From Association to Partnership*. Saxon House.

Twitchett, C. C. 1981 *A Framework for Development: The EEC and the ACP*. Allen & Unwin.

Udo, R. K. (ed) 1979a *Population Education Source Book for Sub-Saharan Africa*. Heinemann.

Udo, R. K. 1979b 'Population and politics in sub-Saharan Africa' in Udo, R. K. (ed) *Population Education Source Book for Sub-Saharan Africa*. Heinemann, pp. 172–81.

Udo, R. K. 1982 *The Human Geography of Tropical Africa*. Heinemann, Ibadan.

Ukaegbu, A. O. 1977 'Fertility of women in polygamous unions in rural Eastern Nigeria', *Journal of Marriage and the Family* vol. 26, 397–404.

United Nations 1978 *Transnational Corporations in World Development: A Re-examination*. New York.

United Nations 1983 *Statistical Yearbook 1981*. Department of International Economic and Social Affairs, New York.

United Nations 1984 *Demographic Yearbook 1982*. Department of International Economic and Social Affairs, New York.

United Nations Economic Commission for Africa 1974 'Review of population policies and programmes in Africa'. E/C No. 14/POP (12). Expert Group on National Population Policies and Programmes in Africa, 11–15 November, Addis Ababa, Ethiopia.

United Nations Secretariat 1980 'Immediate measures in favour of most seriously affected countries'. *Report of the Secretary-General*, United Nations General Assembly, June.

United Republic of Tanganyika and Zanzibar 1964 *Tanganyika Five-Year Plan for Economic and Social Development 1964–69*. Government Printer, Dar-es-Salaam.

Valentine, C. & Revson, J. E. 1979 'Cultural traditions, social change and fertility in sub-Saharan Africa', *Journal of Modern African Studies* vol. 17, no. 3, 453–72.

Van Binsbergen, W. M. J. & Meilink, H. (eds) 1978 *Migration and the Transformation of Modern African Society*. Afrika: Studiecentrum, Leiden.

Van Der Wiel, A. C. A. 1977 *Migration Wage Labour: Its Role in the Economy of Lesotho*. Mazenod Book Centre, Mazenod.

Van Velsen 1960 'Labour migration as a positive factor in the continuity of Tonga tribal society', *Economic Development and Cultural Change* vol. 8, 265–78.

Vengroff, F. 1977 *Botswana: Rural Development in the Shadow of Apartheid*. Associated University Presses, East Brunswick, New Jersey.

Vierich, H. 1980 'The implications of drought for non-village populations living in remote areas of the sandveld', in Vierich, H. & Sheppard, C. *Drought in Rural*

Botswana: Socio-economic Impact and Government Policy. Rural Sociology Unit, Ministry of Agriculture, Gaborone, Botswana, pp. 143–54 (Appendix F).

Vierich, H. & Sheppard, C. 1980 *Drought in Rural Botswana: Socio-economic Impact and Government Policy.* Rural Sociology Unit, Ministry of Agriculture, Gaborone, Botswana.

Wallerstein, I. 1970 'The colonial era in Africa: changes in social structure', in Gann, L. H. & Guignan, P. (eds) *Colonialism in Africa 1870–1960* vol. 2. CUP, pp. 399–421.

Wallerstein, I. 1976 'The three stages of African involvement in the world economy', in Gutkind, P. C. W. & Wallerstein, I. (eds) *The Political Economy of Contemporary Africa.* Sage, pp. 30–57.

Wallerstein, I. 1977 'Class and status in contemporary Africa' in Gutkind, P. C. W. & Waterman, P. (eds) *African Social Studies: A Radical Reader.* Monthly Review Press, pp. 277–83.

Ware, H. 1976 'The motivations for the use of birth control: evidence from West Africa', *Demography* vol. 13, 479–93.

Warren, B. 1973 'Imperialism and capitalist industrialisation', *New Left Review* vol. 81, 3–44.

Warwick, D. P. 1982 *Bitter Pills: Population Policies and their Implementation in Eight Developing Countries.* CUP.

Waterman, P. 1982 'Division and unity amongst Nigerian workers: Lagos Port unionism, 1940s–1960s'. *Research Report Series no. 11,* Institute of Social Studies, The Hague.

Watson, W. 1958 *Tribal Cohesion in a Money Economy: A Study of the Mambwe People of Northern Rhodesia.* Manchester University Press.

Watts, M. 1983 'Hazards and crises: a political economy of drought and famine in Northern Nigeria', *Antipode* vol. 15, no. 1, 24–34.

Weaver, J. H. & Kronemer, A. 1981 'Tanzanian and African socialism', *World Development* vol. 9, no. 9/10, 839–49.

Wellings, P. A. & McCarthy, J. J. 1983 'Whither Southern African human geography?' AREA vol. 15, no. 4, 337–45.

White, A. 1981 'Community participation in water and sanitation: concepts, strategies and methods'. *Technical Paper no. 17,* International Reference Centre, The Hague.

White, G. F., Bradley, D. J. & White, A. U. 1972 *Drawers of Water: Domestic Water Use in East Africa.* University of Chicago Press.

Wiles, P. 1982 *The New Communist Third World.* Croom Helm.

Williams, G. 1976 *Nigeria: Economy and Society.* Rex Collings.

Williams, R. 1981 *Culture.* Fontana.

Wilmsen, E. 1981 'Migration patterns of remote area dwellers'. Paper presented at the National Migration Study Conference, 7–11 December, Gaborone, Botswana.

Wilson, F. 1972 *Migrant Labour in South Africa.* South African Council of Churches and Spro-cas, Johannesburg.

Wilson, G. 1941–42 *An Essay on the Economics of Detribalisation in Northern Rhodesia.* Parts 1 & 2, Rhodes-Livingstone Papers nos. 5 & 6.

Wolff, R. 1974 *The Economies of Colonialism: Britain and Kenya 1870–93.* Yale University Press, New Haven.

Wood, A. P. 1982 'Population trends in Zambia: a review of the 1980 census' in Findlay, A. (ed) *Recent National Population Change.* (Conference Proceedings) Department of Geography, University of Durham, pp. 102–25.

Wood, A. P. & Smith, W. 1984 'Zambia up for grabs? The regionalisation of agricultural aid', *AREA* vol. 16, no. 1, 3–7.

Woods, R. I. 1979 *Population Analysis in Geography.* Longman.

Woods, R. I. 1982 *Theoretical Population Geography.* Longman.

World Bank 1974 *Nigeria: Options for Long-Term Development.* Johns Hopkins University Press, Baltimore.

World Bank 1975 *Kenya: Into the Second Decade.* Johns Hopkins University Press, Baltimore.

World Bank 1978a *Ivory Coast: The Challenge of Success.* Johns Hopkins University Press, Baltimore.

World Bank 1978b *World Development Report 1978.* OUP, New York.

World Bank 1979 *World Development Report 1979.* OUP, New York.

World Bank 1983 *World Development Report 1983.* OUP, New York.

World Bank 1984 *World Development Report 1984.* OUP, New York.

World Health Organisation 1981 *Global Strategy for Health for All by the Year 2000.* WHO, Geneva.

World Water 1978–79 *Water Decade Dossier Nation by Nation.* December 1978, pp. 37–42; July 1979, pp. 23–26; August 1979, pp. 29–32.

Wrigley, E. A. & Schofield, R. S. 1981 *The Population History of England: 1541–1871 A Reconstruction.* Arnold, London.

Yansane, A. 1977 'The state of economic integration in North West Africa south of the Sahara: the emergence of the economic community of West African States (ECOWAS)', *African Studies Review* vol. 20, no. 2, 63–87.

Yeager, R. 1982 *Tanzania: An African Experiment.* Gower, Hampshire & Westview Press, Boulder, Colorado.

Young, C. 1982 *Ideology and Development in Africa.* Yale University Press, New Haven.

Zartman, I. W. 1976 'Europe and Africa: decolonisation or dependency?' *Foreign Affairs,* vol. 54, no. 2, 325–43.

226

INDEX

227

DATE DUE

MAY 2 1 1990		
OCT 1 0 90 OCT 0 1 1990		
APR 1 5 1991		
MAY 6 1991		
MAY 2 7 1991		
MAR 8 1993		
JUN 0 1 1996		
APR 0 6 2000		
		PRINTED IN U.S.A.
GAYLORD		